The Journey
of One Buddhist Nun

The Journey
of One Buddhist Nun

Even Against the Wind

Sid Brown

State University of New York Press

Published by
State University of New York Press, Albany

For information, contact State University of New York Press, Albany, NY
www.sunypress.edu

Production by Michael Haggett
Marketing by Patrick Durocher

Library of Congress Cataloging-in-Publication Data

Brown, Sid.
The journey of one Buddhist nun : even against the wind / Sid Brown.
p. cm.
Includes index.
ISBN 0-7914-5095-3 (alk. paper)—ISBN 0-7914-5096-1 (pbk. : alk. paper)
1. Wåbi, Maechi 2. Buddhist nuns—Thailand—Religious life. 3. Monastic and religious
life of women—Thailand. I. Title.

BQ6150 .B76 2001
294.3'91'092—dc21
[B]
                                                                    2001034165

HC 978-0-7914-5095-6
PB 978-0-7914-5096-3

10 9

To my brother

Michael James Brown

12 March 1954–26 November 1995

Contents

Contents

Acknowledgments

I am deeply indebted to a large number of people for assistance of all kinds in writing this book. My deepest thanks go to my parents, Charles A. and Nadine M. Brown, who supported my work and my dreams for many years. Their willingness to indulge me in my fantasies and to trust that something would come of them and their concerned guidance and enthusiastic appreciative joy have helped me form an interesting and a rich life. I will also be forever indebted to the woman known herein as Māechī Wābī for the many hours of serious discussion, reflection, and friendship that revealed to me and now can reveal to others what the nature of a Buddhist struggle for an honorable life can be.

To the guides of my doctoral program, I extend my thanks. Professor Karen Lang as well as Professors Susan McKinnon, Paul Groner, and Jeffrey Hopkins, generously gave their time and energy.

Many of my friends helped me along the way. Helen Benet-Goodman has always been and continues to be willing to lend me a supportive ear in listening to my troubles as well as to join me in laughing at them and to offer helpful insights and views. She also generously shared her family with me, so that I can now count among my friends her daughters Tess and Maggie and her husband Carey. In addition, Carla Reid, André Hakes, Catherine Gillespie, Rajal Cohen, and Rose Mary Drake assisted me over the years.

Joining these friends are some people who, while being supportive through friendship in many different ways, went so far as to give me places to live when I was in need. They are: Phil Gates, Jackie Reynolds, Clare Lyons (and her housemates Craig, Katie, and Jeanne), Michael Cross, David Disinger, Gay (Rattanaporn Niyomtham), Māechī Bunchuan, and Māechī Darunī. These people provided me with beds in their houses or with space on their floors when I was essentially homeless.

Many of my Thai language instructors were excellent; none surpassed the dedication, skill, and passion of Professor Janpanit of the University of Wisconsin, one of the most inspiring women from whom I have had the pleasure to learn.

Two people helped me with the more challenging translation problems. Many thanks to Professor Warang of Chulalongkorn University and Wimonkarn Kosumas of the University of Virginia.

In addition to the māechī found above, Māechī Bramoon, Warī, Siri, Amphai, and Khūnmāe Prathin helped me enormously, especially when I investigated the Institute of Thai Māechī and Dhammacarinī Samnak.

Māechī Dārunī, Surī, and Noy took the time to educate and befriend me when I stayed at my first Thai samnak in the north. The man who introduced me to these women, Professor Poinsilrat, was kind, attentive, and encouraging, and he also put a roof over my head when I most needed it.

Māechī Kanittha, Sunsanee, and Thongpet, as well as Khūnying Kanok, are some of the strongest women I have ever met. I thank them for their inspiration and gifts of wisdom.

To Māechī Tassanī, I also extend my thanks. She was my first friend at Dhammacarinī Samnak, willing to extend her hand and to share her talents, as was her younger sister Būnghā, whom I always called "Elf."

This book was also made possible by several institutions. The Charlotte W. Newcombe Doctoral Dissertation Fellowship allowed me the year of concentrated work necessary to write it. Foreign Language and Area Study grants for four summers of Thai language at the Southeast Asia Summer Study Institutes at Cornell University, the University of Wisconsin, and the University of Washington allowed me to develop the language skills necessary to interview māechī, who rarely speak English. The Graduate Schools of Arts and Sciences and the Department of Religious Studies of the University of Virginia supported me with various grants and fellowships, including the Commonwealth and DuPont Fellowships.

In one of my favorite Buddhist texts, the *Sigālaka Sutta*, the Buddha gives his view on the qualities of good friends: "The friend who points out what is good for you can be seen to be a loyal friend in four ways: he keeps you from wrongdoing, he supports you in doing good, he informs you of what you did not know, and he points out the path to heaven."[1] Such a loyal friend is Rebecca Barnhouse, known to all of those who know me as The Barn. She supported me in the most difficult periods of research and writing, not only with kind, sympathetic words but with practical action, advice, and thoughtfulness that only the most admirable can offer. She creatively shared in the joys of this work, and her editing skills improved this book immeasurably. I do not deserve the excellent friends I have, but I hope that I have learned enough from The Barn to serve my other friends more carefully. I have become a better person because of her friendship, and there is surely no higher praise than that.

The publishers have given permission to use quotations from the following copyrighted works.

Bhikkhu Bodhi, 1995. *The Middle Length Discourses of the Buddha: A New Translation of the Majjhima Nikāya,* with the permission of Wisdom Publications, 199 Elm Street, Somerville, MA 02144 USA, www.wisdompubs.org. Cited in the text as *Majjhima Nikāya.*

Harischandra Kaviratna, 1980. *Dhammapada: Wisdom of the Buddha,* with the permission of Theosophical University Press, P.O. Box C, Pasadena, CA 91109-7107 USA, www.theosociety.org. Cited in the text as *Dhammapada.*

Maurice Walsh, 1987, 1995. *The Long Discourses of the Buddha: A Translation of the Dīgha Nikāya,* with permission of Wisdom Publications, 199 Elm Street, Somerville, MA 02144 USA, www.wisdompubs.org. Cited in the text as *Dīgha Nikāya.*

Introduction

*The fragrance of flowers does not travel against the wind, be it
that of sandalwood, tagara, or jasmine. But the fragrance of the
virtuous person travels even against the wind. The virtuous
person pervades all directions with his or her purity.*

—*Dhammapada* 54

On the day before the full moon, I walked across the grounds from my room
to visit Āromdī, a small black cat the nuns had encouraged me to befriend.
When I entered the area of the nuns' residences and called his name, he
popped his head up from the fur mound of seventeen cats sleeping underneath the shading tree, looked at me, and then disentangled himself and
trotted over.

On the balcony above me were Māechī Wabī and her roommate, obviously amused to see me visiting Āromdī once again. The only other person
who paid such attention to the cats was a nun everyone called "Māechī
Māeo" or "Sister Cat." There were many māechī, Buddhist nuns—the honorific
is also the singular and plural noun—in the area washing their white robes
and cleaning their rooms, but there was a singular group milling around
Māechī Wabī. Curious, I absentmindedly petted Āromdī on the head only a
few times as I looked up to figure out what was going on. I watched as
Māechī Wabī took a single-edged razor blade and brought it along another
māechī's skull from forehead to neck, clearing off the black crew cut—a
month's worth of hair. The blade scraped across her friend's head with an
audible scritching noise but evidently caused no discomfort. When her head
was once again clean shaven and her eyebrows were gone, the friend rinsed
her head and face in a large aluminum bowl and then rubbed her pate vigorously, thanking Māechī Wabī. Māechī Wabī then waited for the next nun
to sit down for her monthly shaving. When I noticed that a new blade was
being used for each person, I summoned up the Thai to ask why—only to
have three māechī grin broadly at me, hold their shining blades aloft, and
chorus: "AIDS!"

1

Of course. This is modern Thailand, where HIV is spreading rapidly. The shaving procedure is bound to draw blood, and these women are educated about preventing the spread of AIDS.

Māechī Wabī is one of about one hundred residents of this Buddhist nunnery, or *samnak*, in Pāktho, a small village in the province of Rātburī, about seventy-five miles southwest of Bangkok. While it is not far from the capital of Thailand, she and her fellow māechī and the girls from around the country who attend the samnak school do not often travel there because it is not easy to reach—the train is very slow, the buses inconvenient and unreliable. Unless you were born in this village, there is not much to draw you here except this samnak, though the surrounding area, as the people here are eager to point out, is quite beautiful.

Most people in the area farm, so the fields are being worked. In the early morning hours in the beginning of the rainy season, colorful sunrises are reflected in the flooded rice fields, interrupted by the frames of mounded dirt paddy pathways. The sunsets are equally beautiful, often threatening with stunning deep purple and black clouds filling half the sky. The wind at dusk blows cool and erratic across the fields, hopping the wall surrounding this samnak and coming in through the upstairs windows of the main building, where at this time of night you would find twenty māechī and several other women meditating in darkness mitigated only by two tall yellow candles on the altar in front of them.

This huge room, the center of the most overtly religious activity of the samnak, features a red-carpeted, raised platform covering much of the floor in front of the large, ornate altar. Among the carefully organized and dusted shining symphony of mostly golden objects, a large, shimmering Buddha sits in meditation. The monk responsible for popularizing the kind of meditation many practice here also sits in meditation, simply framed in his black-and-white photograph. Windows, open for all services, line the walls; fans cover the ceilings. On the evenings of religious holidays, such as the day commemorating the Buddha's birth, death, and enlightenment, or the cremation of his body, the entire community, each holding a single candle, three sticks of incense, and at least one flower, circumambulates the large room, lighting its outside balcony.

Among them is Māechī Wabī. When she walks, she walks carefully and slowly. In meditation, she sits with her body relaxed but erect. Her back is straight, her shoulders gently sloping. Her white robes are spotless and drape diagonally from her left shoulder down to the right side of her waist, just as the similar yellow robes do on countless statues, paintings, and other representations of the Buddha. Her face is calm. Māechī Wabī's skin is light for a Thai, and her eyes are small. She is quick to laugh and to catch herself laughing, covering her broad mouth with her hand as the skin where her eyebrows would be raised in embarrassed glee. In few ways does she stand out, though her presence at the very front of the room nearest the Buddha statue and altar in any ceremony indicates that she has been ordained as a māechī for a relatively long time, though she is only twenty-seven years old.

Māechī Wābī, like the other māechī here, has "abandoned colors"— given up the colors most of us wear every day, colors that call attention to beauty and attractiveness, that respond to the desires that these māechī are trying to abandon, desires that lead away from nirvana toward more rebirths in samsara. Like all of the other māechī, she wears the standard garments closest to her body: a white tube skirt held up by a belt and a tight-fitting vest. While a tight-fitting vest is a traditional Thai undergarment, the vest Māechī Wābī wears has only one shoulder—a design unique to Buddhist monks and nuns. For the monks, it means their right shoulders are bare. For Māechī Wābī, it means that the mildly translucent white of her shirt gives no hint of anything underneath that might distract the observer from the modesty inherent to māechī. A bra strap showing underneath would be unacceptable. Over this shoulder-to-foot whiteness, Māechī Wābī wears her white long-sleeved outer shirt with the requisite simple neckline and five buttons. Covering the skirt and shirt from shoulder to foot is her draping translucent outer robe. Her covering effectively removes much of her outer individuality, as it is meant to. She is one of fifty māechī here wearing the exact same clothing.

Māechī Wābī and the other residents of this samnak schedule their lives according to the traditional lunar calendar, so the equivalent breaks in routine that laypeople take on Saturdays and Sundays are taken here on the day before and the day of important moon phases: new, full, and half-moons. Daily at 3:30 A.M., Māechī Wābī joins the other māechī to chant and meditate; the girls who attend the samnak school sleep until 5 A.M. and begin the day with fifteen minutes of physical exercise. After the 3:30 session, fifteen māechī go out on traditional Buddhist *binthabāt*, collecting food, to provide an opportunity for the villagers to develop generosity and support serious religious people in their practice. Villagers, following a tradition over 2,000 years old, wordlessly and solemnly offer a variety of foods—often wrapped in small plastic bags so the food will not become mixed in and spoiled with other food offerings in the large, traditional begging bowls. The very poor are likely to give small bags of water secured in plastic with a tightly wound rubber band. This daily contribution of food and water is small compared to the needs of the community, but the abbess is reluctant to put a greater strain on the village by allowing more māechī to go out, nor is their going out primarily motivated by samnak needs. These fifteen māechī a day allow the villagers to support Buddhism and the samnak without overly taxing them.

Later in the day, many of the māechī join the fifty young girls as they study secular subjects in the samnak high school. The girls and the māechī also have allotted times to learn traditional Thai arts and chanting and to practice meditation. The samnak schedule is strict to ensure time for study, meditation, simple religious rituals, samnak upkeep and improvements, and service to others.

I arrived at Dhammacarinī Samnak in 1995.[1] "Dhammacarinī" is a term used for women who are serious in their religious aspirations, women who take a number of vows. "Dhamma" refers to Buddhist truths; "carinī" indicates women who walk in righteousness. "Samnak" has many meanings. It usually refers to spaces such as offices, residences, or institutes, but among māechī it refers to the space of māechī—whether within male-dominated temple grounds or, as in this case, outside of temple grounds: a nunnery with no monks in residence. The majority of the population of the samnak consists of the girls and māechī who work side by side cooking, cleaning, farming, and, perhaps most significantly, studying. All-women samnaks are rare in Thailand; most māechī live in monk-dominated temples, where a few māechī cook and clean for the larger male population, which is allowed time for study and meditation. This samnak is one of only two in Thailand that run their own schools—for underprivileged girls and for māechī to study at the junior high and high school levels.

I began teaching English as a way to make myself useful as I learned more about māechī in Thailand. Māechī Wābī was among the first group of māechī whom I formally interviewed in order to write the dissertation that would complete my Ph.D. in religious studies. She was also a student in my beginning conversational English class. She had been accepted to join the samnak and study at its school, so she had come two years earlier, eager to continue the education that had been interrupted by family duties when she was twelve years old.

I write of some of the highlights of her life and the route that brought her to become a māechī and to come to the Dhammacarinī Samnak, because coming to understand Māechī Wābī can mean coming to understand māechī in modern Thailand. I also write of her life because she is living a noble, honorable, exemplary life as a Buddhist. She is not a teacher who dazzled me with pithy Buddhist truths or the sternness of a master. Her claims for spiritual development are humble; her claims for secular education are humble too—she was studying to finish high school as she ended her third decade. But after years of studying Buddhism, I found in Māechī Wābī a friend about whom I can simply and honestly claim: she lives a noble life using Buddhism as a foundation, lens, and tool. She seeks to live honorably. You could say that her fragrance, being that of a virtuous person, "travels even against the wind."

Early on in our acquaintance we agreed to an exchange: she would tell me about her life, helping me understand any difficult Thai in which she told it, while I would supplement her classroom English lessons with private ones.[2]

Chapter 1

A Young Buddhist Goes Forth

And what is suffering? . . . Birth is suffering; ageing is suffering; sickness is suffering; death is suffering; sorrow, lamentation, pain, grief, and despair are suffering; not to obtain what one wants is suffering; in short, the five aggregates affected by clinging are suffering. This is called suffering.
—*Majjhima Nikāya* 9.15

The story of Siddhattha Gotama,[1] the man who became the Buddha, is a story of a rich prince, husband, and father who enjoys the life of wealth for many years until one morning he wakes up to find the revelers of the previous night sleeping around him in disarray. Some of their mouths are open, and saliva drips out. Some are muttering to themselves in their sleep, their clothing disheveled. Some are not covered properly. Disgusted, and remembering the calm, peaceful monk he had seen once, he decides to go forth from home to homelessness, to leave the life of a householder and seek religious understanding. He is repulsed by the indulgences of the worldly life and drawn to the calm wisdom of the homeless life. After some years of religious seeking, Siddhattha Gotama sits under a tree and realizes in meditation some basic principles about how the world works and how humans are part of that. With this realization, he becomes the Buddha, or the Enlightened One.

Most Thai Buddhists know the story. They have heard it in sermons, read it in religious books—including children's and comic books—heard it on the radio and television, and seen temple murals depicting it. The stories of Māechī Wābī parallel those of Siddhattha Gotama's; they reflect a disgust with the world and an attraction to the holy life such as that of Gotama

Buddha, but they also, of course, reflect many differences, notably related to gender and socioeconomic class.

Wābī learned and loved meditation practice early in life—her introduction to meditation is one of her first memories. When she was seven or eight years old, she went to a temple with her mother on the weekly sacred moon day. She and her mother sat in a large group of people as a monk talked about the practice of "Buddho," the internal repetition of the term for "Enlightened One," referring to the Buddha. This internal repetition of "Buddho" is a popular meditation used throughout Thailand; it falls under the category of calm, or *samatha*, meditation, as distinguished from the other major form of Buddhist meditation, insight, or *vipassanā*. One must calm oneself and develop concentration (samatha), as well as use Buddhist categories to analyze one's experience (vipassanā).[2] While the lines between calm and insight meditation are not always clear, it certainly makes sense that a child would be drawn to a simple, calm meditation taught by a priest on a moon day; Wābī tried it that day and said, as she remembered the experience, "After that whenever I ran anywhere I was with 'Buddho Buddho Buddho' all the time. I ran, 'Buddho Buddho Buddho,' when I ran for fun with my friends. I was always with 'Buddho'—all the time. I liked it a lot. When I ran, repeating 'Buddho Buddho,' I was at ease (*sabāichai*). No one knew. I didn't tell anyone what I was doing." Like the Buddha, who is said to have entered a meditation state at a young age while watching his father plow a field, Wābī was quite young when she began to discover the benefits of concentration.

Perhaps if Wābī had not gone forth, if Buddhism had in the end played a smaller role in her life, this memory of early meditation experience and the comfort it brought her would have been forgotten or would have diminished in importance, excused as a childlike fascination. Māechī Wābī, however, views this as the beginning of her interest in the teachings of the Buddha, and of her experiential learning of their truths. Running about the village with her friends, silently repeating, "Buddho Buddho Buddho," brought Wābī peace, and interest in peace brought her further along the road of the Buddhist renunciant, traditionally described as going forth from home to homelessness, just as the Buddha did in leaving his palace and its pleasures.

When Wābī was about seven or eight years old, she was friends with a bright, loving girl named Porntip. Porntip's family, like hers, included children from two different fathers, but, unlike hers, the family was not split emotionally because of it. Both Porntip's and Wābī's families were poor. Wābī's family's farm had not produced enough rice, so the family had no rice to eat except that which they bought daily through a rice-sharing and storage program administered by monks in a local temple. In an effort to stretch their resources, the family often added water to the rice—sometimes an absurd amount. Wābī's mother worked hard to support her children: she worked in the fields, cared for the children, and at night she cut the hair of people over age fifty-five, without charging, as a way of "making merit."

Obviously Wābī's mother had to make money to support her children. Also obvious—to her and to other good Buddhists—was that she had to "make merit," a phrase often used among the religious. The Thai phrase (rooted in the language of the ancient Buddhist texts, Pāli) *tham būn* means "to do a good thing, to do something auspicious." It refers to performing a helpful or skillful action, one that, in the natural workings of the law of karma, cause and effect, will result in good. The Pāli word is *puñña*: auspicious or fortunate. Some actions, such as donating food to Buddhist monks and listening to someone expound on the Dhamma (Buddhist truths) simply result in good. Ideally, a person gives with no idea of return, but to give in any way is auspicious. Even if one gives to reap the karmic benefits of giving, giving is good. But most highly valued are gifts given from motivations such as joy in supporting the holy life or simply the joy in which giving necessarily results. Large gifts, such as building a temple, are of course valued highly, but intentions can make up for the smallness of a gift, hence the good merit that results from giving a bag of water to religious practitioners. As one scholar writes, "A person with nothing to give can act auspiciously by simply rejoicing in another person's giving. In Theravāda lands, this is expressed by uttering the ritualized expression *sadhū*, meaning 'it is good!', when others give."[3] As Wābī's mother had no time to go to the temple, cutting the hair of others was a way to perform the kind of auspicious act that Buddhists prize; it was a convenient way to make merit.[4]

Māechī Wābī told me about her mother at this time: "Sometimes she'd work past midnight, and get up at 3 A.M. to go buy food (*gap khāo*) to sell in the mornings and then in the evenings." In Thailand, much of the food is divided into two main groups: rice and that which goes with rice. Thus when you sit down to a Thai meal, you are apt to find a huge platter of rice (khāo) and small bowls of different foods to go with it, what are called gap khāo, or "with rice." While Wābī's family had these different foods but no rice, Porntip's family had rice but nothing to go with it. Wābī began stealing some of her family's food and giving it to Porntip to go with her rice. Looking back on the incident, she laughed at her good intentions, precociousness, and mixed feelings of right and wrong, excusing herself: "I didn't take much—just a little." In her telling of the story, it is clear that she now forgives herself for stealing from and deceiving her family when she was so young, and she looks upon it as the kind of dilemma typical in children. When she was actually doing it, however, she struggled with the ethical aspects of the situation.

Meditation and the draw to peace was one early theme in Māechī Wābī's life. Related to that was another theme, that of dissatisfaction with her family, a family that often seemed divided and whose members seemed unnecessarily harsh. Also related to this dissatisfaction was the theme of a desire to help others and to cultivate careful relationships. This story of Porntip also reveals an ethical struggle as she tried to respond compassionately to the poverty around her, in particular, the poverty of a girlfriend, without being dishonest to members of her own family. In telling the story, she also focuses on her disillusionment with the everyday world of householders, a world in which looking out for one's own is often seen as an acceptable alternative to the moment-by-moment generosity to which she aspires now as a māechī.

Porntip's father had died, and her family was larger than Wābī's. Not only that, but they lived so far from school that the children had to walk two hours each morning and two hours back home in the afternoon. Wābī was moved by the seemingly greater circumstantial suffering that Porntip's family suffered and by the obvious love that Porntip had for her siblings and her mother. In her own family, Wābī felt underappreciated, unloved, and drained of energy, so she helped Porntip's family, driven by a developing sense of compassion, her loyalty to her girlfriend, and her respect for those who help each other face the difficulties of the world by uplifting the hearts of others. Her gifts to Porntip's family also show her disillusionment with her own kin—her family clearly suffered many of the same problems that her neighbors suffered, but Wābī felt that her family members (at least her siblings) responded less helpfully to these problems. Her response to this friend in need foreshadows her later dedication to those in her life with whom she chooses to have relationships (such as her māechī friends) over those with whom she is culturally expected to have relationships (such as her family members).

Wābī's mother, upon learning of Wābī's gifts to the family, gave her permission to give those gifts, and Wābī was relieved not to have to sneak the food anymore. Clearly, Wābī's mother saw her gifts as a way her daughter could make merit, learning generosity and helping others as Wābī's mother herself did in cutting the hair of her elderly neighbors.

Māechī Wābī's disenchantment with her family and later with others is related throughout her life to the "heat" that she felt in response to the harsh tongue of her older sister. Māechī Wābī's older sister claimed that Wābī and her younger siblings, the children of Wābī's mother's second husband, were favored over the children whose father had died before the second husband arrived on the scene. Wābī said, "My older sister always said that since the coming of me and my younger siblings she had not had happiness. My father and I and my younger siblings, she said, had claimed all of our mother's love. I often thought that such a feeling made heat in the heartmind."

In Buddhism, as in most Asian religions, the heart and the mind are one; thoughts and feelings often are located in one place, called the "heartmind." In Thai, the words "heat" and "hot" have many different meanings. In this context, "heat" refers to a feeling of urgency, anxiety, negative excitability, and impatience, as opposed to the more highly valued detached calmness to which one aspires in Buddhist practice. In Buddhism, it is desire, hatred, and ignorance—highly related—that keep us in samsara, the round of rebirth and suffering in which gods, animals, humans, hell beings, and ghosts all turn. The ideal is outside of this round of rebirth—*nibbāna* (or, in Sanskrit, *nirvana*)—"the complete destruction, fading away, giving up, and relinquishing of cravings"—to use the typical phrase from the Buddhist texts. Māechī Wābī associates her family with hot, disturbed energy and the life she seeks with cool, calm energy. When the life she makes for herself as a māechī becomes hot, she explores what she can do to make it cool again.

Wābī's generosity to the seemingly cool family of Porntip reveals not only her disillusionment with her own family and her admiration of those she perceives as being more caring but her early admiration of hard work, her association of the idea of making merit by serving others, and her love of peace.

Wābī was disillusioned with the world and her family not only because of her sister's bitterness but because of her father's comings and goings. When she was young, her father left to live with another woman. For five years he did not contact any member of her family. He sent no money and wrote no letters to his wife, his three stepchildren, or his own three children. Then, with no warning, he returned. Wābī was nine years old and counts his return as among the ten most formative events of her life. "I remember . . . that day when my father returned, riding up on a bicycle. I was running around with my brother and sisters. And he said, 'Come to your father.' I didn't recognize him as my father. I ran, fleeing. I ran. I didn't remember him because he'd left when I was four or five."

Māechī Wābī referred to this incident and the situation surrounding it repeatedly during the time I lived in her samnak. She had few memories of when her father lived with the family before he left the first time, but his return to the family, his short stay, and his farewell were significant parts of her childhood. She seldom spoke of this time without crying.

She said he returned to help care for the children, that he had missed them, though he had never communicated these feelings during his absence. Before he returned to the family, he visited the older relatives of Wābī's mother to recognize publicly that his earlier departure had been wrong and to declare publicly that he wanted to come back: "He promised to care for the children and not to leave again unless it was to go forth as a monk. He wouldn't go with another wife." If he were to leave the family again, it would not be in response to the samsaric desire that brings a man to another mate. Rather, it would be in response to the same desire that inspired Gotama Buddha to leave his wife and child: the desire for religious understanding.

After Māechī Wabī's mother had had another child with him, within a year of his return, he left the family, going forth as a monk.

When I asked Māechī Wabī if, when her father had first returned, he thought he would stay long with the family, she talked about her father's lack of trust. When Wabī was nine, she heard a fight between her mother and father—her father accused her mother of having a lover. Wabī was shocked and determined to watch her mother carefully to see if what her father said was true. "I watched my mother for a long time—she didn't have another lover. She just cared for me and my siblings. Even after he went forth as a monk, he'd tell others that she had a lover, but I knew she didn't. I could watch her and know the truth. He would tell all these other people, but it wasn't true. It was a story he made up. . . . Seven, ten years after my father went forth, still my mother had no one. I knew that; I lived there. That was proof enough, wasn't it, that my father's claims were untrue? She never had another man."

Her father's departure from the family led Māechī Wabī to generalize about men: "I think all men are like this—they don't like responsibility. I don't like men. I can't try to get close to them. Maybe they won't love us. And then I wonder why they had us at all." On another occasion, Wabī said, "Children usually feel at ease with the opposite sex, you know, but I couldn't stand to be near men. The only men who'd been in my life were my brothers. The closest I got to them was when I had to ride on the back of their motorcycles to see the doctor. Besides that, I'd never been close to men— only my brothers. I didn't like them. I'm prejudiced against them. All men, they don't take responsibility—I don't like them."

These sorts of misanthropic remarks are not uncommon from Buddhist religious women through the ages. For example, a Japanese nun wrote, "I absolutely couldn't stand men! A man to me was some kind of disgusting jet-black panther."[5] They parallel similar remarks made against women by men who seek the religious life. Misogynistic statements litter the Buddhist texts, presumably in an effort to help monks appreciate the value and rewards of their religious vows of celibacy.[6] People of the opposite sex are seen as a threat to the pursuit of the religious life, so monks are encouraged not to see women as evidenced in this dialogue between Gotama Buddha and Ānanda, his gentle follower: " 'Lord, how should we act towards women?' 'Do not see them, Ānanda.' 'But if we see them, how should we behave, Lord?' 'Do not speak to them, Ānanda.' 'But if they speak to us, Lord, how should we behave?' 'Practise mindfulness, Ānanda.' "[7]

Clearly, Wabī's father's lack of dependability contributed to her fear and dislike of men. But even though I heard her speak like this about men many times, and even though she made a life for herself that involved very few men, she highly respects some men—especially monks under whom she has studied meditation and others who have seriously embraced Buddhism. I watched Māechī Wābī interact with men, and she never displayed any nervousness or fear with religious-minded men. I only saw her apprehension and "prejudice" when I walked with her on village streets and more ruffian types passed; sometimes they took an inappropriate interest in her, me, or the other māechī with whom we walked. At times like those, I watched her face transform from its usual expression of repose and calm and acceptance to a combination of fear and dread that was impossible to ignore, and I watched her glance about her as though she were seeking refuge.

Yet that generalization about Wābī's comfort with religious men and her discomfort with nonreligious men was proven wrong on one significant occasion. She had decided (evidently with the emphatic agreement of various other residents of the samnak) that I needed a haircut, so we went in search of a hair salon in the village. There were many small home salons, and it was difficult to choose between them. I made it clear to Māechī Wābī, in case there was any doubt, that I was unwilling to have a man cut my hair; I did not want that sort of physical intimacy with a man while I lived in the samnak. After all, I had taken, as all residents of the samnak do, some basic vows, including a vow against sexual misconduct; I was celibate. Māechī Wābī chose the salon and, knowing that as a Thai she would be more likely to succeed in this area, she bartered for a reasonable price. It was only after we sat down—she in the waiting area and I in the only chair appropriate for hair cutting—that we realized simultaneously that the loud, colorfully dressed, sensual woman cutting my hair was actually a male transvestite, almost certainly homosexual. I looked closely at Māechī Wābī in the mirror to see if she was catching the irony. A lot of work and walking had gone into our search for a salon with a woman who would cut my hair for a reasonable price, and that work had been for naught. I found her face composed but a little red as she tried to restrain from laughing. But even as the salon filled with other loudly flirting transvestite friends of the owner, Māechī Wābī did not show any of her usual discomfort with nonreligious men. Later, in fact, she told me how comfortable she had felt with the very feminine man who had cut my hair. The men she trusted most were not necessarily celibate or traditionally religious; they were the men from whom she was protected— men whose religious vows or sexual preferences kept them from viewing her with sexual, intimate, or romantic interest.

When Wābī's father left the family permanently, she was ten years old, with two years left of her elementary education. The seeds for her eventual going forth had been sown. Her loyalties had begun to lie with those outside of the family, people with whom she more freely chose to associate; she had seen aspects of family life that were painful to her as well as to her mother and siblings. Further, she had already begun to meditate and to recognize the benefits of that practice. And her father's departure from home to homelessness left a big question for her: What would inspire a person to leave the only life she then knew—the life of the family? She wondered why he had "thrown away" his family, why he lived as a monk, and what his feelings were in choosing that life. What were the negative feelings that drew him away from being a householder? What were the positive feelings that drew him to live as a renunciant? Her father's letting go of the family for the life of a Buddhist monk led her to consider life outside of the family and drew her to it. While it is traditional for young Thai men to go forth for a period of time in their lives, fewer do this as monks, as Wābī's father did—for life.

The departure of Wābī's father meant more burdens for her mother. With one child only two years old and two more under ten, and with no husband to help her earn the living necessary to support the children, she was forced to depend more on her children, especially on Wābī. Bearing more and more of the family burden, Wābī was in a good position to realize the restrictions and oppressions of the oft-praised life of the family. As one philosopher notes, "Subordinate status, economic dependence, denial of economic rights, rape within marriage, and wife battering are just some of the past and still-current examples of problems that family relationships have posed for women."[8] While Maechī Wābī was blessedly spared direct knowledge of the last two, she certainly experienced the first three. In the years after her father left and after she had finished her own schooling, the huge burdens of the family became hers; she slowly became aware of the less attractive aspects of family life.

After Wābī had finished sixth grade, her family required her not only to go to work making money to help support them but to care for her younger siblings as well. The family sent Wābī's oldest brother on to a secondary school, an expensive undertaking which, at the time, she and her sisters were denied. Wābī's attendance of secondary school would have meant one fewer worker in the family field, in the small food-selling business, and in caring for the younger children. While elementary schools are spread throughout the country, upper-level schools are more sparsely dispersed; the government currently only requires education through grade six, and when Wābī was young, only through grade four. Thus transportation to the secondary school and back not only meant more hours away from the work of the family but the expense of the daily truck ride. There were uniforms, books, pencils, and notebooks to be purchased as well. Poverty, the cultural standard of delegation of child care to women and girls, and the related tradition of giving greater priority to educating the oldest male over other family members led to the end of Wābī's formal education when she was twelve.

She was then surrounded by her younger siblings and by visitors to the small family-owned shop, but she also was largely alone—her playmates continued school or helped their own families, as she helped hers. Wabī worked in the fields, raising the family crops of rice and vegetables, and often riding her bicycle out to the fields alone in the lovely mornings. Then she would return home to help her mother. To supplement the family income, she sold sweets at the school she had once attended. The feelings of isolation, hard work, and lack of attraction to the family dramas that seemed to satisfy or at least involve her siblings in the household life led Wabī to explore profound questions related to the meaning of life and the answers provided by Buddhist renunciants. "I had a lot of time to consider the way of my heart because I was alone often. I thought I was very unlike the people around me because I really didn't like men, and I didn't like to chat, and I didn't like talking. I didn't like being close to others. I didn't have fun; I didn't have others around me of my age. I was still young. . . . I liked to work quietly alone. I liked to sit in meditation in the forest. I didn't feel that I would farm in my future. I didn't want to do that sort of thing any more. I didn't know what I'd do or where I'd go, but I felt often that I would not do what I saw all the people around me doing." When she told her mother about her feelings, her mother said that this was normal. "I was kind of scared by that— I didn't think it was 'just normal' for me. Farming, raising rice, raising food, it was the same story again and again, there was nothing better. It was boring. What was all this? 'This is all normal, this is what we have to do,' they'd say. And I'd think, this isn't normal, this isn't what we have to do!"

Dissatisfied with what was considered "normal" life and afraid of other aspects of that life, she worked in the service of her family without reward. "I felt it was odd not having anything better. We eat, work, sleep, eat, work, sleep. I'd asked my friends what they had to do, and they told me they had to care for their families, to care for those they loved, to have children. But I was scared of these things—scared to have a family, scared to have a life like my mother—who cared for all these children alone—I was scared of marrying, having all these children, and then having my husband run away for a second wife, leaving me to care for all these kids—I was scared of the stories of the world. . . . I was scared of living alone, caring for a bunch of kids as my mother had had to do when my father left."

Though Wabī was only twelve, now that she was out of school many social forces were working to compel her to marry and build a family. She hardly had a choice to do anything else; with societal forces so strong and consistent, there were no other options in any substantial sense of the word. Wabī, however, was ensuring that her life would be different from the lives of those around her. A woman with aspirations outside of the compulsion to marry, notes one feminist, often has or forces an "unconscious 'fall' into a condition where vocation is possible and out of the marriage plot." In relation to this "fall," a woman may sense an inarticulate call to something outside of the life of one who puts "a man at the center of one's life and [allows] to occur only what honors his prime position." Such a woman may be unable to identify the call clearly, and those around her may decide that she has "been dealt a poor hand of cards," but in fact she is "forming . . . a life in the service of a talent felt, but unrecognized and unnamed."⁹ This was the case of Māechī Wābī—although she was dissatisfied with her own life and the lives of the people around her, she was as yet unsure what else there might be, what other path she might take. In the meantime, she defined herself religiously more and more, removing herself from the norm: the possibility of marriage.

While Wābī's workload increased and her sense of the worth of the family life declined, some of the many facets of her father's decision to leave the family and go forth in the manner of Gotama Buddha became more clear to her. Wābī's mother had had three children with her first husband, who was long gone by the time Māechī Wābī was conscious enough of the family situation to ask about him. She was born from the marriage to a man her mother consistently described as "good." When he left the family to live with another woman, Māechī Wābī's mother explained that their own karma had led to his absence and the sudden lack of financial and emotional support. The natural order of their lives was tied to the moral order in the order of karma—thus removing individual responsibility and blame from husband and father. Karma seen in this way helps as one tries to accept one's lot in life. Her father's departure and the need for Māechī Wābī and her mother to work so hard was their fate, a fate decreed by their wrongdoings in this life and in earlier lives. In Māechī Wābī's mother's interpretation, the father's second departure did not reflect poorly on him—he chose a highly regarded spiritual path. (As one thinker notes, "It is not mothers who free women from their fathers."¹⁰)

While one might be horrified by Wābī's father's abandonment of his family, one might recognize or even admire him following in Gotama Buddha's footsteps. Siddhattha Gotama left his wife and child to pursue a religiously significant life.¹¹ When I asked other māechī about the tension between fatherly responsibilities and going forth, most were uncomfortable and quiet on the issue; they were reluctant to find fault with Gotama Buddha for deserting his family, yet they had difficulty accepting his desertion as morally exemplary. Those who talked about this issue with me indicated that the financial stability of the family gave Gotama Buddha the freedom to go forth; his wife and son were provided for.

While Māechī Wābī never explicitly condemned her father for his choice, she once discouraged her sister from following his example. Her sister had married and had had a child, and she came with Wābī's father to visit Māechī Wābī, considering going forth as a māechī. Māechī Wābī objected: "She had a baby to take care of—that baby was still under a year old, still red. She was

going to give that baby to my mother, but I thought my mother had already
had enough of her own children, had already cared for them for years. It
wasn't fair to saddle her with this other child who wasn't even hers. If my
sister had worked hard first, and taken care of her child, then okay, [she
could] go forth. But she needed to teach the child, raise the child, prepare the
child for its future and then she could go forth, not before." Her sister left the
samnak without going forth, seeing clearly that Māechī Wābī thought that her
obligations to the child disallowed her to do so.

Wābī's responsibilities grew as she entered her teens and as her siblings
had children of their own, and her consideration of the lives of those around
her deepened. She was exhausted and often thought of death. "In the early
mornings, I'd have to get my younger siblings to go with me and go get a
bus to get the food to sell. My younger brother was a wanderer—he had no
mindfulness and would just walk anywhere. I was constantly worried that
he'd fall into a ditch or something. I had to watch him closely. After I'd get
the food, I'd have to keep the younger ones with me and have them close or
else they might hurt themselves. He might just walk into a pond or something. He loved just walking without thinking. I had to think about the kids
constantly, and I was tired all the time, and I didn't want this for my own
future. I was tired all the time." The hard work and isolation left her with a
large question: " 'Why must all people die?' I wondered."

During this time she took up the pious practice of wearing white and
observing more religious vows on holy days. In general, she tried to ob-
serve religious precepts more strictly, to live an admirable Buddhist life.
Māechī Wābī began behaving more and more like a māechī, and she had
experiences that supported her turn toward the religious life. For example,
shaving one's head is a significant event in one's initial going forth, a
procedure repeated once a month on the day before the full moon as long
as one remains a monk or māechī. Māechī Wābī told me, "One time I heard
the sound of a razor scraping across a skull. I hadn't gone forth yet, but I
heard this sound of shaving. Craeck, craeck, craeck. All the time. It was
very loud. I asked my mother, who's shaving their head? My mother said
I was alone in hearing that noise—no one else heard it. Where was it
coming from? Craeck, craeck, craeck. At that time I had long hair; I hadn't
cut it yet. I felt very odd, very alone. I heard things that others did not hear;
I felt things other people did not feel. I often heard that sound of shaving,
craeck, craeck, craeck, for a long time—for about two years before I went
forth as a māechī. The noise was very loud, but when I asked others if they
heard it, they just laughed."[12]

When I asked Māechī Wābī how she felt about these incidents, she said,
"I felt sad, sorry—not good. I heard these things that others didn't hear. I felt
sad. There were a lot of things like this, so I kept them to myself. I didn't

tell others." The more isolated she felt in her religiosity, the more she turned from her family, while simultaneously trying to convince them to follow her. She wore white and followed more Buddhist precepts on the holy day of the week, and daily she led her family and friends in evening chanting in her house at the altar she had built. These visible practices allowed her to present herself as a model for a different kind of life, one with values different from the mainstream. Instead of a young girl in the market for a husband, she was a woman dedicating her time to spiritual activities. Further, when Māechī Wābī was sixteen years old, she went forth as a māechī for the first time— for seven days, bringing her mother to the temple with her. She had finished sixth grade at age twelve and had worked hard for four years to help support her family. During those four years, Buddhism had played a larger and larger role in her life. Outside of her religious practices, her life revolved around caring for the children and selling food to help support the family. The time as a māechī was a welcome break.

Like men who go forth as monks for a short time, some women go forth as māechī briefly. Wābī went forth for seven days for a number of reasons, including as a gāebūn, the fulfilling of a vow or the making of a thankful offering. Māechī Wābī explained, "It's a tradition in Isān, Northeast Thailand. It was fulfillment of a vow. When we're not well, or we have some problem, we of Isān will go forth." Māechī Wābī had had difficulties with her throat, a painful illness that sometimes did not allow her to speak. (I once explored out loud to her the metaphorical implications of a problem that led to her silence and also to nunnery life, ripe with possibilities for analysis. Most obviously, I noted that perhaps living as a householder she could not speak because what she most had to say were criticisms of the householder life—something that those around her could not hear. Māechī Wābī looked at me as though I had gone crazy, but the next day she came back and said that I might be right.) The throat problem did not disappear after the seven days, but as Māechī Wābī said, "That doesn't mean I wasn't supposed to fulfill the vow. And it was the first real happiness I had ever known. . . . I didn't have to spend any money. We walked collecting food (binthabāt) every morning and ate that. I felt peace, cool."

The samnak she went to, unlike Dhammacarinī, where she lives now and where I met her, was a serious meditation samnak. Whereas Dhammacarinī has its school and a variety of activities throughout the day, this samnak encouraged only meditation. There was no talking and no chanting. Residents were encouraged to sleep only a little. The nap is a common practice in tropical areas, where afternoon heat can be paralyzing, and also in contemplative samnaks, but this samnak allowed no sleeping during the day and only three hours at the most at night. "Some nights we didn't sleep at all," Māechī Wābī said. The meditation was the calm one of "Buddho."

Going forth in fulfillment of a vow is sometimes not respected because it is "based on beliefs which some would argue are not totally in accordance with orthodox Buddhist teachings, i.e., the power of deities to intervene on one's behalf to effect changes in circumstances which might be held to reflect one's karmic state."[13] I also have heard laypeople less involved in Buddhism criticize vow-inspired going forth. Māechī Wabī, however, views the fulfillment of a vow as a respectable reason to go forth. And her willingness to go forth because of her physical health led her to religious happiness, the greatest happiness she recognizes, thus justification for her reason is even less necessary. Other māechī I spoke with referred to the fulfillment of a vow as a perfectly acceptable motive to go forth.

More generally, however, when I asked Māechī Wabī why she was interested in becoming a māechī at all, she referred to her bitterness, confusion, and curiosity about her father's going forth: "I wanted to go forth to find out why my father had thrown [his children] away. Why did he live this way? What feelings did he have living this way? I never knew his real feelings." This aspect of her desire to go forth adds a dimension to some of the scholarship done on women renunciants in the early Theravāda texts. For example, Liz Wilson argues against earlier scholars' assessment of Mahāpajāpati, the woman who raised Siddhattha Gotama, and other early women renunciants as being independent. According to the texts, Mahāpajāpati's husband dies, and she and a large number of persons go forth. In the texts, these women ask Gotama Buddha to be allowed to go forth as bhikkhunī, the female equivalent of the male bhikkhu, monk, but he refuses to allow the women to go forth—twice. Only after they enlist the aid of Gotama Buddha's gentle-hearted disciple, Ānanda, are they allowed to go forth, legitimately living their lives as religious women. Thus some scholars have argued that Mahāpajāpati and the women who accompanied her to seek the religious life are independent women—they sought their rights to ordain with tenacity. Against this conception, Liz Wilson argues that Mahāpajāpati "places herself in the care of her son. The five hundred women of the Sakyan clan who accompany her into the *sangha* (the community of bhikkhunī and bhikkhu, nuns and monks) are also reacting to a loss of male authority in their lives: their husbands have all renounced the world and left them virtual widows." Wilson is correct to balance analyses that do not take into account the brahmanical conception of women and how that affects women renunciants, but Māechī Wabī's statements remind us not to simplify such assessments too much. While she may not have been a fully developed, independent woman—whatever that is—she was not simply reacting to "a loss of male authority." She watched her father go forth and was curious about his experiences as a renunciant.[14]

When Māechī Wabī went forth for the first time, her mother went to stay with her, going forth as a *phrām*. In Thailand, a phrām is a person who wears white. Usually, for women, this means a white skirt, a white blouse, and a small white robe. The blouse (unlike that of the māechī) is sometimes very ornate and expensive, made of or punctuated by lace—and sometimes with shorter sleeves than the usual blouse of a māechī. The robe does not fall almost to the ground, like that of māechī; it often is only a foot wide when folded and arranged over the left shoulder in a manner similar to that of the māechī. A phrām does not shave her head or eyebrows and may take a smaller number of vows; in general, a phrām is not expected to follow the stricter code of the māechī with its rules of deportment and other behavior. Translating phrām as "novice" would be inappropriate because that term leads one to believe that the person plans to go forth as a māechī when in fact often this is not the case at all. While going forth as a phrām is sometimes a step toward going forth as a māechī, more often it is not.[15]

The basic vows with which any Buddhist is familiar are the five precepts: to abstain from killing, stealing, sexual misconduct, false speech, and intoxicants. A Phrām takes these five precepts and sometimes three more: to abstain from eating after noon and before dawn; to abstain from dancing, singing, listening to music or seeing shows, and wearing perfumes; and to abstain from using high chairs and beds. Māechī usually take all eight, as do many laypeople on each week's holy day. The other traditional set of precepts is the set of ten—which includes these eight precepts but is divided differently, with one additional precept—that of abstaining from handling gold or silver.[16] Some māechī take these ten, as do male novices.

Often a person goes forth temporarily as a phrām (for one week, one month, three months, or so), as Wābī's mother did, simply because she wants to have an experience as close to that of a māechī as possible without having to shave her head. If a woman wants to understand more of the religious life, she might take time from work or family to go forth as a phrām, keeping her hair and eyebrows so as not to attract attention when she returns to her home and work later. Wigs are expensive in Thailand, and the appearance of a nonreligious woman without hair is rare. So if a woman were to go forth and shave her head, she would be faced with awkward situations as her hair grew out after the period she spent living the religious life. This is what Wābī's mother did, what Wābī did on many moon days in her young adulthood, and what I did while I lived at Dhammacarinī Samnak.

Māechī Wābī compared the time to a vacation for her and her mother; others took care of the household work that she found meaningless, while she and her mother engaged in comparatively meaningful religious work. The period was even more special, since at no other time had she and her mother enjoyed anything similar to a vacation. When Māechī Wābī reflected on the time, she could not restrain herself from rapture. Her eyes were wide: "I had never before felt the feelings I felt during those seven days: peace, contentment, joy, coolness in my heart. In all my life, sixteen years, I'd never felt such things. It was the very first time. I knew then why a person like my father would go forth."

When the seven days came to an end, Wābī reluctantly returned home with her mother; it was clear that she was happy with her taste of the religious life. "I felt very good; my suffering was much less." The problem with her throat lessened (perhaps partially because in the circumstance of a contemplative samnak she had fewer things to say that would be difficult for her compatriots to hear), but that was not the main point for her. Her bodily suffering was a hint of larger suffering: "My throat was sore, for a long time. But really, it was always more than that. People would think that I had a sore throat, but I always knew it was more than that. It was the feeling of being bored of the world, bored of the family, bored of so many things, bored of caring for children. Bored. . . . I disrobed after the seven days, but I knew something had changed—it was the greatest happiness I'd had. [People who live in temples] work in the temple, you know—they do many of the same things that people do outside, but they do it while training their heartminds in the religion of Buddhism. I said to myself then, if I have good merit, if I am virtuous, I will have a chance to go forth again—this time, to go forth forever, until I die." Māechī Wābī watched the young women and men around her pair up to marry, but she resisted the pattern. She saw the idea of a compatible marriage and satisfying work as a wife and mother as exactly that: an idea, not a reality. "I didn't want to have a family as others did because I just couldn't. Suppose I had a child? I wondered. Could I care for the child as well as my mother cares for children? I thought, No, I can't. I can't set my heart on doing that sort of thing as my mother does. Care for children? I just couldn't. And my heartmind was hot, could my heart be cool in caring for children? No, it would be hot."

When she was about seventeen, a young man took an interest in her and asked her parents if they could marry. "I didn't like this at all," she said. "He liked to buy things and he'd seen me selling things, taking care of my siblings and such; he wanted to marry me. I said no, no way. My mother accepted this. I told [my mother] if I was made to marry I'd flee and go forth as a māechī. My mother said fleeing wasn't necessary—I didn't have to marry him." Many young women I spoke with did not have mothers who would have spared them the attention of a man. Most women, especially less educated village women, were (and are) expected to marry.

Māechī Wābī watched her sister return pregnant to her mother's house; the father fostered doubts about whether the child was really his or that of some other man. Māechī Wābī watched again as her sister gave birth to a child in her family's house with no guarantee that the father would help raise the child. She watched, remembering her mother giving birth and her father departing, leaving her mother to care for the infant as well as for the other children. The situation was complicated by her brother's lack of acceptance and compassion, his concern for the family's reputation. When she told me of this incident, she laughed loudly, looking directly into my eyes: "Giving birth, you know, having a child when there's no father means that the woman is bad. She'll give the family a bad reputation. But I empathized with her. I empathized with the child, too—who couldn't know what was going on. And I empathized with my sister. She was my older sister. But my brother remained angry. He didn't accept her—he wanted her out of the house."

Her sister soon thereafter got together with another man, and Māechī Wābī watched her sister's quick change of interests and her own increasing workload. "She didn't think. She wanted a child, wanted a baby. At that time I was living, you know, with my older brother's daughter on one hip (here Māechī Wābī mimicked carrying a child on her left side, braced at her hip), and my older sister's daughter on the other hip. I was tired, tired. Taking care of these two children." She laughed an overwhelmed, amazed laugh. "Taking care of what kids were there and selling things in the store. It was pretty rough, keeping the kids under control and selling things. Difficult. . . . Caring for my younger siblings and nephews and nieces! But I empathized with them. I loved them too. [My siblings] didn't help care for the children; they didn't help sell things for the store. They bought stuff for themselves only. They went here and there for fun as they liked. If they didn't help, I knew I'd go forth. I was tired. I was tired. You have to care for kids a lot until they're past seven or eight years old; and I'd cared for them for a long time. Now I was looking after these other two babies. I knew I'd go forth."

Neither Māechī Wābī's mother nor her siblings, nor her father wholeheartedly approved of her going forth. Her mother, she claimed, "didn't want me to go because there was too much to do at home. My older sisters had married already and moved elsewhere. And here I was, going forth. The Thai way is for the child to stay home and help mother." But she was dissatisfied with the life of the householder: "I was hot all the time; I was upset all the time. . . . I'd go to a temple and give money, and it still didn't satisfy me; I'd go to another temple and I'd give some money—only [when giving to temples] did I feel at ease. Only then did I feel like I had happiness." Only in engaging in the righteous acts of making merit was she at peace. When she explained her desire to go forth, her mother cried. "My mother felt that if I left she'd have no one. My younger siblings were still young, and my older siblings all had their own houses—they didn't live in our house." Wābī wrestled with her sense of obligation to her mother: "But I just couldn't live there anymore. I was hot all the time. I never had any happiness. I kept thinking of when I'd go forth."

When Wābī was considering going forth, she had had little contact with her father for some years. He was then living in a different village as head monk of a district, where he taught Pāli and Dhamma (Buddhist teachings), two government-standardized areas of Buddhist education. The third area is Buddhist philosophy (*abhiddhamma*). There are three degrees offered in the first two areas, each requiring about one year of study: beginning, intermediate, and advanced. In Pāli, there are nine levels of competency.

Wābī and her father had neither corresponded nor visited. When he invited her younger sister to come and live at the temple and to earn her high school degree, Wābī accompanied her in the move, seeing her father again for the first time in years. Her sister was to stay with the one māechī there, cooking for the monks during the day and studying for her degree at night.

Wābī was hurt that her father had not asked her to come live at the temple and to continue her own education. Why was her sister chosen for the gift of education and not her? She had already gone forth once and tasted the fruits of meditation, however, and at the time she saw meditation and merit making as the two most rewarding aspects of life. She did not think that she was capable of studying for a higher degree. Her strengths, she thought, lay elsewhere than in worldly education: "When I was there with [my sister], I helped out with the temple. I already liked to make merit—I already had experienced happiness [in meditation]. But I was still a greedy person . . . I was greedy to go forth. It made my life unhappy and difficult—I had no time to meditate. . . . I wanted my parents's permission to go forth."

Māechī Wābī has never asked her father why he did not take her into his temple to allow her to continue her education as he did her younger sister, but she thinks it simply never occurred to him. By the time he was in a position to make such an offer, Māechī Wābī was older and had discontinued her education four years earlier. Further, as a woman who was no longer in school and who had remained unmarried, it was assumed that her duties lay in caring for the children of the family, as she had been doing.

When her mother grudgingly gave permission for her to go forth, Māechī Wābī approached her father for advice. As a person who had gone forth himself, her father understood the appeal, but initially he too was against her leaving home: "He pointed out that going forth as a māechī is not the same as going forth as a monk. Thai society does not accept māechī." The only māechī her father had known was the one who lived at his temple. The temple had 500 monks and novices (*sāmanen*) and only one māechī.[17] "She worked every day in the kitchen, cooking for all those people, she had to cook breakfast and lunch. The novices helped, but everyone else had to study. It was difficult. And she never chanted—she only cooked." The māechī her father knew served the monks, having little time to develop spiritual practices such as chanting.

After expressing these concerns, however, Wābī's father supported her decision. He recommended she go live at a temple near Bangkok known for its strength in insight meditation where a student of his had gone, and he offered to take her there. Now Wābī could take the step from the simpler calm meditation of Buddhism to the more complex insight meditation. Neither she nor her father, however, knew much about the lives of māechī. They had seen only a few: her father knew only the hardworking cook at his temple; Māechī Wābī had seen only a few outside of the temple walls and only that one māechī cook within the temple walls. She had never spoken at length with a māechī. She was unwilling to return to where she and her mother had gone the year before because practice there was limited to meditation. Reading books and other sorts of learning were not allowed.

Neither Māechī Wābī nor her father suspected that living as a māechī might require money; going forth as a monk did not require money outside of the ornate ceremonies, and as there was no ornate ceremony for māechī, neither had considered the issue of finances. Thus they had a rude surprise when they arrived at the temple near Bangkok and asked about Wābī living there as a māechī: "I was told that if you want to be a māechī near Bangkok, you have to have money. You have to have a lot of money or else you can't live there. . . . I had 270 baht at the time [when I left Isān]. The price of getting to the temple was 115 baht, so I arrived with almost nothing. I had nothing."

The rent and utility costs for a māechī to stay at the temple were 500 baht a month, and Wābī had, by the time she arrived there, only 155 baht. She tried not to panic as she considered her alternatives—should she simply throw herself into the bustling materialism of Bangkok in the hope of making money in order to go forth? Should she return home to work and save money? Returning home meant more months of living a life that she found meaningless in order to save enough money to go forth; going to her father's temple meant living with and cooking for monks, both of which she found unhelpful to her practice. "I had no place to go. My father was a monk—I didn't want to live with monks. . . . I only wanted to live together with women."

Further, she would not have received the education at her father's temple that she felt she needed as a person who has gone forth. She knew of no other place to go. "I wanted to go forth, to live as a māechī. I would go anywhere; it didn't matter. I just wanted to live as a māechī. I was very, very desirous of living as a māechī." A māechī who lived at the temple near Bangkok suggested Wābī practice meditation for seven days, going forth as a phrām. So Wābī decided to remain there for seven days, meditating on her problem and hoping that a solution would present itself to her. Her father left her, returning to his temple, and for the first time in her life she was alone, isolated from all relatives.

Chapter 2

Who Gets to Drink in the Dhamma and How

> Just as a woman—or a man—young, youthful, fond of ornaments,
> with head bathed, having received a garland of lotuses, jasmine,
> or roses, would take it in both hands and place it on the head,
> so too there are clansmen who have gone forth out of faith . . .
> not drivellers. These, on hearing the . . . discourse on the
> Dhamma, drink it in and eat it, as it were, by word and thought.
> Good indeed it is that he makes his fellows in the holy life
> emerge from the unwholesome and establish themselves in the
> wholesome.
>
> —*Majjhima Nikāya* 5.33

Māechī Wābī's difficulties when she simply wanted to go forth as a māechī make perfect sense as one of the results of the ongoing problems related to Buddhism which, like most of the world's religions, has deeply ingrained patterns of sexism that daily affect the religious lives of both women and men. Thai women seeking to focus their lives on religion are in an entirely different situation than Thai men seeking to do the same.

Many young Thai men become monks for a short period of time upon reaching early adulthood; others go forth to remain monks for the rest of their lives. Families of young Thai men going forth as monks temporarily or permanently almost universally support the decision and often throw huge parties the night before and then orchestrate elaborate ceremonies as the monks welcome the young men into their order. A young boy or man from a poor family may best prepare for his future and his family's by going forth as a monk and guaranteeing himself an education and a place in a well established

24

hierarchy—the hierarchy of monks. Boys in the countryside who have economic and familial problems can be sent to live in a temple, and the monks there care for the boys; these boys ordain as *sāmanen*. As sāmanen they take ten precepts, live and are schooled in the temple, and have daily duties related to cooking, cleaning, and maintaining the temple. So a boy whose family cannot afford to care for and educate him may go forth as a sāmanen and receive a free education even past the high school level and may in that time make helpful friends from wealthy families as they come to stay in the monastery for a period.

Significantly fewer girls and women go forth than boys and men, and of those who do, most have little if any family support for and recognition of the event. Reasons for this vary. On the one hand, māechī lack the textually recognized status that monks have. While the categories of phrām and māechī seem to parallel those of sāmanen and bhikkhu, in some ways they do not. Buddhist texts recognize four categories of followers of the Buddha: *bhikkhunī* (nuns, taking several hundred vows) and *bhikkhu* (monks, taking several hundred vows), laywomen and laymen (taking five to ten precepts). In the Theravāda Buddhism of Thailand, three of the categories remain strong, but the bhikkhunī or official nun lineage died out in the twelfth century. While one needs only monks to perform the ordination of a monk, one needs both monks and bhikkhunī for the ordination of a bhikkhunī. There being no bhikkhunī in the Theravāda tradition, some say that women cannot go forth as bhikkhunī—they cannot be recognized as Buddhist nuns.

Another reason fewer women go forth as māechī than men go forth as monks and why so few enjoy family support of the choice is that unlike Thai boys and men becoming monks, girls and women do not enjoy the possibility of an education by going forth, nor are they guaranteed a place in a hierarchy by going forth. And as far as most people know, māechī are simply poor women who have lost in love and have nothing better to do with their lives, thus it is not surprising that the families of the māechī I knew objected to the woman's desire to become a māechī and did not attend the ceremony as a group. Usually only one or two members attended, if anyone.

If Wābī had been a young man wanting to become a monk, it would have been a very easy process, one with which many people are familiar. Temples carpet the country, so even if Wābī's own family had been unfamiliar with the ordination process, countless local monks would have been ready to provide information. She would have had many resources available to her to learn what needed to be done. Comparatively fewer women-dominated samnaks exist. Māechī are rarer than monks, and most live on the periphery of monk-dominated temples, making merit by serving them. In sum, everyone knows what a man needs to become a monk, but very few know what a woman needs to become a māechī. Everyone has at least a vague idea of how monks spend their time, but very few have a realistic conception of how māechī live.

On the other hand, however, if she had been a man, the attractions to the religious life may well have included those related to material concerns and status. Becoming a monk is a way to get ahead in Thai society, so men who may or may not have inclinations toward living careful, reflective, ethical lives that embrace the best aspects of Buddhism become monks, thus diluting the sincerity of a group that officially aspires to go "forth out of faith from the home life into homelessness, who are not fraudulent, deceitful, treacherous, haughty, hollow, personally vain, rough-tongued, loose-spoken; who are guarded in their sense faculties, moderate in eating, devoted to wakefulness, concerned with recluseship, greatly respectful of training, not luxurious or careless, who are keen to avoid backsliding, leaders in seclusion, energetic, resolute, established in mindfulness, fully aware, concentrated, with unified minds, possessing wisdom, not drivellers," as a passage from the Theravāda texts elucidates.[1]

Currently māechī lack many of the advantages of persons gone forth and also lack the advantages of laypeople. For example, unlike monks, māechī do not unquestionably receive medical treatment for free or discounted rates. They are not consistently excused from paying bus fares, nor are they customarily given the reserved seats for clergy on buses. A male government worker is by law invited to take three months on one occasion during his employment to go forth as a monk; his job is not in danger. A female government worker who wants to develop spiritually, on the other hand, risks losing her job by taking such a leave; no legal protection of her employment is offered to her if she chooses to go forth as a māechī during a rainy season. In these ways, māechī are not recognized as persons gone forth but are treated as laypeople; in other ways, however, they are treated as persons gone forth, such as at the polls. Monks do not vote, māechī who try to vote are refused.

Because of the many material and status concerns that may motivate a young man to become a monk and because of various scandals, there is in Thailand a perceived decay of the *sangha*, technically the community of Buddhists, but usually seen as simply monks. Monks are often seen as overly traditional, political, hierarchical, and unresponsive to the problems of fast-changing Thailand. Media coverage of deceptive monks, more frequent in recent years, leads people to consider monks as being not only irrelevant but in some cases offensive. Accusations against monks such as the vastly popular Phra Yantra, whose many followers are trying to make sense of the several charges of rape against him, have led to growing questioning of and disenchantment with representatives of Buddhism.

So although it is easier to become a monk in Thailand and to get an education in Buddhism as one does so, it is perhaps more difficult to be a sincere and careful monk in Thailand motivated less by political and materialistic concerns. While it is more difficult to become a maechī in Thailand and to get an education in Buddhism, one is certainly less likely to be motivated by political and materialistic concerns when one chooses to go forth as a maechī. Thus maechī suffer for their lack of societal recognition, while monks suffer for their great societal recognition. Further, Thai Buddhism, defined largely by men and powerful in its influence on Thai society, despite growing skepticism about the motivations and ethics of monks, is unbalanced by its lack of input from religious women and blinded by its own power.

The bias toward conceiving Buddhism in Thailand as the monks, as the sangha, is carried on in Western scholarship: little is said in scholarship of Thai women's spiritual development. Most scholarship on Buddhism in Thailand concerns what men are doing, often focusing on the government-defined and government-catalogued Buddhism—a hierarchy of ordained men making up what is sometimes called "establishment Buddhism."[2] This group is, of course, just one kind of Buddhism in Thailand, a kind in which women cannot yet play a role.

So what are the religious possibilities for Buddhist women in Thailand? The most famous scholarly debate on this topic is that between Charles F. Keyes and A. Thomas Kirsch. Kirsch sets aside concern about the spiritual path of women, and Keyes sees it as being available in Thailand through motherhood. Kirsch claims that, "In Thai society women's religious roles in general and Buddhist roles (e.g., the 'nunhood') in particular are not only poorly developed but are also not highly regarded."[3] The highest religious role in Thai society, Kirsch notes, is that of a monk, a male ascetic who gives up attachment to the world. Women cannot aspire to this role in their current lives—at least in part, writes Kirsch, because they are considered inherently more attached to the world than are men in Thai culture. Women are seen as being more strongly related to samsara, the round of rebirth. Men are perceived as being less related to samsara and so are more easily associated with the ultimate goal of Buddhist practice: nibbāna.

According to Keyes, however, pious Buddhist women can aspire to be mother/nurturers, a role admired and respected in Thailand. The rural cultural texts that Keyes examines show, he claims, "the relationship of woman as mother to that supremely cultural product, the Buddhist religion."[4] Women nurture Buddhism by providing sons who go forth as monks and by feeding monks, argues Keyes, and he compares the temporary going forth of a young Thai man to the lying in of a new mother, when she is required to lie by the household fire and ingest only certain medicinal foods.[5] "A basic status change occurs . . . when a woman gives birth to a child; from that point on she will be known by the title 'mother' by all."[6] A boy who goes forth as a monk is considered "ripe" when he becomes a householder—he is ripe for marriage, ready to accept the responsibilities of family life. A woman who gives birth is now similarly complete and ready for responsibilities. So the only religious possibility of a woman in Thailand is to become a mother.

Not to become a māechī? Keyes notes the existence of māechī, calling their role one of "lay devotee" and dismissing them in importance by citing one scholar's claim that they are often called "elderly, poor, and without kin to take care of them."[7] He notes further that other scholars report that māechī are not a field of merit—one does not gain a more positive reward by giving to māechī than by giving to any other person, whereas giving to monks gains one a more positive reward than giving to non-monks.[8] Of the women who formally drop lay roles and devote their time, and sometimes their lives, to a spiritual quest outside of familial obligations, Keyes brings them up only to dismiss them by defining them as laypeople who are not members of the mainstream, who are not exemplary.[9]

Popular discourse in Thailand reveals similarly varying perspectives on women's spiritual development. On the one hand, most Thais I met through channels not related to māechī were surprised to learn that I would be interested in māechī—clearly because they did not consider them worthy of study. Understanding that my project involved learning about Buddhism, they recommended that I turn to monks, the agreed-upon experts. When I explained that I was interested in women and Buddhism, they often simply asked why I was interested in that. Sometimes they explained that in Thailand women's duties in relation to Buddhism are to sustain the monks, the true practitioners. One particularly exasperating conversation began when I asked one monk about the relation of women to Buddhism and he replied, identifying Buddhism with monks and monks with recognized sangha, "Women are very helpful to the sangha. They can help the sangha very much because they can do things that monks cannot do, like cook." Neither of the two māechī who were with the monk and me at the time of this conversation—sitting right there with us—lived among monks. Neither cooked for monks. One lived in a samnak made up of women only; the other lived alone in an apartment. (It is rare for a māechī to live alone, outside the walls of a temple or samnak, but this particular māechī preferred the independence of living alone, stating that she did not want to have to ask an abbot or abbess for permission to leave her abode every time she had business that took her out, a standard code of conduct in temples and samnak.) When I indicated these two māechī beside us and asked how women such as these serve Buddhism, he said, "It is the same, they can cook for the monks, too." He laughed and continued, "You know what we call monks, yes? The belly of Buddhism." He did not see any discrepancy between his words and the reality sitting right there in front of him. Another monk noted that in Thailand "a woman's power is in birth, and māechī are not exercising their power . . . they've failed at it. And that's the stereotype: heartbroken, old maids."

A Thai professor of social work I met astonished me with her lengthy emotional diatribe against māechī. They are lazy, they are ignorant, and they have no energy for work, she claimed. When I asked her about her experience with or research on māechī, I found that she had none. She recognized no conflict in the two points she had made—that she had a bad impression of māechī, and that she had nothing but hearsay on which to base her impression. Another well educated Bangkok woman, devoted to feminism, expressed her opinion of māechī by responding to the going forth of a famous feminist activist by shaking her head in frustration and saying, "Well, she just gave up, gave up! She was defeated!" This woman could not imagine the going forth of a māechī as a courageous, much less a courageously feminist, act. For her, a woman goes forth only when there is nothing else that she can do.

On the other hand, the people I met through māechī, often women who came to make merit by giving to māechī, talked to me excitedly about how impressive the māechī were—how seriously rooted in spiritual practice they are, what generous gifts they give to their local communities and to Thailand and Buddhism. These māechī are clearly considered fields of merit. Some samnaks such as Dhammacarinī regularly send groups of māechī out on early morning binthabāt; most welcome groups of people at least once a week to serve the midday meal; most are somehow involved in local funerals; and all receive deliveries of fruit, rice, and other foods and gifts from pious Buddhists. Some people whom I met through māechī saw them as holding a unique role in Thailand's spiritual as well as economic development. Monks, they said, monitored by the government and often motivated by competition for higher positions in the monastic administrative hierarchy, lost the true spiritual gifts of Buddhism. Māechī, on the other hand, ignored and with no legitimated hierarchy to climb, could focus their lives on nobler activities such as meditation and helping others, especially helping women and children who are so often ignored by development concerns.

When I turned to Thai media reports, I found what seems to be a similar disparity between those who did and did not have contact with māechī. A survey of ten years of newspaper articles revealed that those on specific māechī were generally admiring (becoming more so in more recent years), while those on māechī as a social category (such as articles addressing whether māechī should have the same privileges as monks) were less so. The more abstract the focus, the less complimentary the report. It is possible that newspaper reporters who had less or no direct contact with māechī wrote less complimentary reports. P. Van Esterik notes this as well: "While individual [mãechī] may be admired for their good acts or meditation skills, as a category they are not particularly admired or respected."[10] In short, if a person had little or no contact with mãechī, that person often considered them unworthy of note or worthy only of derision. Those who had contact with mãechī, however, often had very favorable opinions.

The view of the all-male sangha as corrupt has been represented in the media too. Newspaper articles on monks have become increasingly less complimentary over the years. While more and more articles about mãechī focused on the achievements of individual mãechī, more and more articles on monks have focused on incidents of fraud and sexual misconduct. In 1989, the issue of monk misconduct was so well recognized that quite a stir was created when the periodical *Krungthep 30* represented the problem on its cover with a picture of a smiling young man in a monk's robe (with his head but neither his mustache nor eyebrows shaved) sporting a personal stereo, carrying an issue of *Playboy*, and holding his right hand in the sign symbol for "love."

In light of popular opinion and media coverage, I wanted to gain a better understanding of the history of mãechī in Thailand. How did Mãechī Wãbī and the difficulties she had going forth fit into the big picture of mãechī in Thailand? What heights and valleys were the terrain of mãechī in the past, and where did Mãechī Wãbī fit in the landscape? Gaining an understanding of mãechī history, however, is extremely difficult. Mãechī have long been ignored officially, so few government records are available to help. Further, since most mãechī live in temples dominated by monks and serve the monks of those temples, in the past mãechī seldom had contact with and knowledge of other mãechī. They know little of their own history and the activities of their colleagues. Wãbī and her father's ignorance of what might be required for Wãbī's ordination and life as a mãechī is unexceptional; the ignorance is a reflection of, among other aspects of the social situation, the isolation of mãechī. Only recently has an organization been formed to unite them—the Institute of Thai Mãechī.

The institute is comprised of mãechī from all over the country. Its central headquarters in Bangkok, a small combined shop and office, is tucked away beside the boy's school on the grounds of the Bowonniwet Temple.[11] White mãechī clothing and handbags sewn by mãechī and sent to the institute—one of the ways the mãechī support themselves is by the money they earn from this sewing—fill ancient wooden and glass-doored cabinets that extend from floor to ceiling. Three desks crowd the small floor space; institute documents fill file cabinets in the back. To rest after the last meal of the day at 11:00 A.M., the mãechī who work in the office lie down behind the desks on mats. There is no space in which to retire apart from where they work.

At the time of my research, two māechī ran the institute, Māechī Waree and Māechī Laksana, as secretary general and assistant secretary general. Similar to many Thai organizations, the president and vice president of the institute, technically higher in status than secretary general and assistant secretary general, are largely figureheads. They are quite respected but are not responsible for the daily administration of institute activities. Māechī Waree and Māechī Laksana work with a team of māechī to call meetings of central committees, to organize the annual meeting, and to see that the *Māechī Sān*, a journal, is published and distributed to māechī throughout the country every three months. They are also responsible for producing the identity card for māechī and for publishing and distributing the discipline handbook for them. Māechī Waree and Māechī Laksana do not live at Bowonniwet Temple; they travel from Chonburī to work in Bangkok and return to their home temple every week for the holy day and the day before. The traveling is difficult and time consuming; the office/shop is far too small for the amount of work and the varied activities of the institute.

Two main committees are at the core of the institute: one is an administrative committee (limited to twenty-five members) and the other is called the Foundation of the Institute of Thai Māechī (with an unlimited number of members). All members of the administrative committee must be heads of samnaks, whether samnaks on temple grounds or not, and they must have gone forth at least ten years earlier. Committee members hold the position for four years. The president of the administrative committee represents the institute, supervises the secretary general, and is assisted by a vice president. The foundation is simply the financial arm of the institute and works in concert with its administrative committee.

Space is a large issue for the institute, as is travel and communication. When the main administrative committee heads assemble every three months in Bangkok, Secretary General Māechī Waree must arrange to use the large room next door to the small shop/office, a room the institute also borrows for the annual meeting and other activities. The committee members, many of whom are older women, must travel from their home samnaks, often using the most basic public transportation and spending many hours in discomfort. Institute members are spread throughout the country. The institute has only one phone, and many of its temple and samnak members have only one phone as well—sometimes serving as many as 500 monks and māechī. All business for the samnak or temple is conducted through the one line, and Thai phone lines are low quality—one is as likely to be disconnected as not. There are no computers and no fax machines. These are some of the challenges of the institute, ones that would be more easily met with more money, but the government does not support māechī as it supports monks.

In the 1970s, the institute slowly began to establish more samnaks separate from temples—places for māechī to live independently of men in general and monks in particular.[12] It also worked to welcome more temple samnaks as members and began several training programs in Thai handicrafts, one of which led to the establishment of a samnak in Bangkok specifically for Buddhist contemplation and training in handicrafts. Skills in such handicrafts are often seen as being important for cottage industries as well as for the preservation of Thai heritage. The institute also trains māechī as hospital aides, cooperating with Chulalongkorn and other hospitals, and it trains māechī in early child care. Over the years, the institute has established twenty branch nunneries throughout Thailand, including two that run their own schools for Thai girls and māechī. One of the most successful of these is Dhammacarinī Samnak, where I met Māechī Wabī.

As I explored the institute's programs, projects, goals, historical roots, and methods of functioning, I found its central purpose to be the development of māechī spiritually, intellectually, and physically, so that they can be better religious people and better serve others (primarily other women and children). This purpose includes greater exposure of māechī, so laypeople can learn to respect them as religious practitioners instead of denigrating them as women who are socially unfit. In short, the institute works not only to develop māechī to give their gifts but to educate laypeople so that they can accept the gifts of the māechī.

The history of the institute indicates how its formation was the creative response to emotional, social needs. The institute allowed people to act responsibly with freedom and power to some societal problems.[13] It now responds to other societal problems as well: the lack of attention to the education and empowerment of young girls and the lack of care for older women with no families.

Because of the general disinterest of monks in māechī, I was surprised to learn that the official head of monks in Thailand, the sangharaja, called for the first meeting of māechī.[14] Letters were sent out by the small group of māechī in Bangkok, which had first been approached by the head monk. Hundreds of abbots in temples all over the country were invited to send māechī to the first meeting of māechī.[15] Some abbots refused to send anyone, but still hundreds came, and the annual meeting was established on August 24, 1969. One māechī estimated that perhaps a thousand māechī came to that first meeting. It was, by all reports, an amazing experience for those who participated. For the first time, māechī were able to get a sense of their numbers, to see themselves as part of a strong, nationwide force. An interview with Māechī Prathin Khwan'on, who helped prepare the temple for that first large meeting and who was present for the meeting (and who is now head of the institute), reveals an interesting aspect of the origins of the institute not mentioned in official institute documents. This māechī studied with ten other māechī at Mahamokut Buddhist University when a leading monk called the group together and asked, "Do you want to have a meeting of māechī?"[16] She laughs at the limited view of her group at the time—their reply to his idea was to ask, "What for?" He explained that māechī would then come to know how māechī live in temples and samnaks all over Thailand and learn their concerns.

When I asked this māechī why the monk took an interest in māechī, she answered that people from foreign countries had become interested in Buddhism and had come to Thailand to learn more about the religion. When they asked the head of monks about the number of monks and novices, he could reply readily; but when asked about women and Buddhism, such as why there were no women who had gone forth (nak būat), he had no answers at all.[17] No one knew how many māechī there were and what place they held in the history of Buddhism in Thailand. This māechī concludes, "Back then we didn't know anything. We didn't know how other māechī went forth or how they lived. We didn't know anything about each other." The roots of the foundation of the institute, then, include increased ease in communication across the globe, Thailand's openness to influence from different countries, and Western feminism.

The institute, however, may or may not answer why māechī are not accorded the same rights and benefits and status as monks in Thai society and how māechī might gain these rights and benefits. Answers to these questions vary. Some begin the discussion noting that the texts recognize bhikkhunī (nuns) and bhikkhu (monks) as members of the sangha, the clergy. There are rules governing how one goes forth as a bhikkhunī and bhikkhu, and those who, following those text-established rules, go forth can be recognized officially and given the status and rights as nak būat, those who go forth. Thus if a woman wants to have the status and rights of one who has gone forth, she must go forth as a bhikkhunī. Since there are no living Theravāda bhikkhunī, required for the ordination of a bhikkhunī, there can be no more going forth as Theravāda bhikkhunī. Therefore, women simply cannot have the status and rights of those who have gone forth in the Theravāda tradition.[18]

Some, on the other hand, respond to the problem of the lack of living Theravāda bhikkhunī by inviting bhikkhunī of other Buddhist traditions to participate in the going forth ceremony. Their argument is that though the Theravāda bhikkhunī lineage has died out, in some ways it has been preserved in the bhikkhunī lineage of Mahāyana Buddhism, thus bhikkhunī of this other branch of Buddhism can be used to restart the lineage in Theravāda Buddhism. Once this is done, women can have the status and rights given to monks as people who have chosen to go forth.

Others view the problem somewhat differently. Reestablishing the bhikkhunī lineage is not important, they argue. Rather, the problem is somehow allowing women the status and rights of those who have gone forth. Thus instead of reestablishing a lineage that is dead, people should recognize māechī, who have gone forth, as among those who have gone forth. Thus māechī can then be given the rights and status of others who have gone forth, monks. This answer appeals to one high-profile māechī in Thailand: Māechī Kanittha.

Māechī Kanittha, a lawyer, is prepared to seek the ratification of a law that recognizes māechī as among those who have gone forth like monks, either through the Parliamentary Council on Religion, Art, and Culture or through the ecclesiastical hierarchy. She hopes that giving māechī legal status will allow for helpful differences in samnaks but will encourage standard education for māechī. She is establishing a college that will serve māechī who are at different levels of religious and secular education. Educated at a Catholic convent school, Māechī Kanittha knows what respect for nuns can be like, and she has always admired the Catholic emphasis on social service.

The biggest problem for māechī in Thailand, Māechī Kanittha says, is that "they don't care. And they don't think they have any problems. . . . And they don't know what to do with themselves." She credits her education as a lawyer with sensitizing her to the importance of an official title. When examining an official government identity card and finding no recognition that a woman might have a title other than "Miss" or "Mrs." such as "Māechī," Māechī Kanittha sees the large implications, for women and for māechī. Too often women become māechī because they need to, because they need peace in a samnak or temple, and, finding that peace, they "accept their fate," she says. They lack the education to discern the societal problems of māechī and to work to solve them.

In deciding that māechī ought to have legal status, Māechī Kanittha approached the institute, seeking its approval of her plan. She wrote to the ecclesiastical council on behalf of the Association for the Promotion of the Status of Women, an organization that "looks at women who are discriminated against, who need to be supported." Māechī Kanittha has "found that māechī are a group of women who are not supported and who deserve to be recognized." Her work, however, is proving to be more controversial than she had hoped; many members of the institute do not support the law that she designed (and that would immediately benefit the college that she is establishing). One of the problems is her dependence on the 1962 Monk's bill, which many feel has left monks in Thailand in an overly bureaucratic structure that emphasizes unhelpful aspects of the monk's life. Monks have a strictly defined ladder to climb, and reaching higher rungs is not dependent on sincere Buddhist practice. Writes the monk Santikaro: "Over the last century, the politicians and bureaucrats have gained control over the monastic hierarchy and administration in Siam. . . . This has had disastrous consequences for the ability of the monks to manage their own affairs, to adapt to changing social realities, and to be a moral voice within the very immoral Thai polity."[19] Maechi, ignored by officials, have not suffered from these difficulties, but some think that they may begin to if the bill becomes law. Maechi Kanittha worked with Prime Minister Chuan Leekpai, who went to law school with her, and with the Department of Religious Affairs to draft a bill. The institute considered the bill in 1996 and eventually voted to support it. Interestingly, the proposed law suggests a hierarchy of maechi that puts maechi under the control of the ecclesiastical council—the head of monks would be the peak of the pyramid; below him would be the ecclesiastical council of thirty monks; and under that council the monks and the maechi would form two different hierarchies. There was some discussion about the need for placing the maechi under the control of the monastic ecclesiastical council. Why not have the maechi form their own ecclesiastical council, just as monks do? As the proposed law stands, the maechi are under the head monk but not under any other monks. The biggest changes that will occur legally if the draft bill is passed is that all maechi will be under the umbrella of the institute, and the institute will no longer be a private foundation. In short, the maechi who currently reject the institute and its rules and bureaucracy will no longer be able to reject it legally.[20]

One of the key issues related to the bill is how to define the category of maechi. Maechi Kanittha sees the maechi category as a suitable substitute for the category of bhikkhuni. Though she admires and respects those interested in reestablishing the bhikkhuni line, she thinks Thailand should work with what it already has: maechi.[21] And maechi can determine which vows they need to take. She notes that even if 100 of the 311 bhikkhuni rules were deleted, the women would still be unable to follow them because modern society is so different from the society in which the rules were first created. Those in the institute grappling with issues related to the law also address this question, wondering if any law for maechi might be defeated by monks who not only are legitimized by their lineage but also by their taking of so many vows.

The problem of defining maechi as nuns, as religious women in a way that laywomen are not, highlights the unique position of maechi. They have the structure of those who have gone forth, living in temples and samnaks and following monastic schedules and rules, but they are not restricted in their behavior as are monks, who reach back 2,500 years to a very different society to legitimize their lives. Maechi, lacking such rigid and ancient definitions of their place in society, can respond more easily than monks to the differences in modern society. Unlike monks, for example, they can work in the fields, farming their own food. They are therefore less dependent on their lay neighbors, who are often the more burdened rural population of Thailand. Although work such as this can earn them respect from villagers who also farm their own food, some argue that this practice can cause loss of respect, because māechī do not act as the monks do. My own fieldwork indicates no lack of respect for māechī who grow their own food. They are, rather, complimented on their resourcefulness, knowledge, and hard work by people who are familiar with them.

In explaining why she took on the torturous process of proposing a law giving legal status to māechī, Māechī Kanittha laughs and says, "I think it's my job because no one else can do it." Recent developments in the institute, however, are proving that other māechī may indeed be able to do it and may define themselves against leadership offered by a *khunying* such as Māechī Kanittha.[22] Some leaders of the institute and at least one monk involved have fought the law, and this battle may be the most significant and dramatic one in which the institute has been involved.

The samnak at which Wābī's father left her is associated with the institute; its māechī were connected to others around the country through the only umbrella organization of māechī in Thailand. This connection would later play a large role in Wābī's life: Dhammacarinī Samnak was established by the institute.

Chapter 3

A Friend in Need

The helpful friend can be seen to be a loyal friend in four ways:
he looks after you when you are inattentive, he looks after your
possessions when you are inattentive, he is a refuge when you
are afraid, and when some business is to be done he lets you
have twice what you ask for.

—*Dīgha Nikāya* 31.21

Regardless of how much the institute would affect her later, at the time of her own going forth Wābī knew nothing of it and its work. She had no money and was alone at a strange samnak, uncertain of her future. Having been left by her father at the samnak to meditate for seven days, Wābī tried to put aside these concerns and get to work. She meditated. Following the schedule of the samnak, she rose early, joined the others for meditation followed by chanting and tried again and again to put aside her concern about her future: where she would live, how she would live, whether she would be able to go forth as a māechī then or be forced to live the life of a householder. She had been advised to meditate, so she meditated. Reflecting on her distractions at the time, she said, "I was scared—if I waited, what would happen? A man would look at me. Before I knew it, I'd have a family! Children! I had to practice! I was scared, desperately afraid. I wanted to go forth. I didn't want [a family]. I was afraid."

Though Wābī herself spoke with no one at the temple where her father left her, promising to return for her in a week, others heard of her strong desire to go forth and of her lack of money. One day, Māechī Senī, a meditation instructor at the samnak where Wābī was staying, approached her. She

37

also ran a samnak in northeast Thailand and now divided her time between running her own samnak there and teaching meditation at the samnak in Bangkok. Her father and sister lived in her samnak in northeast Thailand. Before beginning her work near Bangkok, Māechī Senī had had enough time to care for her relatives, but now she did not. She offered Wābī a deal. If Wābī would agree to care for two of Māechī Senī's relatives for a small salary and free room and board, she could live in a small, women-led, women-dominated religious community. "She said she had an elderly father—very old—and a mentally retarded sister, and she said, 'If you want to go forth, you can go forth to live in my samnak and care for my father and sister.'" It was a good match: Wābī had no money but a desire to live in a samnak, and Māechī Senī needed a helper and an assistant at her samnak.

During this, one of Māechī Wābī's most difficult times, she met one of the people most influential in her life. Practically penniless and among strangers, she met Māechī Senī, who lifted her up, giving her food and a place to live and providing her with acceptable work and the opportunity to meditate in a peaceful environment. Having decided to live among women, she now made her closest woman friend. Māechī Senī's offer to allow her to live in her samnak to care for her father was, in Wābī's mind, a rescue in one of the most desperate moments of her life. She clearly relives the feelings that she had back then, summarizing her repulsion from the worldly life and her attraction to the life of a māechī: "It's a story of what I didn't want, of wanting to go forth, of my fear."

Māechī Wābī's ceremony of going forth was short, simple, and not well attended. She does not share the memory easily or joyously, though she was certainly relieved to go forth. She received robes to wear. In standard ritual form, she held a lock of her hair as another māechī shaved her head. She tried to reflect on her new religious life as the blade scraped across her skull. She had no money to give to the monks on that important occasion; when she showed me the one picture she has from that day, she cried, speaking of her disappointment in being unable to give.

Māechī Senī's samnak, where Māechī Wābī would live for seven years, was small and located in a rural area. When Māechī Wābī first arrived, there were thirteen māechī, one uninfluential monk, and two laypeople. While most would assume any monk present would be running the samnak rather than a lower-status woman, Māechī Wābī said that the monk was such a recluse that the samnak was run by the women led by Māechī Senī. Besides regular chanting and meditation, daily the inhabitants cut wood from the trees to be dried and used as fuel for cooking in the kitchen; they helped keep the main worship and practice area clean, and they maintained the grounds. Those who wanted to study aspects of Buddhism took the classes offered by Māechī

Senī. Maechī Wabī finished the advanced degree in Buddhist teachings (*dhamma*) and the intermediate degree in Buddhist philosophy (*abhidhamma*) there.

Maechī Wabī's arrangement with Maechī Senī was good: Maechī Wabī could study seriously anywhere she wanted during the three-month rainy season and then return to Maechī Senī's samnak to care for the latter's father and sister the rest of the year. This arrangement of spending the rainy season at another samnak is a popular one among maechī in Thailand and was satisfactory to Maechī Wabī: "I had time—at that time I was working in many different ways, but I still had time to pay respect to the Buddha, wash clothes; and the father, he'd gone forth before, he was at ease, he was very much at ease. He was a devout layperson, living in the temple—he took five precepts, not eight. He was weak, you know, so he had to take food in the evenings. As for the sister, she didn't know much. She'd sit anywhere, you had to help her and help her to the restroom and make sure she was dressed properly before she went out." Maechī Wabī counted herself lucky to have the opportunity to go forth and to show her gratitude to the woman who enabled her to do so.

> I was very fortunate, I felt very fortunate. I was so happy to go forth; Maechī Senī had given me that opportunity. I had been thinking and troubling over my inability to go forth for a long time.
>
> I had to cook two meals a day for [Maechī Senī's father and sister]—dinner was pretty much the same as lunch, and they'd go to bed at around eight at night, so I could meditate from then until two or three in the morning. I liked it. I could meditate alone anywhere on the temple grounds and everyone was asleep and I could stay alone and meditate. It was wonderful. I liked being alone like that. . . . Sometimes I'd just sleep a few hours at night and then from one to two in the afternoon.

Elderly parents (especially mothers) occasionally come to live in the samnaks of their daughters who have gone forth, usually taking the five precepts and living quietly among maechī. No maechī with whom I spoke on the issue ever expressed disapproval of this practice. Combining caregiving and contemplative activities was considered natural and good.[1] The practice is often frowned upon by monks, however, who view the taking in of such laypeople as a sign of lack of seriousness by maechī; monks consider the duties of caring for those who have not gone forth (are not nak būat) more appropriate for householders. Maechī Wabī dealt with such objections. The hermit monk at Maechī Senī's samnak once "asked why I had to care for these people. He said it wasn't an appropriate activity for a person who has gone forth. But I said, 'This is Māechī Senī's father, he is a man very important to Māechī Senī, and she is my teacher (*ăčhān*) and my friend, and taking care of her father is a small thing for me.' Caring for them I was at ease. I didn't have any problems."

Her feelings of indebtedness to Māechī Senī were strong then and remain so today. When I asked Māechī Wābī to provide a pseudonym for her teacher, she decided on "Senī" because it means "leader," and Māechī Senī was, she said, "the first person to give me light." From the initial kindness of Māechī Senī, which was also beneficial to Māechī Senī herself, the friendship between the two grew and strengthened.

During most of the time Māechī Wābī lived in Māechī Senī's samnak, the latter lived near Bangkok. For seven years, Māechī Wābī cared for Māechī Senī's father and sister, five years while Māechī Senī lived much of the time in Bangkok and two years after Māechī Senī returned and they moved to a different samnak. Māechī Senī had been responsible for these relatives for many years, since before she had finished school. Before she went forth, they lived with her in her home. After she went forth, they moved to her samnak. Against objections to this arrangement, Māechī Wābī points out that Māechī Senī's sister was the latter's responsibility from someone else's doings from early on. The woman "is mentally retarded; she wasn't a brand new child—she wasn't Māechī Senī's newborn child—she was her sister, already born, already living, no plan of Māechī Senī's." Just so with her father.

For seven years, Māechī Wābī lived peacefully in the samnak and the next one, caring for Māechī Senī's father and sister and meditating nine months a year, usually spending the rainy season at a serious meditation center elsewhere. Her friendship with Māechī Senī was rewarding and grounded her as a māechī. While the cultural norms of Thai society dictated that Māechī Wābī marry and become a mother, her friendship with Māechī Senī gave her support for rejecting the cultural norm and embracing and developing her role as a renunciant. The friendship, perhaps especially because it was voluntary, "[supported] independent standpoints and unconventional pursuits."[2] While Māechī Wābī's friendship with Māechī Senī began and continued with certain inegalitarian aspects that make me reluctant to call it simply a "voluntary" relationship, it certainly helped Wābī develop her understanding of what a māechī is and does and discover more of the rewards of the life of a renunciant. Māechī Wābī said, "Māechī Senī helped me a lot. She is a person I've talked to a lot. She allowed me to go forth that first season—she led me out of bad circumstances." When Māechī Wābī was sick, Māechī Senī cared for her: "She washed my clothes for me. It was the first time anyone besides my mother and my siblings had done this sort of thing for me. Māechī Senī was the first one." It was certainly wonderful that Māechī Senī as a *person* would care for her. But for Māechī Wābī, the experience was even more significant because Māechī Senī, her *teacher*, cared for her: "I had never seen a teacher (ăchăn) anywhere take care of a follower (lūksit, pupil, disciple) like that. At that time, I was just a follower. It was the first time I'd met a person like that—especially for me: one who would care for me. Usually it's the follower caring for the teacher. I knew then that outside of my mother and father I had another person, Māechī Senī, who was a *pubakărī* to me. A pubakărī is the person who cares for you, whom you respect, whom you love."

Māechī Wābī summarized the seven years she spent in Māechī Senī's samnaks. "At that time, my heart was very much at peace because the incidents of the future had not occurred. At this time when I had first gone forth, things were very peaceful."

This peace, in fact, would last some years, but there were undercurrents of difficulty, and eventually Māechī Wābī would undergo a religious crisis that would change her life.

Chapter 4

The Beginning of a Crisis in Faith: Harsh Speech

Now, Cunda, here effacement should be practised by you:
(6) 'Others will speak maliciously; we shall abstain from malicious speech here': effacement should be practised thus.
(7) 'Others will speak harshly; we will abstain from harsh speech here': effacement should be practised thus.
—*Majjhima Nikāya* 8.12

After seven years as a māechī, Māechī Wabī almost threw away her robes and left the religious life. It was the most significant crisis she had ever faced, one that involved peripheral related events, as religious crises generally do. While the main crisis began with disappointment in representatives of religion around her and peaked with their betrayal of her trust, other factors such as the failure of her own health, incidents in her meditation, and calamities in the lives of her loved ones all worked to try her dedication to the homeless life.

With so many factors related to Māechī Wabī's crisis of faith, we might wonder which was the true determining factor, which account the true one. Such a question, however, can be misleading. Consider your own life and its shifting stories. The list of reasons to take a certain job, to participate in a certain program, or to become involved with a certain person written on the eve of your doing so may differ utterly from the list you give five years later. Trying to determine which reason is the true one may falsely reduce your life and the decisions you made. The more accounts for an important life incident that you can give, the more you make that life choice "coherent within the entire fabric of [your] life." Having many accounts for an important life story

42

"helps guard against the chilling possibility that one's life is random, accidental, unmotivated."[1]

Māechī Wābī gives many accounts of her considering divestiture of her white robes, and investigating these accounts entails examining key issues in her life and faith. Faith here cannot be seen as if it were merely an intellectual holding of a belief. As one scholar remarks, "A theory of religious development is a circling about the unreachable center of our own lives and the lives of all creatures."[2] By examining Māechī Wābī's crisis with an eye to what caused the problem, how the problem affected her, and how she worked to resolve the problem, we find underlying concerns about Buddhism, about the representatives of Buddhism, and about her way of life; we circle her life's unreachable center. During the crisis, but mostly through its resolution, Māechī Wābī clarifies what she values about her life as a māechī.

While living in Māechī Senī's samnak, Māechī Wābī was content: she had a job she accepted gratefully as a duty toward the person who had given her the long-sought-after opportunity to go forth. She had plenty of time to meditate. Māechī Senī was a skilled teacher of meditation, and Māechī Wābī embraced her instruction enthusiastically. Until this time, she had exclusively practiced *samatha,* or calm meditation, repeating "Buddho" in her mind. Calm meditation is very important in the Buddhist tradition; it develops the one-pointedness of mind that allows a person to turn her or his attention to Buddhist truths and to understand them deeply and experientially. This turning of attention to Buddhist truths and understanding them deeply is the second kind of Buddhist meditation, that which it is said the Buddha taught as distinct from other teachers—*vipassanā* (from the verb meaning "to see clearly"), or insight meditation. Scholars of Buddhism have long debated over the relationship between calm and insight meditation. Writes one scholar, "They may be seen as basically complementary rather than as mutually exclusive methods." Calm meditation contributes to the control of the mind and to the experience of deep tranquility. Insight meditation leads to seeing the world clearly, to the profound understanding of Buddhist truths, such as the three defilements, obstacles, or roots of unwholesome behavior: attachment (desire, lust), hatred or anger, and delusion. These obstacles are extinguished in the realization of nibbāna (nirvana). Both calm and insight meditation are necessary for enlightenment, nibbāna, for release from the round of rebirth and suffering.[3]

My understanding of the relationship between samatha and vipassanā meditation was first formed through teachers in northern India at the very start of my learning about Buddhism and meditation. Samatha, I understood, is a good way to be focused and to develop what is needed to do the real work of Buddhist meditation—vipassanā. Vipassanā, however, was never far away. My understanding of their interdependence was further solidified five years later, when I did a three-month meditation retreat in Sri Lanka. My meditation instructor told me that meditation has not only these forms but these aims: calm and insight. "They may be practiced jointly, but not simultaneously. You don't need to be completely calm before you get insight, nor do you need to be perfectly insightful before you become calm." I was told to analyze my state immediately upon sitting down to meditate. If my body was tired and my mind was not alert, I should do insight meditation. If my mind was overly alert and my body was in decent shape, I should do calm meditation.

Through calm meditation you can attain the eight absorptions (the four jhānas and the four immaterial states); calm meditation can take a number of forms: you can, for example, meditate on a bowl of water, the flame of a candle, or a blue, yellow, or white disk. You can meditate on your breath, simply internally saying "out" whenever your breath leaves you. You can also meditate on what are called the four divine abodes: boundless loving-kindness, compassion, appreciative joy (joy in the success of others), and equanimity.

A meditation on loving-kindness, for example, might proceed like this: you begin by saying repeatedly and slowly to yourself: "May I be peaceful and happy." When you are settled into that practice (depending on your situation, this could mean minutes, weeks, or years), you consider a mentor you have had, someone for whom you have uncomplicated gratitude, and you repeatedly and slowly say to yourself, "May [that person's name] be peaceful and happy." When settled into that practice, you consider someone about whom you feel neutral and wish them well similarly. Finally, you consider someone who may have caused you harm, someone who has made you angry or sad, and you wish them well similarly.

While in some ways these practices, like anything one does, can be boring or easy, overall, my experience is both that they are often very difficult—certainly at the beginning—and sometimes inexpressably rewarding. These practices do not necessarily lead to immediate swells of peacefulness and joy for most, but performed regularly, they can yield vast results. For example, once when I was filled with enmity toward a colleague, I meditated, sending him loving-kindness. While it was not easy and certainly not immediately rewarding, over months I found myself less inclined to disparage him, less frequently defining him as the source of my problems. One day my understanding of our different contributions to the institution and the people we served was radically changed in one sitting—I came to understand our interconnectedness a bit better. And after that, my colleague's best qualities were more often in my mind. I understood them more deeply and remembered them more consistently. I could see why we were involved in some way, how our involvement revealed a particular karmic nut that I had to crack. Meditation and its rewards are often like this: both dramatic and utterly undramatic—even this kind of meditation, known for its development of concentration more than insight.

One learned Buddhist monk writes of the two basic forms of meditation:

> Whereas in serenity [calm] meditation the meditator attempts to focus upon a single uniform object abstracted from actual experience, in insight meditation the endeavor is made to contemplate, from a position of detached observation, the ever-shifting flux of experience itself in order to penetrate through to the essential nature of bodily and mental phenomena. The Buddha teaches that the craving and clinging that hold us in bondage are sustained by a network of "conceivings" (*maññita*)—deluded views, conceits, and suppositions that the mind fabricates by an internal process . . . and then projects out upon the world, taking them to possess objective validity.[4]

Insight meditation is when a meditator uses Buddhist categories to analyze his or her experience. One can contemplate the nature of body (noting sensations) or of feelings (noting them as simply pleasant, painful, or neutral). Thus contemplating, a practitioner becomes aware of the three characteristics of everything, including the body and feelings: all experiences are impermanent (*anicca*), suffering (*dukkha*), and without an essential self (*anattā*). As a canonical Buddhist text tells us,

> There are . . . three kinds of feeling: pleasant feeling, painful feeling, and neither-painful-nor-pleasant feeling. On the occasion when one feels pleasant feeling, one does not feel painful feeling or neither-painful-nor-pleasant feeling; on that occasion one feels only pleasant feeling. On the occasion when one feels painful feeling, one does not feel pleasant feeling or neither-painful-nor-pleasant feeling; on that occasion one feels only painful feeling. On the occasion when one feels neither-painful-nor-pleasant feeling, one does not feel pleasant feeling or painful feeling; on that occasion one feels only neither-painful-nor-pleasant feeling.
>
> Pleasant feeling . . . is impermanent, conditioned, dependently arisen, subject to destruction, vanishing, fading away, and ceasing. Painful feeling too is impermanent, conditioned, dependently arisen, subject to destruction, vanishing, fading away, and ceasing. Neither-painful-nor-pleasant feeling too is impermanent, conditioned, dependently arisen, subject to destruction, vanishing, fading away, and ceasing.

Seeing thus, a well-taught noble disciple becomes disenchanted with pleasant feeling, disenchanted with painful feeling, disenchanted with neither-painful-nor-pleasant feeling. Being disenchanted, he becomes dispassionate. Through dispassion [his mind] is liberated. When it is liberated there comes the knowledge: "It is liberated." He understands: "Birth is destroyed, the holy life has been lived, what had to be done has been done, there is no more coming to any state of being."[5]

For the person with no meditation experience who lives in a culture that ignores the value of contemplative practices, meditation may seem strange or simply boring, but someone who meditates with diligence soon learns how difficult, how active, and how helpful this sort of practice can be—as Māechī Wābī did when she was sixteen. Unlike, however, how I learned the relationship between calm and insight meditation—as being closely connected—Wābī learned the two forms as separate. For years she practiced calm meditation without ever tasting the rewards of insight meditation. Her chance to study insight meditation under the guidance of Māechī Senī was a great opportunity indeed. And she was properly grateful. In addition to rewarding work and rewarding meditation, Māechī Wābī at this time also had the satisfaction of a close friendship with Māechī Senī, whom she deeply respected. Further, the samnak was peaceful and the grounds beautiful. One incident, however, disturbed her and later contributed to the major religious crisis of her life.

She had felt since first going forth that her friendship with Māechī Senī, the first person to hear many of the stories that made up Māechī Wābī's personal history, was very important to her. She also had felt, since that time, that her friendship with Māechī Senī complicated her relationship with another young woman, Māechī Mīna. Māechī Senī and Māechī Mīna had been friends for some years. Like Māechī Senī, Māechī Mīna had worked outside of her home for years and was in her thirties when she went forth. The two were close: Māechī Mīna had decided to go forth to live in Māechī Senī's samnak before Māechī Senī had even met Māechī Wābī, and Māechī Mīna viewed herself as Māechī Senī's protégée.

While both Māechī Wābī and Māechī Mīna were devoted to Māechī Senī and had similar rural backgrounds, and had even gone forth together in the same ceremony, Māechī Wābī's lack of worldly experience and her poverty set her apart. Māechī Wābī had never lived away from her family until immediately before she met Māechī Senī, and she had gone forth with no money saved for her life as a māechī. Māechī Mīna, jealous of a competitor for Māechī Senī's attention, did not appreciate Māechī Wābī's dependence on

Māechī Senī and blamed her for not saving money before going forth. "Māechī Mīna said often how I liked to live 'clinging like a leech.' 'Clinging.' She said this word often," Māechī Wabī told me. She felt at these times ill at ease and sad. Māechī Wabī also noticed Māechī Mīna's tendency to save up small events, such as a brief interchange over who should do which task in the morning while Māechī Senī was away from the samnak, and to present them to Māechī Senī as big problems or incidents upon her return. What were unimportant incidents to Māechī Wabī were evidently of greater seriousness to Māechī Mīna.

The deeper undercurrents of Māechī Mīna's dissatisfaction came to the surface in a dramatic episode. Buddhist monastics count their years of ordination in "rainy seasons"—this incident took place in Wabī's third rainy season, when she was about nineteen years old. It was the season of *loy grathong*, a water festival of Southeast Asia held on the full moon night of the twelfth lunar month (generally November).[6] One day Māechī Wabī was stung by wasps so many times that her life was threatened. "It had just rained the night before. I was taking the trash out after breakfast and was passing a coconut tree. I stirred up a nest of them, I think, and thirteen of them stung me. . . . I fell in some water. I couldn't speak—not much noise came out of my mouth, but Māechī Senī and Māechī Mīna heard and ran to help me. They didn't walk, as is the custom in a samnak; they *ran* to help me."

I have never seen an adult run on samnak grounds. "Graceful, restrained" deportment—restricted range of movement that is slow as well—is highly prized in samnaks as well as in Buddhist temples throughout the world, and there is an explicit rule in the handbook for māechī that prohibits running.[7] That the abbess and a fellow māechī ran indicates how seriously they took the call for help. Māechī Wabī found herself unable to walk, unable to do anything. She stayed in the hospital two days, receiving oxygen. Had she arrived fifteen minutes later, her doctor said, she would have died.

While both Māechī Senī and Māechī Mīna cared for her and indeed saved her life, there was a moment during the incident when Māechī Mīna irrevocably communicated her dislike of Māechī Wabī. Māechī Senī had run to get a car from the village, and Māechī Wabī was lying in a painful stupor. Māechī Mīna was to care for Māechī Wabī as Māechī Senī got the car, but she did nothing as Wabī struggled for her life. In growing pain and fear, Māechī Wabī lay on the ground, and her face began to swell. As Wabī lay there and Mīna sat in a chair looking down at her, Māechī Mīna simply and clearly said, "Serves you right."

When I first heard this story, I speculated that perhaps Mīna had been paralyzed by the sight of Wabī's severe injuries and allergic reaction—that she had not helped because she could not help. Māechī Wabī disagreed and explained further: "She just sat in a chair casually; she just sat in a chair. And then she said, 'Serves you right.' I was very sad. That's all she said; she said nothing else." I asked if she thought Māechī Mīna knew that Māechī Wabī had heard her comment. "I don't think so; I think she thought I couldn't hear. They helped me put on some clothes and took me to the hospital. After two nights I returned to the samnak. I was still sorrowful; that feeling hadn't gone away."

For Wabī, this event was the climax of the difficulties she had in living at Senī's samnak. The difficulties were made harder to bear because the person to whom she normally turned for advice was simply too close to the situation to be of help, and Wabī felt that she would have made the situation worse by involving Senī. Soon after returning from the hospital, Wabī's meditation gave the incident added meaning and depth.

The incidents that follow happened over several months while she was on retreat, meditating intensely at another samnak. Wabī spent most rainy seasons, three to four months, at other samnaks in retreat, following a pattern of serious meditators by removing herself from her everyday residence to meditate many hours a day in a temple or samnak known for its encouragement of serious meditation. She tells the incidents as one story, a story with several sections. Each section begins with an emotional or a physical feeling or vision, or a combination of those, and moves to the noetic aspect of the experience gained by applying a Buddhist analytical tool to the feeling or vision. Exploring Wabī's meditational response to the incident with Mīna elucidates not only the kind of place the incident took in her life but also her experiences of meditation and how they can be interpreted in the Buddhist context and thus incorporated into one's understanding of one's life as well as one's understanding of Buddhist ideas.

Not long after her hospitalization, Wabī was on retreat and was, as usual, alternating between walking and sitting meditation. One can meditate in any of the bodily positions, of course. There are many different styles of both sitting and walking meditation—most meditation instructions are related directly to sitting or walking with the understanding that one can lie down or stand while meditating too. In her practice at this time Wabī attended to each foot as it moved and stopped in a standardized, slow, walking movement. She divided each step into two parts and labeled them "righting," "stopping," "lefting," and "stopping." Such a practice allows one to be mindful of exactly what one is doing. When she sat in meditation, she used a form of meditation in which the practitioner notes parts of her body in a particular sequence. This systematic attention to the parts of the body is a meditation technique often applied when a practitioner is overattentive to the aspects of pleasure that the body can provide, such as lust. Seeing the body as simply a group of parts helps a practitioner dissolve attachment to the body and to the pleasures the body can provide. The entire list includes "head-hairs, body-hairs, nails, teeth, skin, flesh, sinews, bones, bone-marrow, kidneys, heart, liver, pleura, spleen, lungs, mesentery, bowels, stomach, excrement, bile, phlegm, pus, blood, sweat, fat, tears, tallow, saliva, snot, synovic fluid, urine" and sometimes the brain. When I first learned this meditation method in Sri Lanka, the instructor explained that I should first visualize the object of my lust and instead of indulging in a fantasy related to that person, I should mentally divide the person's body into body parts, visualizing each part one by one on the floor in front of me. After dividing the body into parts, I should then look at the entire pile and say, "Now what was it that I was attracted to in this pile? Was it the liver? The heart? The intestines?" and so forth.[8]

Wābī, however, was engaged in the shortened version often given as a meditation subject for new practitioners. The body parts are arranged in an order from driest to wettest, and the first five—skin, teeth, nails, body hair, head hair—are the list with which Wābī was working. She sat in meditation and attended to each body part in the sequence, going through it a number of times, and then she walked in meditation—alternating between sitting and walking meditation. She told me about this meditation, saying:

> After some days of this, I felt as though as I thought of each part of my body, that part went away. It fell onto the ground as I attended to it. [Each part] peeled off from head to toe—the hair on my head, the hair on my body, fingernails, toenails, teeth, skin, and then it would all return: skin, teeth, finger and toenails, hair on my body, hair on my head just as I attended to the word "skin," skin peeled off every time. . . . It wasn't a true thing, right? It was just a feeling. And my internal organs felt all turbulent—like my stomach was upset.

Wābī's larger understanding of the event focused on the Buddhist division of the world into name and form (nāmarūpa), a natural shift because dividing the body into parts can be one step to dividing everything in one's experience into name and form: name, nāma, are those things of the mind; form, rūpa, are those things that are corporeal, material. In Buddhist understanding, this division does not necessitate a valuing of one aspect of experience (that of the mind, for example) over another. In the Buddhist understanding of reality, one's experience is varied—a changing, shifting pattern. The failure to see the changing nature of experience leads to a false dichotomy of self and everything else. There is no essential self separated from the essential world. Things of the mind and corporeal things shift constantly. The world as one experiences it can be simply divided into name and form.

The five constituents of existence recognized in Buddhist thought can also be divided into form, the body; and name, feeling, perception, mental formations, and consciousness. Wābī says,

And at the same time I understood form and name, because I felt that my body and mind were separate parts. I felt the separation of body and mind. Suffering was in one part—I had peace in another part, in my heartmind. . . . I felt their separation. The parts—it was like I had a consciousness that understood the difference in mind and body—and could determine suffering from happiness. My heartmind was at peace for the first time as much as it had been at peace during those first seven days when I first went forth.

The noetic content of the feeling of her body parts dropping off, then, was an understanding of name and form. Her experience proved to her that bodily sensations—painful, odd, or at the least distracting—did not necessitate mental pain, that she could find mental peace amid physical turmoil and action. The bodily experiences were separable from her mental experiences. She saw reality, experience, as a shifting pattern, then composed of bodily pain and heartmind peace. Her primary experience of the world was not the false delusory one of "I" on one side and everything else on the other. In Theravāda Buddhist philosophy, at the ultimate level of reality, there is no "I" separate from the world.

The word that Māechī Wābī uses, which I here translate as "consciousness," is one that she uses again in describing her meditation experience. While it can be translated as "permanent soul," it is best understood here as a consciousness present with the bodily and mental experiences. This consciousness allowed the understanding of the Buddhist tools relevant to understanding the experience: name and form. In describing her experiences, Wābī went from the feeling of the body parts falling away to the Buddhist understanding of name and form.

This experience of feeling her body parts fall off as she sat in meditation continued every time she meditated for approximately a week. Then one night, about two weeks into her retreat, she heard a loud noise like thunder. She knew it was not real; she knew no one else heard or felt it at the time. Then her body began shaking and shivering, and she felt a blow to her face: "My face was struck horribly—it was as though a person were slapping me very hard: it felt numb as though a big heavy hand were slapping my face. It was like someone hitting me with the flat part of the blade of a knife. Slapping, slapping." The blows to her face then dwindled, becoming less severe, but for six days each time she sat in meditation she felt as though her face were being slapped.

After that, she got a sharp, darting pain in a tooth and was unable to eat for three days. "But at that time when I couldn't eat, at that time while I was sitting in concentration, there appeared to me a fruit, a delightful fruit, gorgeous. I'd never seen [such a fruit] before. It floated directly in front of my face and then it entered my stomach. It was strange; I never felt hungry or thirsty during this time. I felt full."

When Māechī Wābī asked the instructor of insight meditation at the retreat about the meaning of the fruit, she advised her to simply attend to any visions as she would other stimuli: be mindful of them. The instructor warned her not to cling to them. This experience of the fruit, the instructor said, allowed her to see for herself the three characteristics of existence recognized by Buddhism: suffering, impermanence, and not-self.

In Buddhist thought, everything one experiences has these three characteristics. Recognizing them leads one to a greater understanding of the root of one's samsaric entrapment: desire. If, for example, I want a piece of chocolate cake, I see the world through that lens of desire; things are either helping me reach fulfillment of my desire or they are obstructing my path to the fulfillment of that desire. At one level, the world as I experience it is just a running list of this sort. Led from desire to desire, I am deluded into thinking that *I* really exist. If you take the last piece of cake, for example, I *really* exist—and so do you: very separately. Understanding the three characteristics of existence leads me to let go of that desire: I understand that really the cake can never fulfill my desire—I will always have a desire, whether for chocolate cake or the milk that ought to accompany it or the book I like to read after dessert. Another desire will come. That is the nature of dukkha, of suffering, of samsara. This continuing flux of desire and seeming fulfillment is anicca: impermanence. In this shifting pattern recognized through Buddhist practices, where is "I"? There is no essential "I" according to Theravāda Buddhist thought—as one realizes suffering and impermanence, one also realizes anatta: that fundamentally there is no separation between some "I" and everything one ordinarily defines as "not-I" or everything else.

On the topic of the fruit, the meditation instructor told Māechī Wābī, in accordance with Buddhist emphases, that visions of this sort "don't stay, they are suffering, they are without self. We cannot control them." So Wābī was advised not to dwell on (a form of grasping, acting out of desire) such visions (that is, seeing the fruit), because "it would make me lose my way."

The fruit came as an answer to her suffering, but its relief of her suffering, was temporary and carried with it inherent dangers of attachment. Her instructor urged her to remember that it was not in some way more essential than other experiences—it was without self, as all other elements of her existence are. Though the powerful meditation experience could have been quite enjoyable, enjoying it or otherwise overly attending to it would merely add to the suffering of existence. The vision was temporary, therefore it is suffering. It disappeared, therefore it is subject to change. It is no more essential than anything else. It is subject to the same laws of karmic cause and effect, therefore it is not-self—it does not indicate an inherent separation between Wābī and the world.

Maechī Wābī's fruit was a fruit of the homeless life—wisdom to help her along the path that she had chosen. She gained an experiential and clear understanding of the three characteristics soon after her understanding of name and form deepened: "This fruit showed me things don't last. It is all suffering, not-self. . . . In reality we have nothing." As I once gained a greater understanding of karma and interconnectedness through loving-kindness meditation on a colleague, Wābī gained a deeper understanding of Buddhist truths, such as the three characteristics through her meditation related to the fruit.

The pain and peacefulness, and the fruit, with the Buddhist analyses using name and form and the understanding of the three characteristics they inspired, were the context for meditation experiences more directly related to the wasp and to the larger problems of her relationship with Māechī Mīna. During this time, feelings of anger, resentment, and hurt about Mīna arose in Wābī. In describing their presence, she used the word "ferment"—these feelings "fermented in a profound part of my heartmind." They did not lie dormant but became stronger.

Wābī wondered about the cause of her anger. She had experienced anger while living in the small samnak and dealing with Mīna on a daily basis, but here she was in a completely different samnak, miles and months away from her life with her, and blinding anger was welling up inside of her. She talked about its cause and the reason that it was so profoundly rooted to her many previous lives. Living a normal life without dedicating oneself to Buddhist teachings, Wābī explained to me, a person daily experiences anger and resentment: "This bitterness, anger [is great], but we see it as a little thing." Distracted by mundane concerns, one is blind to the rootedness of this anger in one's previous lives. Through meditation, one sees that a feeling of anger one moment in this life has roots in one's other hundreds of previous lives. A feeling of annoyance is just a tip of the karmic iceberg. The habit of anger had become ingrained in a fundamental part of Wābī's heart, she said, as she had been born, had lived, and had died over the rounds of her rebirths. That her anger toward Mīna, small in everyday life, would become so large while in a meditation retreat was not surprising if understood in this way. In the protected atmosphere of a retreat, significant karmic difficulties revealed themselves to her. The advantage of the negative feelings arising while she was on retreat was that they were not so easily excused or put aside. The feelings became an area of questioning. When she felt small-hearted and angry about Mīna while living in the samnak with her, Wābī had work to distract her from the anger and its source in her previous lives. On retreat, however, meditating all the time, she would find peace and then be shocked by an onslaught of anger—seemingly from nowhere. The anger was no mere smallness of heart—she was angry.

When telling me this story, Wābī made the sounds of a cataclysmic wind and said, "Angry. Very angry. Very, very angry. And I thought, when, from where does this come? It doesn't come from living in this temple, does it? Working, studying, we talked all the time, but then I felt this anger out of nowhere. How did this feeling come along?" In retelling the incident, she laughed at the hugeness and its coming from seemingly nowhere—such is the way of the karmic world.

The feelings of anger also became an area of work. To counteract feelings of anger, a Buddhist practitioner often generates loving-kindness (*mettā*), the natural antidote to anger (as I did with the colleague).[9] Mettā can be translated as love (a spiritual love, not a sexual one), friendliness, sympathy, benevolence, or kindness; it indicates active kindness. A practitioner, faced with her own anger, also seeks to realize her own obstacles or defilements (*kilesa*). Kilesa are the obstacles or areas of work in one's path to nibbāna; they are what one gets rid of as one travels a Buddhist path. The obstacles are often listed as three: greed or lust, hatred or anger, and delusion, but they can include characteristics such as conceit, wrong view, doubt, sloth, restlessness, shamelessness, and lack of moral dread.

Wābī tried to calm her heart, but there were difficulties. The anger came and went in waves, fluctuating quickly. Her meditation required her to concentrate on the anger, to discern its nature and origin. But the fluctuations were so great and so fast that just as she thought she grasped it, the anger slipped through her fingers. She slept only two hours each night and continued to walk and sit in meditation, beginning to realize that while the anger seemed to come and go, it was actually always present.

"Usually [when at Māechī Senī's samnak] if I felt bad, if I felt small-hearted, or not at ease, maybe I'd cry a little. If I talked a little, it went away." In the quiet of the meditation samnak she could recognize that this anger was not a surface feeling—it indicated her obstacles. "I observed that my own body and feelings, for example, are not good, are unhelpful (*bāp*), and tried to think of the good points of Māechī Mīna. She was a person with benevolence just like me and others."

Mīna had helped Wābī and her family often in the years since they had gone forth. She had helped Wābī's sister find a job in Bangkok, and she traveled with her there. She had also helped Wābī's older brother find work when he finished high school. In trying to get rid of her obstacle of anger, Wābī practiced generating loving-kindness:

Every time that I felt anger toward her I tried to consider these good things in order that my mind would calm down and be at peace. A lot of energy came: feelings of anger, feelings of forgiveness toward her, and next feelings only of anger. I hadn't yet caught up with "feeling anger" and extinguished it. That's how it was every day and every night. . . . Finally I felt the anger going away just like going down a lot of stairs, down a long staircase. The anger extinguished like that. Finally I almost couldn't grasp any; I didn't feel any anger toward her any more. Really, there was still anger, but it is so fine [small] that I almost couldn't grasp it—that feeling.

What was clear was that my obstacles had not disappeared—I had a lot of obstacles. And I knew when I returned to my samnak, I would still be dealing with this anger—that it would come again and again and disappear too. I tried to be mindful "hearing, hearing." With mindfulness, it would be okay, never mind. But when my mindfulness was weak, up it would come. This happened all the time.

That Wabi felt anger did not surprise her. What did surprise her was the strength of that anger and its persistence as well as its changeability. Using the anger to understand the profundity, the deep-rootedness of such obstacles in general, and generating loving-kindness to reduce the anger, she was surprised when another strong feeling arose, one seemingly unrelated not only to her samnak and to Māechī Mīna but to anything around her: "I felt the arising of a kind of lust—strong, excessive lust and it arose strongly and intensely and just as suddenly and intensely, it went away." Wabi was stunned by this—she had not seen a man nor even a picture of a man. There was no one around, no one with whom she was in love. So why was she feeling lust? Where did the lust come from? She asked these questions and compared it to her feelings of anger: "This feeling arose in me, and like the anger it arose with no outside stimulus and then I understood this: you don't need any outside stimulus to bring up this sort of feeling. It is here in us already. There doesn't have to be another form [rūpa] for it to arise—it is already in our forms already. We don't know it usually, but there it is. I saw that it was in our minds, our mind-consciousnesses. I mean, there I was sitting all day alone in my room—I never saw anyone, so I could think, 'Where did this anger and lust come from?' Really, these feelings had been in me for a long time, but I just hadn't known it. There were a lot of them." The juxtaposition of the anger and the lust, one with a more definable and removed cause, one with less connection to the daily life that Wabi led, made her consider their commonalities; having found their common roots, she could see more about the workings of obstacles and practice:

To improve ourselves rightly, we must see them [anger, lust] as impermanent, just as the Buddha said, because at the time when I was angry at Māechī Mīna I had only suffering, but as soon as [my] heartmind forgave her what she said, I had excessive happi-

ness. . . . The characteristics of the feeling of lust were the same—
it arose and extinguished, it came and it went, it stayed like that.

Understanding their commonalities and, paradoxically, realizing the causes of
the arising of these feelings as she realized their seeming spontaneity led
Wābī to experience great joy:

> It was strange that I felt my body was lighter and the mind that had
> felt like it was suppressed by heaviness, now it was lighter. It was
> a feeling of great happiness. The mind could open and close to lust
> miraculously, automatically.[10] Finally, I almost couldn't grasp that
> lust at all.

The lust was so small that she knew how to make it disappear so there
was no lust anymore. Wābī kept these understandings and experiences to
herself, unsure whether telling another person would benefit anyone or not.

During this same period of retreat, she had another important meditation
experience, part of which was longer and more intense than the previous
ones. The experience took the knowledge she had gained from her previous
meditation experiences and gave her more knowledge—experiential knowledge of Buddhist principles as well as knowledge that would direct her away
from the samnak where she lived and broaden her understanding of the world.

She had been on retreat for over a month when a large ceremonial gathering of more than 500 monks, 100 novices, 140 māechī, and about 50 devoted male and female laypeople took place at the samnak. She was sleeping
outside under the trees, using a meditation umbrella and net, standard tools
for forest contemplatives—an umbrella that suspends a net to the ground
under which a practitioner can sleep and meditate, protecting one from bad
weather and insects and allowing an element of privacy. In her years of living
as a Buddhist, she had never before heard the sound of many monks and
novices chanting. "It was a beautiful sound, and it entered my heart and I
cried in appreciation. I was deeply impressed. The place where they chanted
was very close to where I sat, so there were many people around, but I felt
like everything was very still; I felt free from all things with life. I felt like
even I didn't exist, that there was nothing else with life in this world. It was
as though perception extinguished completely, and I couldn't remember where
I was, who I was, what my name was. It was really empty of all things."
(Perception, sañña-khandha, is the third constituent of five, into which one
can analyze experience and so remove the false conception of self and realize
anattā, one of the three characteristics of reality: body, feeling, perception,
mental formations, and consciousness. In most explanations, the difference
between feeling and perception in the Buddhist framework is quite distinct

from that in Western frameworks: at the level of feeling, the experience is simply good, bad, or neutral. At the level of perception, one has a more detailed sense knowledge, of color, for example. Wābī's use of the term, however, seems more general.)

Her use of the term "empty" refers to the sudden lack of all of the things that had been present previously—she and all of her surroundings and the perception of these things. The beautiful sound of so many chanting people elated her and helped give her a glimpse of what lies outside of the karmic patterns of cause and effect, outside of the round of rebirth and suffering (*samsara*). Suddenly there were no normal phenomena and no Māechī Wābī. The line between self and other, a line that Buddhist philosophy recognizes as delusion, disappeared. Wābī was seeing the world as it is, not somehow separated fundamentally from some false but seemingly more essential Māechī Wābī. Later that night, as the ceremony continued, she sat in meditation and suddenly,

All sounds around me extinguished completely. I could hear nothing else because the noise in my own body was so loud. It wasn't like a noise about which you'd say, "Hey, what was that?" It was a noise in the body, like the blood of my body. This noise in my body was like the noise of a waterfall, the sound of pouring water, but it was noisier than just one waterfall could be. It was like the sound of all my blood in my body making a huge number of waterfalls, sometimes loud, sometimes soft. The sounds were like a cascading waterfall, the sound of pouring water, but different from that of a cascading waterfall, for in a waterfall the water falls only down, and this sound of water in the body, it was as though the water was going both up and down. It rose and fell both. After that, the sound extinguished.

She underwent this primarily auditory experience and then began experiencing a haptic event, during which she applied mindfulness techniques, observing her physical sensations: "After this sound in my body stopped, I was thrust out of my body; there was a sudden sharp pain in my chest. During all this time, I was still mindful, attending thus: 'thrusting pain,' 'cool(ing),' 'cool(ing),' because seemingly as a result of being thrown, shoved so suddenly, out of my body, I was very cold." In labeling her perceptions as she does above, Wābī here describes mindfulness meditation—of being mindful to the stimuli that enter one's consciousness. As she feels the pain in her chest, she labels the experience "thrusting pain" in such a way as to recognize the experience without becoming attached to it and without forcing the experience away (another way of being attached: being attached to *not* having the experience). One often uses the "-ing" form of verbs when being mindful in this manner in order to recognize the immediacy and temporariness of any experience. The Thai terms used are *yen nǭ*—"cool[ing]." As she experienced noise, pain, thrownness, she labeled them so as not to become attached to these but to allow myriad changing experiences to come and go. "I felt this stinging, smarting pain on the front of my body. Sometimes the feeling was overwhelmingly strong, sometimes it died down. It was a feeling like you have, Ms. Brown, when you're riding your bike fast and the wind is hitting the front of your body and you're cold, cold. 'Cool(ing), cool(ing)'. . . . Sometimes it was like my face and chest collided with something because it felt painful on my front." Leaving her body sitting in meditation, Wābī then went on a journey that reveals some of her actions in a previous life.

> Outside of my body, I sometimes moved up high, sometimes I floated forward. . . . By then it was the middle of the night, but the light was not like that; it was the light of the full moon and there was a forest, a dense forest and in it was a deserted house with a yard about ten meters by ten meters, with two guardians. And these men were crying. They said I'd killed them both. I hadn't been a māechī [then, when I'd killed them], I'd been a man. Their bodies were large, but at that time [when they said this] I felt that I *had* killed them— because it was necessary, because it was my duty. I didn't hear what followed because the individual who had led me there told me time was up, and I was gently returned to where I'd been sitting. I [was thrown] back into my body, feeling faint, almost losing consciousness. First I returned to the umbrella, then I reached my body. Once I returned to my body, I felt very tired. It felt as though only a few moments passed, but after I could move my body, I looked at my watch, and it was past two in the morning. I felt faint, tired, very, very tired.

While Wābī gives many physical details of her experience, the feeling of peace amid the chanting by so many people, the sounds of water, the pain and the cold, the removal of her mind or spirit from her body, and the vision of the two men she had killed and the feelings that went with that vision, she does not dwell on them. From her earlier, less complex experience with the fruit, she draws from the lesson of the meditation instructor: one ought not cling to experiences such as this.

After Wābī first told me of this meditation experience, she mentioned it to me in different contexts several times. Her emotions about it varied. For example, she was somewhat taken aback to learn that she had at some point been capable of killing another person. She was also a little disbelieving—

when she notes above that the bodies of the men were large, she is calling attention to the difficulty she had believing that she, a small-bodied person (and a woman at that, she implied) in her present life, could ever have been big enough to kill these large men. But during the experience she *felt* that she had, in fact, killed the men—it is the feeling she had in the situation, during meditation, that battles the doubt in face of the present physical facts. Further battling the doubt is the feeling of why she had killed the men. Hers had not been a crime of passionate hatred, an act that arose from strong emotion, which would have been more difficult for her to believe. She had killed the men because, for whatever the reason, that had been her duty. Being a dutiful person, this reason for killing in her past is not alienatingly distant from her reasons for doing many of the things she does now. In a sense, the vision was largely about the inexorable workings of karma: she acted out of duty, but the action was still one that created negative karmic seeds. I never heard her refer to the experience as a deeply personal opportunity to apologize to the men she had killed; she never described it as a dramatic personal confrontation with old friends she had wronged. Rather, these men were simply two of the many people with whom she had had contact in her previous lives. In this way, the vision broadened and deepened her understanding of herself in the world—in the different worlds at different times. Her many lives had been full of various experiences and people and emotions and duties. She was not simply a village girl with a strangely serious inclination toward Buddhism. She had now experienced herself in a much larger context, and this context was decidedly Buddhist: she had gained at least a partial experience of what the Buddha had attained at enlightenment—knowledge of past lives. In fact, her experiences here in some ways mirror Gotama Buddha's enlightenment experience wherein he is described as realizing three things: details of his past lives, karmic implications of helpful and unhelpful conduct (karmic interconnectedness: *paticca samuppada*), and the four noble truths: that there is suffering, that it has an origin, that there is a cessation of suffering, and that there is a path to that cessation.[11]

Wabī's experiences—of a world suddenly empty, of visiting the men whom she had killed—and her attention to them led her to realize a larger Buddhist principle, perhaps best translated as "suchness" (Pāli: *dhammatā*), the connectedness of all things in cause and effect. She described it:

> I continued to meditate until dawn, and all the monks and māechī were very frightened—I had been sitting very still, not moving at all, for so long. But I myself was peaceful, still. In that incident I felt suchness. From that day on I've been able to understand the meaning of the [Thai] word *thamatā*, suchness. As my mother used to say, everything follows its cause.

Though Wabī uses the Thai term *thamatā*, which usually simply means normal or regular, she clearly means to use it in a specifically Buddhist sense, referring to nature, the law of nature, the connectedness of all things—the Pāli *dhammatā*. In Buddhist texts, this recognition of the connectedness of all things is a glimpse of nibbāna and is called "escape from this whole field of perception."[12] (My loving-kindness-inspired realization of my colleague's and my interrelatedness in serving our college is a humble version of this kind of recognition of suchness.) Understanding suchness so clearly for the first time led Wabī to reflect on education in general:

> And I began to have the feeling that I should get more education than I had because whether it's the worldly life or the contemplative life, both can continue as we progress. . . . If you lack education in Buddhist doctrine already, then it's hard to benefit others, to complete the cycle of benefiting others, to give Dhamma to others, completing the circle of tasks.

Wabī felt that her experiences of the most fundamental Buddhist truths, name and form, the three characteristics of existence, her obstacles, rebirths, and suchness, provided her with a gift to give to those around her. Rather than conceiving of her progress as a straight line, a trajectory, Wabī sees it as the completion of a circle.[13] The gift of understanding implies the sharing of the gift with others; that sharing is the completion of a circle of tasks. Now she had something unique to offer to the world—her understanding of Buddhist truths—but the gift required that she receive further training, because there were societal restrictions on how well her message could be heard. Her sixth-grade education would be an obstacle to other people benefiting from her knowledge. "Educated people couldn't respect me because I have no education," she said. She had learned a lot about life and Buddhism. She wanted to study both meditation and secular subjects.

> I have more of an understanding of men and women, understanding that in the past I've adhered to illusion—in fact, men or women are comprised of parts, name and form. The state of the heartmind: love, anger, bitterness, envy, these are all parts that are there already in our characters, whatever—they or we are not different from each other at all. The only difference lies with which mind can control its form. . . . For sure you can know that we and they still have obstacles that have fermented in our characters. Such obstacles will very soon be shown and others will see them—one day, this day, the next day, or another day.

Her new understanding is related to name and form, in particular its application to men and women. Further, Wabī sees the similarity of all of us at the level of karma. She was reminded repeatedly through her meditation experiences that given the matrix supplied by one's karma, one has the freedom to train the mind to work with obstacles skillfully. Everyone has their own set of karmic difficulties, and everyone can have the tools needed to reach a better existence.

This series of understandings was rooted in the wasp incident with Māechī Mīna. Wabī still cries when she relates that incident, but she also expresses her indebtedness to Mīna:

> I think now that it was good for me that Māechī Mīna said that thing ["Serves you right."], because if she'd never said it, I never would have thought about my future. I never would have considered my life and the state of my education, knowledge. I would have lived satisfactorily at the samnak, helping out, just living. Many things came out of what she'd said.

Wabī saw that in gaining a deeper understanding of Buddhist truths, she could gain different kinds of freedom—the freedom to live anywhere, for example. This ability to live anywhere, she said, "is the life of the person who has gone forth, observing the eight precepts."

She felt that she caused problems between Māechī Mīna and Māechī Senī; she was particularly concerned about Mīna's obvious disdain for and disapproval of her. Further, she was somewhat alienated from her close friend and mentor, Senī, because she felt she could not confide in her about the difficulties with Mīna without causing unhelpful confusion for everyone involved. When a number of other factors came into play, she would move from her permanent residence at Senī's samnak, responding in part to Mīna's dislike and to the knowledge that she had gained from her long retreat. Her ideal as a person who had gone forth was to live unattached to her surroundings, a person truly free to live anywhere. Until her rude awakening through Mīna, she had been able to believe that she could live anywhere, and that she simply chose to live where she did. But now she saw her own blindness and restrictions: she could not just live anywhere. That was an ideal to strive for. This knowledge of herself pushed her out into the world toward an even greater knowledge of herself. As she pointed out:

> At Māechī Senī's I couldn't be at ease because of what Māechī Mīna had said about my being a leech. This was the thing that was really hurting me, and from it came many obstacles. She said it, and I'm sure she forgot it soon thereafter. But I didn't forget. I had many bad

effects from it. I needed to make heartminds better, especially my own; I could see that. I heard it, and I was angry; the obstacles were clear. She said it and forgot, but I remembered. I heard; I was angry.

Chapter 5

Hellfire and Karma

Next the wardens of hell take him feet up and head down and plunge him into a red-hot metal cauldron, burning, blazing, and glowing. He is cooked there in a swirl of froth. And as he is being cooked there in a swirl of froth, he is swept now up, now down, and now across. There he feels painful, racking, piercing feelings.

—Majjhima Nikāya 130.14–15

Māechī Wābī's meditation, intensified since she had become a māechī through daily practice and through three or more months of retreat every year, became the most important aspect of her life. Her experiences were varied and fruitful in her quest to understand the Buddhist teachings, especially in deepening her understanding of karma. Besides the experiences examined earlier in this book, she had others as well that helped her find her way as a religious woman.

For example, one time in meditation she suddenly plummeted into a deep state and found herself falling into a big copper cauldron of the sort in which wrongful persons boil in Buddhist hell. It was, she said, a visit to a past life, where she had suffered for her own wrongful acts. In Buddhist cosmology, beings can be born as humans, animals, ghosts, gods, and hell beings, depending on their karma. The most religiously helpful rebirth is as a human, because humans suffer enough pain (*dukkha*) to recognize the need to escape samsara but not so much pain that they are unable to act on this knowledge. Gods, in the Buddhist understanding, are both a desirable and undesirable rebirth. Gods have a lot of fun—both bodily, if they take some kind of corporeal form, and mentally. But it is harder for them to make spiritual progress, because they do not suffer enough pain to motivate them to escape samsara. Actions that are unhelpful and unkind will cause a being to be born in hell, where suffering is so great that it is difficult to maintain a spiritual practice. Similarly, such actions can cause one to be reborn as an animal or a ghost.

Through Wābī's meditation experience of encountering the men she had killed in a previous life, she had been reminded that her sufferings in the present life were at least partially the result of deeds she committed in past lives. She had been forced to face the very people she had obliterated previously. One of the most basic Buddhist truths—that you karmically reap what you sow—was brought home to her with strong and unforgettable meditation experiences.

These experiences of hell are indeed reminiscent of descriptions of hell from Buddhist texts. In these texts, practitioners ask the Buddha what hell is like, and he claims that one can only begin to imagine the pain and suffering experienced by hell beings. To begin to understand, the Buddha suggests, imagine a king commanding that a robber be struck with 100 spears in the morning, noon, and evening. He asks his listeners if they think that man would experience pain and grief, and they predictably answer yes, even one spear would be enough. The Buddha then takes a stone the size of his hand and says that just as that small stone is to the Himalaya, so that man's pain is to the pain suffered by hell beings. Even that comparison is only a beginning: the Buddha imagines the speared man then tortured with red-hot iron stakes through his hands, feet, and belly. Next he is pared twice—once with axes and once while hanging by his feet upside down with adzes. He is harnessed to a chariot and dragged across fiery ground, then made to climb up and down a hill of burning coals. Next he is drawn up by his feet again and immersed headfirst in a red-hot metal cauldron, where he is cooked and swirled about. Finally he is thrown into the Great Hell of hell, a vast, heated metal box, with flames reaching across the whole interior from every side.[1] The images here are those one finds in Wābī's meditation: red-hot iron stakes, cauldrons, and hooks holding bodies.

Her experiences of hell reminded her that the fruit of karma ripens inevitably; another experience taught her that it can ripen in the same life as when its seeds were sown. One does not need to wait lives before the ripening: "I was [alternately] sitting and walking back and forth in meditation and suddenly I had the feeling of being a fish caught on a hook. The hook came and caught me in the side of my mouth, suspending me in pain—great pain. . . . It wasn't real, but the feeling was real, the pain was real, the suffering was real." She attributed this meditation experience to the karma she gained as a child when she used to fish. She understood not only that karma can ripen and bear fruit in one life but she also received reinforcement of her understanding that even when one does something to help people, if it is a wrongdoing, such as killing something, there is a karmic result. "I enjoyed fishing and bringing fish to my mom to cook and if there were any left over, I would exchange the fish with the villagers for rice." In meditation, she had many opportunities to make offerings to ghosts and to visit hell. Hungry ghosts in the Buddhist cosmology are beings that have very small mouths, long necks, and huge stomachs, thus they are always hungry and desirous but never can feel satisfied, even temporarily. Pictures of them in Buddhist comic books and the like are memorable and graphic. Hungry ghosts approached her, she said, looking at her plaintively.

On one occasion, two ghosts came to her in great distress, and after meditation she made a point of offering candles, flowers, incense, money, and monks' robes at a nearby temple. Later in meditation, they returned to her— wearing better clothes, appearing to be in better physical shape, and thanking her for her kindness. They had received her thoughtful gifts. Such experiences reinforced her understanding of karma and of her power within the karmic round. Because the ghosts came to her, she could help them—they were part of her reality. By serving them as she could, she was able to help them and help herself as well.

One such incident stands out for her as a colorful experience of the whole karmic round.

"One time in meditation I found myself standing near and watching a woman with long, beautiful, flowing hair, wearing a loincloth passed between her legs and fastened at the back with a belt. . . . It was hot and muggy and there was a man, a large man with black reddish skin, beating that woman." The woman screamed and moaned. Watching this scene in hell, Wābī realized that she was each and every person in the scene: the person beating and the person receiving the blows, the person standing watching and the person sitting in meditation. And, of course, seen in the long-range perspective of Buddhist philosophy, she is. We have all been in samsara long enough to play every role in relation to someone else that anyone might play in relation to us in our current lives. Wābī visited hell on many occasions, sometimes watching scenes such as this. "I was in hell another time—at that time I was a man again—without a shirt, wearing only pants, suspended above a fire, being stabbed and beaten. The pain was great—there were no words; I couldn't speak."

By the time Wābī suffered her greatest trials, her meditation had, with years of cultivation, become a richly rewarding garden of understanding for her life. While her temptation had been to blame daily troubles on those around her, her meditation forced her to understand her situation as part of her own karmic lot in life. Just as she was a person who dutifully cooked and cleaned and meditated and chanted at Māechī Senī's samnak, she was also a person who had dutifully killed two people in a past life. Just as she was a person stung by Māechī Mīna's unkind insults, she was a person capable of stinging others—she *was* a person who beat others, was beaten by others, stood by and watched beatings, and sat in meditation on it all. She encompassed all of these realities. Taking time from her daily life in Māechī Senī's samnak to meditate in retreat allowed these truths and sharp, personal images associated with them to enrich her life and to help her become a better, more compassionate, and less prideful person. Thus understanding her karmic situation was not a signal to submit to a cosmic force but rather to understand its workings and to change her karmic interlacement.

Wābī met many beings through her meditation—beings in pain—and she suffered pain with them and because of them, and she inflicted pain on them. She learned of hell experientially, by visiting it. She learned the results of bad actions by boiling in a cauldron and hanging from a hook piercing her cheek. She joined beings in their pain and thus developed a strong empathy. With such reminders—physical, emotional, intellectual, and spiritual—she battled what William Carlos Williams calls his " 'moral drift'—spells when he had forgotten the harm he might have done others and thereby himself as well."[2]

Wābī's demeanor is polite and attentive, and she appears to be not at all self-interested. She was the first person to notice my absence at a meditation sitting at the samnak and to inquire whether I was ill. She is the sort of person who stands a bit apart from most situations and notices the details of what is happening. Yet for all of these fine qualities, she battles pride, a pride evident among those who develop a profession. Robert Coles points out that professional people, in their training, learn a certain language and befriend certain people and exhibit their knowledge among those people in ways that are not always aimed at a greater good: "A professional person's vanity is a critical aspect of his life."[3] Wābī's character and her role as a māechī no doubt invite a similar vanity. She works hard to know her responsibilities and to act on them. She also watches others who are blind to their responsibilities and do not fulfill them. Even these meditation experiences are related to this battle of pride. On the one hand, many of the images were urgings to fully understand the karmic cycle and to act carefully for the good of all within it. On the other hand, who but a very skilled practitioner indeed would be able to see her past lives?

Wābī's meditation experiences and her interpretation of them as well as the relationships she had with those around her contributed to her crisis of faith and the resolution of that crisis. Her meditation was deep and varied and aided her in applying Buddhist concepts to her life, so the concepts became real and useful to her—concepts such as *nāmarūpa* and the three characteristics of existence. Her central understanding of the delights of meditation being as transient as other experiences allowed her to respond to her anger toward a friend creatively. Anger became an opportunity to explore her rootedness in past lives, to develop loving-kindness and examine her own obstacles, and to view the object of her anger as a person as benevolent as she was. She saw the karmic interconnectedness of her life with those around her, including her previous lives, as revealed through her meditation. Her understanding of suchness led Wabī to view herself in a different way: no longer as a person indebted to a mentor but as a person with a gift to give and a need to develop herself enough to give that gift. While Maechī Mīna's comment and treatment of her was negative, Wabī's meditation allowed her to use it and the feelings that arose from it to understand Buddhism better and to thus be able to live in the world more significantly, more carefully. But the incident with Maechī Mīna that led to all of this was only the beginning of what would become a life-altering crisis of faith.

Chapter 6

Like a Corpse-Filled Bowl: Meditation and Māechī

On the gone-forth who abandons unwholesome wishes:
> *Suppose a metal bowl were brought from a shop or a smithy clean and bright; and the owners put clean boiled rice and various soups and sauces into it, and, covering it with another bowl, went back to the market; then people seeing it said, "What is that you are carrying about like a treasure?" Then raising the lid and uncovering it, they looked in, and as soon as they saw they were inspired with such liking, appetite, and relish that even those who were full would want to eat, not to speak of those who were hungry.*
> *—Majjhima Nikāya 5.29–30*

Māechī Wābī enlarged her sensibility, broadened her experience, and deepened her heart through meditation. She rooted herself as a māechī and had experiences that allowed her a perspective of herself in larger spheres: the sphere of the Buddhist universe with its hells and heavens and hungry ghosts and gods and the sphere of public life—her relationships with others close to her and others she did not know.

The stories of the māechī I spoke with reflected how they gained personal strength through meditation, especially during the more significant changes in their lives: when they went forth, established samnaks, and founded social programs. Meditation images such as hungry ghosts often helped them define their struggles and justify their decisions—struggles and decisions that often challenged the norm. Meditation experiences such as Wābī's meeting with the men she had killed in a previous life led māechī down paths of

67

which they could only see the first few steps, providing them with both direction and the confidence to proceed.

Once removed from the standard Thai laywoman's path of marriage and child care, māechī gain more experiences of a broader social world, protected from many of its dangers by their rootedness in the religious life. They meet many whom they would not have met otherwise, and they meet them in ways that invite them to learn and contribute safely.

In order to understand māechī in general and to place Wābī among her peers, we must examine the contemplative practice of meditation building on the foundation of what we know of Wābī's. The roles that meditation plays in the development of māechī are complex, varied, and difficult to study for these reasons and because some kinds of discussion of meditation are discouraged traditionally. For example, practitioners are specifically warned not to brag about special powers attained through meditation. I learned of the meditation experiences only of the māechī with whom I became closest. But to understand māechī, we must understand the roles meditation plays even with these formidable research obstacles because meditation is so important to the māechī themselves and because it has such a large effect on their interactions with others and on the ways in which they live.

Meditation can enforce and give meaning to solitude, deepening one's understanding of Buddhism and one's place in the world. It costs no money and is not merely socially acceptable but lauded.[1] While this first point relating to solitude may seem simplistic and obvious, it is significant and often overlooked. Meditation grounds māechī in being alone, an aloneness often denied women who choose the standard householder path: there are a huge number of social, familial demands on Thai women to interact with and nurture others. Meditation is the most culturally legitimate way to remove oneself from these demands, to make time and space to be alone. Māechī Wābī was, as most Thai women are, raised in a net of responsibilities toward others, a net that allowed little attention to the cultivation of herself and her skills that were unrelated to the family. Once she learned to meditate, she could legitimately be alone and could feel more secure when she was with others. When she first learned to meditate, she enjoyed security and comfort as she ran about with her friends, thinking to herself, "Buddho Buddho Buddho." As she became a young adult, she could secure time to be alone to cultivate her religious practice. Also, she could take a leadership role among the people with whom she was closest—it was she who built the altar in the family house and led the chanting and meditation at it as a young woman. While many consider māechī unworthy of respect, most Thais greatly respect the practice of meditation, considering it difficult and valuable. It would have been awkward at best to fault the young Wābī for meditating.

Scholars have convincingly argued that meditation can improve the status of women in Thailand. One study of women leaders of meditation groups points out that the monk's role is defined very clearly and supported largely according to the ability of monks to follow the rules and to recite texts. Because monks gain respect in these ways, they spend a lot of time learning rules, making sure that they obey them, and memorizing and studying texts.[2] The emphasis is not necessarily on meditation. Women leaders of meditation groups, on the other hand, develop their roles in their ambiguous societal position by studying texts that monks are not studying as much—such as the Abhidhamma texts, systematic treatment of Buddhist philosophy—and meditating as few monks take the time to do. Some explicitly argue that meditation is significant for māechī status and ability to influence society.[3]

Meditation also can encourage a sort of communality. While the meditation experiences of different individuals are, of course, different, they all draw on Buddhist practices, characters, and stories, and in this way individuals share a world in which meditative experiences and Buddhist analyses are seen as valuable. Wābī's experiences of hell included images from the Buddhist texts that all Buddhists recognize. The image of a person dangling over a hot cauldron is one shared by most Thais and certainly by all māechī. Thus māechī, engaged in a private practice, are united in experiencing aspects of Buddhism, even though they may never or may infrequently specifically communicate these experiences. Most samnaks, for example, have scheduled time for residents and visitors to meditate together; they thereby publicly legitimate the private practice—scheduling public time and public space for a practice which, though private, is shared.

There are similarities between this communality and the community encouraged by reading, to which some Western thinkers are turning their attention. Reading "brings [people] together in a way that is constitutive of a particular sort of community: one in which each person's imagining and thinking and feeling are respected as morally valuable."[4] Similarly, when people meditate together or recognize in other ways the importance of meditation (e.g., providing rooms for visitors bare of decorations but holding a mat on which to meditate), they recognize the importance of spiritual development. While not everyone experiences the same things at the same time in meditation, all share certain understandings. Everyone knows, for example, that if you encounter a hungry ghost in meditation, you ought to at least send it loving-kindness or give it something to eat.

In this and other ways, meditation can be an ethical education. Through meditation a person has concrete ways to manage overwhelming and varied emotions and to learn from them. The meditator also has concrete ways to manage the everyday experiences that bring on those emotions. Meditation can remove a person from the nexus causing the emotions and from the tumult of the emotions themselves so he or she can gain greater knowledge from the emotions, allowing them to inform rather than to distract, paralyze, or force a rushed, unhelpful response.

Reexamining in greater depth Wābī's difficulties with Māechī Mīna and how she gained a more helpful perspective on them demonstrates how meditation can bring a wider perception. Wābī was obtuse in not recognizing Māechī Mīna's daily pain in the samnak, pain brought on in part by Wābī's attitudes and actions. Even when Māechī Mīna communicated her pain clearly and directly by causing Wābī pain, Wābī was able to ignore that pain, refusing to see the problems between her and Māechī Mīna and the problems in herself. For years she simply attributed Māechī Mīna's demeanor to Māechī Mīna's karmic situation, brushing away Māechī Mīna's pain and not reflecting on her own responsibilities, her own karmic situation in relation to Māechī Mīna. In this way, as she later explained with humility, she indulged in a kind of moral arrogance. When Wābī went on retreat after the wasp incident with Māechī Mīna, she did not set out to concentrate on her relationship with her and to somehow solve or resolve it. In fact, at the start of the retreat, she would not have claimed that she had much anger or sorrow. Any anger, she would have said, was that of the ill-tempered Māechī Mīna. Meditation practice, however, allowed Wābī's difficulties to reveal themselves, while the practice simultaneously offered her ways in which to understand the difficulties. Daily she had brushed aside the problems, and she looked forward to the retreat as a break from them. But when she was on retreat, huge emotions boiled up during meditation. She could no longer brush aside the feelings and her own responsibilities. She had been lulled into a blind, artificial, and spiritually unhelpful contentment; meditation woke her up and allowed her to see clearly. It allowed her to perceive areas to which she had blinded herself before. She saw her own responsibility in the dynamics with Māechī Mīna. Later she felt indebted to Mīna and to her long retreat for making these problems real to her, inviting her to see them and their greater implications.

This seeing clearly is not just a moral obligation—that Wābī could now see her own karmic problem set more clearly and act on it was a gift of meditation that would allow her spiritual progress.[5] Repeatedly she told me how indebted she was to Māechī Mīna; she struggled to see her consistently in this light. In this way, the clearer perception led not just to a larger appreciation of Wābī's own situation and a call for action but also to a deeper appreciation of another human being. Through meditation, Wābī gained the distance from Māechī Mīna necessary to feel the immediacy of Mīna's pain and to treat Mīna's pain as important. She could no longer dismiss Mīna and Mīna's troubles, and this acceptance of Mīna's pain was a step toward love, toward recognizing Mīna's full humanity and her own. As Nussbaum writes, moral learning begins with seeing, through an image, "some new aspect of the concrete case at hand."[6] When Wãbī saw the two large crying men and knew that she had killed them, she realized the many roles she could play in other people's lives. Reflecting on Mīna's role in her own life in light of this meditation image and the understanding she gained from it, she saw she could no longer dismiss Mīna's pain, nor could she dismiss her as a person. She and Mīna were alike: in the complexity of karmic relations in samsara, she and Mīna both played many roles in relation to each other and to others. In their many lifetimes, they had all played all roles to someone. Wãbī came to see Mīna as fully human and began to work on treating her better.

The Buddhist texts offer lovely metaphors emphasizing perceptual clarity in moral development. The best practitioner is one who, having a blemish—such as sloth and torpor, ill will, envy, avarice—recognizes that she or he has a blemish or one who, not having a blemish, recognizes that she or he does not have a blemish. Someone who, filled with lust, hatred, and delusion, does not recognize herself or himself as someone filled with lust, hatred, and delusion is like an ignored, dirty bowl: "Suppose a bronze dish were brought from a shop or a smithy covered with dirt and stains and the owners neither used it nor had it cleaned but put it away in a dusty corner. Would the bronze dish thus get more defiled and stained later on?" Yes. Thus we know that a person so blind "will not arouse zeal, make effort, or instigate energy to abandon that blemish, and . . . he will die with lust, hate, and delusion, with blemish, with mind defiled." Such a blind person, unable to see a blemish and so unable to allow that blemish to inspire practice, is in samsara and will remain there for a while. A practitioner who outwardly evidences having gone forth from home to homelessness but who harbors qualities such as greed, anger, and delusion is like another bowl: "Suppose a metal bowl were brought from a shop or a smithy clean and bright; and the owners put the carcass of a snake or a dog or a human being in it and, covering it with another bowl, went back to the market; then people seeing it said, 'What is that you are carrying around like a treasure?' Then, raising the lid and uncovering it, they looked in, and as soon as they saw they were inspired with such loathing, repugnance, and disgust that even those who were hungry would not want to eat, not to speak of those who were full." Mãechī Wãbī, able to see that in harboring the three roots of unwholesome action she was like this beautiful but corpse-filled bowl, could now have the zeal and energy to abandon her blemishes.[7]

Through meditation, mãechī are able to care about what happens without getting lost or overinvolved in what happens. They give what happens respectful, quiet attention. This quiet attention invites a person to see what that person might otherwise be unable and/or unwilling to see. We can demonstrate how important this is and the role it can play in the lives of maechi by reexamining aspects of Wabi's going forth.

Wabi chose to go forth to avoid the "heat" of human relations; she thought family relationships were representative of human relations, and she sought to avoid them, cultivating other aspects of her life and character. She had seen what happens to women in families—she had seen them work hard, be abandoned by their husbands, and lack money and sleep. She also had seen them watch as their children's opportunities became smaller and fewer with the growing poverty of the family. And she saw that she could not be the woman she wanted to be in those kinds of relationships. Through her problems with Maechi Mina, she first saw that the religious life was not necessarily a refuge from this "heat." In a way, before her meditation revelations regarding Maechi Mina, Wabi treated people who were unkind to her as inessential to her practice. They were present but ignored; they were not important to her practice. She escaped her family, members of which encouraged her practice only a little: while they chanted before the altar she constructed at home, they otherwise burdened her with large, time-consuming familial responsibilities. When she meditated and saw aspects of her problems with Maechi Mina, she began to fully comprehend other people as being deserving of compassion, just as she was deserving of compassion, and capable of inflicting pain, just as she was capable of inflicting pain.

Through meditation on her anger, she became sensitive to Maechi Mina as a person in her own right, one with whom she could work on her own spiritual development. She could no longer blame the heat of human relations on others and escape it.

Through meditation, maechi allow certain emotions and scenes into their consciousnesses, allowing themselves space, information for their inquiry. They can surrender obtuseness and see things that they might otherwise miss. In this way, a person's meditation experiences are sometimes comparable to the stories a lover of literature collects over time for use in understanding the world and how to behave in it. In examining reading, one philosopher emphasizes "the urgency of our engagements with works of literature, the intimacy of the relationships we form, the way in which we do, like David Copperfield, read 'as if for life,' bringing to the text our hopes, fears, and confusions, and allowing the text to impart a certain structure to our hearts."[8] Just as a person brings to a novel these urgent concerns, and then in a way puts those concerns aside in order to concentrate on the novel, so a person comes to meditation with concerns and puts them aside in order to engage in meditation practice. Yet just as the concerns a person brings to a novel throw into relief certain characters and scenes and plot developments, bringing about certain reading experiences, so a meditator's concerns bring about certain kinds of meditation experiences. By not gazing directly at our deepest personal concerns of the moment, we are able to place those concerns in larger contexts and allow them to reveal profound truths and ways of addressing problems. Meditation removes the "bullwarks of ignorance" when we might otherwise actively refuse knowledge of truth.[9] Removing these areas of ignorance allows perception unclouded by negative selfish emotions.

One of the more dramatic stories I heard relating meditation to crucial times in a māechī's life is the story of Māechī Dārunī's going forth. Dārunī, an extremely independent woman who now successfully runs her own samnak and for some years ran a sewing program for disadvantaged women, had a religious experience that helped her turn away from the household life and fully embrace the religious life. Though the experience did not take place while she was formally sitting in meditation, she said that it was one of the many rewards that meditation has brought her.

At the time of this incident, Dāruni was married and caring for her first child. Her infant daughter was very ill, so ill that her husband's mother thought the baby was going to die. As Dāruni, her mother-in-law, and her husband sat in a room looking over the child, Dāruni watched a māechī enter the room. She quickly asked the other adults in the room to give up a chair so the māechī could sit down. They looked at her in astonishment; Dāruni had been alone in seeing the māechī. She vowed then to go forth if her daughter survived the illness. When her daughter did survive, she went forth for fifteen days at the large temple of an older monk known as a good teacher of meditation.

During this fifteen-day period, Dāruni had several meditation experiences that helped ground her as a spiritual seeker. One evening, when she and others at the samnak were chanting "Our bodies are only skins and bones," she suddenly felt her body become perfectly peaceful. She felt removed from all worldly things, that she could never be a person of the world again. At the end of the fifteen days, her husband and mother-in-law brought her daughter and some clothes so that Dāruni could dress appropriately and come home. But as the family sat in the room, Dāruni saw her husband as a skeleton. He was no longer a live human being to her; the physical space that she knew held her husband had only a skeleton in it, a popular Buddhist symbol indicating impermanence or the change inherent in all existing things. She realized that she could not give up her robes. She could no longer be a wife, condemning herself to more rounds of rebirth by not embracing the opportunity for serious religious practice that being born in a human body gives. Samsara is where we spend many lifetimes, according to the Buddhist conception; we remain in samsara as long as we are gods, ghosts, hell beings, animals, and humans. Thus samsara is referred to as "the flood of tears shed by you crying and weeping as ye fare on" to the "waters in the four seas."[10]

Dārunī refused to go home with her husband and mother-in-law because she had a newfound appreciation of her rare position as a human being—she now had the opportunity to seek release from samsara. Dārunī remained a māechī; her husband raised the baby.

When Dārunī fulfilled her vow to go forth because of her daughter's ill health, she did not know that a central problem of her life lay in her choice to become a householder, yet through meditation during those fifteen days, she learned this and had experiences to ground her in this understanding and to legitimate it. Dārunī did not look directly at her problems. Indeed, she did not even realize that she had problems at the time: her child's illness was finished. She went forth to fulfill a vow. Doing so, it was revealed in meditation that she ought not indulge in the pleasures of the householder life. By not looking at her life and problems, she saw her problems and their implications and solutions clearly and in a Buddhist framework.

Meditation can also broaden the world of the meditator by introducing new characters, worlds, and situations in the same ways that literature can. Just as Nussbaum argues that literature can extend our experience, making it less "confined and parochial," so can meditation. Māechī Wābī's and Māechī Dārunī's hungry ghosts and skeletons are characters in their lives with whom they have creative relationships. Yet because these beings are not part of their intersubjective daily reality, their perceptions of them can be more clear. While Wābī suffered a great deal of pain in meditation, she gained great clarity in her dealings with other people. Dārunī's life is vibrantly populated with hungry ghosts and gods with whom she speaks on a daily basis; they help her as she helps them. For example, I once asked her why gods came to her. I could understand, I said, why hungry ghosts in their suffering would turn to her, a māechī, in hopes of her dedicating merit to them and thus improving their condition. Just as Wābī was approached in meditation by hungry ghosts who benefited from her aid and perhaps hoped to earn a better rebirth for her kindness, so the hungry ghosts who approached Dārunī hoped for a better situation. (The Buddhist texts make the relationship clear when describing a good wish of a practitioner: "When my kinsmen and relatives have passed away and died remember me with confidence in their minds, may that bring them great fruit and great benefit."[11]) When those who knew Dārunī remember her goodness, that remembering is merit for them, a helpful act of the mind that may help them achieve a better rebirth. I could see, then, why ghosts approached Dārunī, but I could not see why the gods would come to Dārunī. When I asked, she looked at me in perfectly open and gleeful appreciation of my ignorance, shaking her head and asking, after a significant pause, "Disney (until my last day at her samnak, she consistently called me "Disney"), when you walk down the street, do you stop and say hello to everyone you meet? No. Well, I don't stop and talk with every god and hungry ghost I meet. Only the ones I know." Dārunī has plenty of gods and ghosts to choose to speak with—but she chooses to speak with the ones she knows. And really, any being who approaches her gains merit in contemplating her goodness—whether that being is in one of the easier realms of being, such as gods, or in the harder realms of being, such as hell beings and ghosts.

Wābī and Dārunī have never met, but much of what they do in meditation is similar, as are the benefits they derive from meditation. They are sensitive, enmeshed in a meaningful, broad Buddhist world, and they respond to and know beings of many sorts who help them as they frame their lives and act.

Chapter 7

A Heart Defeated in Faith:
Crisis and Loss

*What should be done for his disciples out of compassion by a
teacher who seeks their welfare and has compassion for them [to
teach them the Dhamma], that I have done for you, Cunda. There
are these roots of trees, these empty huts. Meditate, Cunda, do
not delay or else you will regret it later. This is our instruction
to you.*

—*Majjhima Nikāya* 8.18.

Meditation played a huge role in Māechī Wābī's life from her childhood, as
she ran about repeating internally "Buddho Buddho Buddho," and her young
adulthood, as she experienced peace doing calm meditation during her first
retreat, and in her varied experiences and deep understandings of Buddhist
philosophy revealed in her practice under Māechī Senī and other meditation
instructors. Through meditation on the wasp incident with Māechī Mīna, she
came to understand both of their places in the Buddhist world more clearly;
the incident and its repercussions also contributed to, though they were not
the core of, a deep religious crisis.

As Wābī and I talked every day for hours about her life and the most
important stories of it, she circled around a central incident. She was reluctant
to tell me about the event. Later she told me that she contemplated for a long
time whether to tell me. She questioned her own motives, where the information would go, and what effect it might have on her life, on the people in
her life, and on the readers of this book. Finally, she told me the whole story.
It was important in her life, she said, and it explained why she had come to
the samnak where I met her. Also, she said, she had come to trust me and my

76

intentions, and perhaps most importantly she thought that telling this story might help others.

She described this incident succinctly: "One time when I was meditating at a temple I had a large shock. I was meditating there, you know, and meditating is very important for me. It has to do with living a real life; it's not a mundane thing. A meditation teacher came in and accused me of a wrongdoing. She didn't know the real story—she didn't know me. There was a group of us meditating there very seriously, and she picked me out and accused me."

Through many conversations at different times over the following months, I pieced together the details. One rainy season, Wābī went to the samnak to which she usually went annually to meditate seriously for three or four months. She had been meditating and living at this other samnak for two months when the meditation instructor, Māechī Noy, who was also the meditation instructor of Māechī Senī, approached Wābī in the hall in the presence of two other practitioners. The instructor asked for Wābī's help because she had an appointment. Wābī, of course, was happy to offer her assistance. Noy asked her to tell the new practitioners about her own meditation experiences. Wābī, she reasoned, had been meditating for some time and could substitute for one day in helping those present at the retreat, especially the newcomers, learn about meditation as they began their retreats.

Wābī, having learned what was being asked of her, was hesitant for a number of reasons. One was that her meditation experiences during this period were painful. Sharp pains racked her body as she sat in the meditation hall. "I felt as if my body were breaking apart, scattering, becoming little seeds the size of grains of sand—the smallest of small, such that you can't even hold them." In meditation, she watched as a traditional food container, consisting of bowls of food layered on top of one another and fastened together to be carried, broke and scattered into parts. "The walls of the room broke apart, and my mind felt as though in each split second it opened and closed—was conscious and unconscious. I think at that time I didn't need to breathe much—my breath was very shallow, tiny, just the same really as at death, but I didn't die. . . . As this continued I suffered a great deal. Courage was required as the fruit of old karma appeared." While these experiences might indicate a particularly fruitful meditation state, relating this pain she was experiencing when she was only beginning to understand it might not be helpful to new meditators. Also, on a day not long before the meditation teacher made this request, Wābī's meditation had been particularly painful and dramatic. She had returned to a past life, when she was a warrior in battle. Around her were many injured and dying people. She herself, then a man, had been stabbed by a long sword.

My body was covered in red blood, and fresh blood gushed out of my nose and mouth and wounds. There was great suffering, but the state at that time of my real body was that I was sitting at the temple, with tears falling and saliva filling my mouth. Tears fell from my eyes and water ran from my nose. There were māechī helping massage my body and giving me medicine for fainting. In the vision blood covered my body; in the temple, there were tears and saliva but no blood.

Wābī was also hesitant to take over teaching meditation—even for one session—because she was disturbed that the meditation teacher disagreed with Māechī Senī's interpretation of Wābī's meditative state. Senī had given her advice on the meditation state, but when Noy had learned of that advice, she had reminded Wābī that she was now at *her* samnak. When at Senī's samnak, a meditator should follow Senī's advice; when at Noy's samnak, a mediator should follow Noy's directives. Wābī was troubled by the disagreement between the two teachers she respected. Not wanting to relate stories of this painful meditation, and not wanting to address the complexity of the dueling teachers problem, Wābī asked the teacher if she could focus on other meditation experiences. Her teacher told her to relate whichever meditation experiences she wanted: "She said, 'Never mind; this is all Buddhism. Traveling, and knowing many different things, that's okay. It's like if you're going to Bangkok, you can go by train or bus—both will get you there.' "

Wābī remained hesitant. Not only was her decision clouded by her painful meditation and the disagreement between the two teachers, it was clouded by lack of experience. She had never taught before; she was unsure about teaching in general and teaching meditation in particular. She asked the teacher, "What if I say something that is bad, something wrong . . . something unhelpful (*bàp*)?" She was concerned about the karmic implications for herself in saying something wrong, but she also was concerned about the implications for the people listening—they might learn wrongly about this important religious practice that had been so helpful to her. Noy replied: "Oh, never mind—at first we all have this kind of problem. Me, too, when I first started training practitioners. I sometimes made mistakes in teaching. It's all practice, so it's okay. It's a time for you to practice teaching. You came here to practice, and you can practice teaching, too."

Reflecting back on her reservations and the teacher's urgings, Wābī does not condone the teacher's decision to invite her to instruct and the teacher's casual dismissal of the dangers and Wābī's concerns. "[Teaching others meditation] is very, very dangerous. A person who has meditated a lot, they understand that this is a dangerous situation. They understand why it's dangerous. They can see what it might cause. . . . I don't think she understood the dangers. If you develop your mind to a certain level, you'd never invite me to do this thing. You'd know what kind of problems might result, what kind of incidents might come about." There are warnings in Buddhist literature, for example, about the dangers of mistaking an understanding as evidence that the practitioner has reached a certain level of practice when she or he has not. Such a misunderstanding can lead at the very least to a waste of time— if the practitioner stalls in a practice that is not moving her or him toward greater insight. Alternately, a teacher of meditation could misunderstand a practitioner's problem and thus suggest a meditation that leads the practice away from insight.[1]

Because Wābī's superior had requested the favor, however, Wābī agreed to teach the practitioners in the instructor's absence. She meditated, as usual, all that day, and at about four in the afternoon, she simply told her fellow meditators about some of her experiences. She did not tell them about some of the more dramatic incidents, such as when she first left her body and saw hell beings. "The teacher had said to talk about my experiences so that they could hear them. So I just told them, normally, indifferently." In recounting the story, Wābī emphasized that she had simply done what the teacher had asked her to do as well as possible. "I didn't know really what she wanted. I didn't know. I didn't have any experience. I'd never taught anyone. I'd never told these experiences to anyone except teachers. I'd never taught practitioners. She had this idea for me to speak. I explained [to her] before-hand: I'll talk about this."

Wābī explained her method of walking meditation and about one time when she had felt her body was covered in fur. She spoke for thirty minutes and then returned to her meditation. Twenty women in the room listened as she spoke. Although the teacher was not there, the teacher's mother was: "She was staring at me, and it made me feel strange and wonder, 'Why is she staring at me like this?' " Wābī remained uncomfortable about having taught the other meditators.

After speaking of her experiences, the other practitioners called her *ačhān*, the term they used to address the teacher herself, a deeply respectful word meaning "teacher" or "professor." She resisted this elevation in her status, asking them not to call her by this term of respect, repeatedly telling them that she was a practitioner, just as they were. Later there were indications that something was wrong.

At around nine that night, I thought something might be happen-ing—an incident was going on. I felt strange. . . . That night I'd showered at nine, and I heard a meeting called for all practitioners. The teacher was very angry; she was showing her anger a lot. She was extremely mad at me. I wondered what was wrong, but I certainly

knew *something* was wrong. That was clear. I didn't have any time
to prepare myself [emotionally]. I could tell by the way she looked
at my face that she was angry at me for some reason.

One of the other people who had met with the teacher and her mother
looked at Wābī and drew her index finger across her throat in a cutting
motion. Wābī was in trouble, but she had no opportunity to learn in private
conversation with the teacher what the problem was. All of the practitioners
gathered in the hall, and when they were seated, the meditation instructor
singled Wābī out, asking and accusing, "Who asked you, who told you that
you could teach the practitioners?" The meditation instructor was obviously
seething in anger; her mouth was very tight, very controlled. "This was when
my shock came. It's not a horrible question in itself, but in the context it was
horrible. I was sick and overcome with shock. She said this in the meeting,
in front of over twenty people, 'Who asked you, who told you you could
teach the practitioners?' "

Wābī had no real opportunity to defend herself. The person with the
highest status in the room had accused her, a person with comparatively low
status, of an inexcusable action: teaching about meditation without permission from the real teacher, elevating herself to a level undeserved. In Thailand's
strict hierarchical society, this self-elevation is not easily dismissed. As one
scholar notes, "To overlook the etiquette of one's station is a first step toward
decline."[2] Wābī was dumbfounded at the accusation and its implications and
could only manage a frozen smile listening to the charge. "I smiled. Why?
Because I couldn't speak. Why? She was the person who'd ordered me to
teach. She'd asked me to do it. Then she pointed at me and asked me who
had asked me to teach! And now she was asking whether I was a practitioner
(*nak patibat*)—[or a teacher]. . . . I couldn't speak." Even as she told me the
story several years after the event, she was nervous, speaking quickly, her
voice rising a pitch. Then she caught herself and tried to calm down. "I have
great compassion for her. It was, she, I pity her. She used me, asked me to
teach. Then she left, and when she returned, everything had changed. She
said, 'Teach the practitioners to practice, to meditate, calm meditation, not
insight.' '-ing,' that style, that's calm meditation, not insight meditation. I
had practiced this way, practiced '-ing,' but I hadn't done it since I had been
practicing at that temple, and then I told them what had happened to me when
I did this practice that I used to do. Then the teacher said, 'A practitioner
came to me and told me what she heard,' but I knew by the way that her
mother looked at me that the 'practitioner' she spoke of was her own mother.
It was her own mother."

Wābī's concerns with status are clear as she indignantly and desperately
referred to the difference between the mother's vows and her own: "Her

mother hadn't even gone forth. She wore white, but she ate in the late afternoons." Because Wābī followed eight precepts and the mother only five, she was incensed that the mother was trusted more and treated better than she.

There were only two other people at the temple who knew that Wābī had not stepped out of line to teach but in fact had responded to a direct request from the teacher herself; they spoke up while Wābī sat paralyzed with horror. "They said, 'Teacher, you were the one who asked her to instruct.' But the teacher said, 'I didn't ask you; I asked Wābī.' " Wābī remained too shocked to say a word.

> The teacher said I'd taught incorrectly. She said I hadn't taught what
> was taught at that place; she said at that place they didn't use the "-
> ing" practice. They taught a different style, name-and-form. I didn't
> have anything to say. I didn't think it was necessary to speak—
> speaking would have no purpose now. She'd told me to teach herself, and then she came back and asked me this. It wasn't necessary
> to speak—there'd be no meaning in it. She was higher than me, the
> head of that place. . . . She'd told me to teach whatever I wanted. I
> had trusted her, I had believed her, but when I heard her ask me this
> question, I knew she hadn't been sincere with me. . . . She said I'd
> taught without her permission, that I'd come to practice but I'd
> taught instead. That I wanted to teach, not practice.

There were many long- and short-term physical, emotional, mental, and spiritual effects of this incident. Almost immediately, Wābī packed her things to leave that temple, though she had originally intended to stay there another two months. She became very ill, however, and had to be taken to the hospital. "At 11 P.M. I drank just a bit of fruit juice because I hadn't eaten in so long—I threw up whenever I ate. A māechī who had seen me and noticed that I was dedicated to meditation wanted to make merit, so she gave me a small bottle of orange juice to drink. I drank it and was violently ill from then until nine the next morning." She was taken to the hospital and hooked up to an IV. She thought she was facing her own death. For Wābī, all of this had to do with meditation, the very center of her life; she had been in a very serious meditation state at the retreat. Now she was in shock: "My heartmind was not okay. My health, my body, my health was suddenly not strong." She stayed several days at the hospital and then returned to the temple. Her fellow practitioners gathered around to say good-bye, to offer some support, but for Wābī life no longer had any meaning or purpose. She remained physically exhausted and sick. She could not even walk to her room after returning from the hospital; she had to stop and rest every few feet. Those around her were frightened that she would die.

Wabī's earlier realizations related to name and form led her to experience parts of this physical and mental crisis in a unique manner:

I wasn't afraid to die. My heart was at peace; my heart had happiness. It was my body that had suffering. It had only suffering. I was not sorry to die. My heart was full, happy; I couldn't be sorry to die at that time. I wouldn't have wasted my life. Before I'd had little merit: I'd had old karma from the past, from other lives, from the past, that was bad; and I needed to do good. I needed to get rid of the bad karma. I needed to do a lot of good. I understood this. But I don't think the people at the temple understood this; they were just afraid I'd die. But I thought: if I die, I won't regret it, I don't have any problems.

A māechī friend took her to the bus station, worried that Wabī would be unable to travel safely because of her illness. Wabī's mental peace in the face of the physical pain did not last long.

That teacher had said, "You've traveled wrong, thinking you are to be a teacher of meditation." Speaking these words is wrong. It's bad. Okay, I thought: I had some knowledge, but it has failed me. This person has misunderstood things. She didn't see the real story. But she is a teacher. But she has done wrong. This is bad. She was a bad person. I suffered, pain, pain, pain. I had no energy or will for practice. Pain, pain, pain. I was sorry. I had to . . . consider everything very carefully.

The teacher's words hurled Wabī to the lowest she had ever been. While different incidents contributed to the form of the crisis and the crisis itself, the words of the teacher left her without a foundation. One aspect of Wabī's cognitive dissonance was caused by utter humiliation and the difficulty she had reconciling two paradoxical ideas: that this person was a teacher and therefore a person who does right, and that this person, a teacher, did something that seemed very wrong. Wabī had placed her trust in a teacher when she was seventeen and that teacher, Māechī Senī, had offered to give her a whole rewarding way of life and guidance in living it; she had had no reason to question her trust in a teacher, and the woman now calling her trust into question was Senī's own teacher. If there were a person she felt she ought to be able to trust implicitly, it would be the teacher of her own worthy teacher—both because of her status as a teacher and because of her relationship with Senī. A central aspect of her faith was called into question: "In the past I had faith. Now my faith was very different, and I needed to take the time to know it better."

Whether this crisis was more a crisis of faith in Buddhism, in a person of higher status within a Buddhist hierarchy, in the Buddhist hierarchy found in Thailand itself, in any Buddhist hierarchy, or in any hierarchy at all is worthy of exploration. Immediately upon speaking about how her faith had changed and how she needed to learn about it, she used Buddhist concepts to interpret the experience: "Now my faith was very different, and I needed to take the time to know it better. Everything really is impermanent, not-self, unsatisfactory." While her faith was very different, it certainly had some of the same components: the three Buddhist characteristics of existence. Quickly thereafter, she reemphasized how difficult the time was: "I have to tell you that this incident really finished off my energy. Telling this story is hard. I was sick for a long time afterwards; I was shocked, very shocked." The quick application of Buddhist principles to understand a situation that she defined as a faith challenge points to the come-and-see aspect of Buddhism, of religions from India—religions that purport that certain practices will inevitably lead one to experience the truth of that religion. On this point, one scholar writes: "A more precise rendering [of "faith"] would be 'confidence (in the truth of doctrines not personally experienced)', since in Buddhism and all Indian religion it is always said to be in principle possible for any individual to experience personally the truth of such doctrines, by himself becoming an ascetic and undergoing the necessary practices."[3] Wābī retained her confidence in Buddhism, in that she used Buddhist categories to interpret the experience that called into question her way of life. On the other hand, she was no longer sure that she could live that way of life.

After leaving the hospital, Wābī felt that she had nowhere to go and no one with whom she could talk. The meditation instructor was close friends with Māechī Senī, the only person Wābī felt she might be able to trust completely. "I had a difficulty that Thais call mouth flood—a thing that you can't be calm about, a thing about which you can't speak. See, my teacher is the follower [lūksit] of this woman, and I am the follower of my teacher. So I couldn't tell her this story of her teacher." Worse yet, Senī, eager to understand and help, was struggling to determine if Wābī's suffering was from the style of meditation that she was doing or from the karmic results of past actions. Wābī, unable, she felt, to tell Senī of the incident, allowed her teacher to guess at the cause of her illness, further alienating her from the people around her who cared. Wābī returned to Senī's samnak three days before entering the rainy season, and she was advised by Senī to practice further. Senī advised her to meditate seriously another ten months so that she would have been on retreat for a full year. The meditation state she had reached was an important one. "This wasn't a state for working—it was a state for meditative practice. I had gained a lot of knowledge, a lot of knowledge about myself. This wasn't knowledge about other things—it was

knowledge about myself, about practice, about meditation. It was better."
Though she realized the importance of the meditation experiences she was
having, she was also very sick; she was resistant to practicing more. Wābī did
not want to repeat the horrible illness that had led her to the hospital. "I just
drank that one bottle of orange juice that that woman gave me and I got so
sick. At first [I said to myself], 'Okay, it doesn't matter.' With such pain in
my body during meditation, when it felt like my soul was being ripped from
my body, [I could discount it]—it didn't matter, Okay, I could stay. Once I'd
drunk that orange juice, though, I didn't know what else might happen. I
couldn't eat any food, I couldn't drink juice."

Living in Senī's samnak, Wābī was still unable to care for herself properly. She could not work, could not go to the toilet by herself. She could not
open her eyes without feeling the room spin. She could not eat anything
without vomiting. "I could only drink ginger juice in hot water. This was all
I ate and drank for three whole months. I didn't die because I drank so much
of the ginger juice. I lost a lot of weight. It was very very strange: I looked
the same, but my face looked white. There was no color in my face." Senī
and another māechī helped her to the toilet, washed her clothes for her, and
brought her ginger tea. She was frightened and uncomfortable having her
teacher help her in these basic ways, ways that defied their relative status, and
the difficulties with Māechī Mīna remained. "I was scared—I was an individual, an adult. Māechī Senī helped me, [another māechī] helped, but I was
uncomfortable with this. Māechī Mīna didn't understand—I couldn't do [these
things] myself. The toilet was far away. She thought I was faking it, that my
illness wasn't real."

She yearned to discuss her difficulties with another who had gone forth,
who might be able to understand her feelings and circumstances, but calamity
had struck the other ordained person to whom she felt she might have been
able to turn. Her father, a dedicated collector of books on Buddhism, had
gone out of town one day and had returned to find his residence and all of
his belongings—most preciously, his books—burned to the ground by a fire
caused by faulty electrical wiring. He was upset, and she did not want to
burden him with her own problems. Further, as a māechī, she did not feel that
she could turn to people who had not gone forth for advice. They lived in a
different world with different problems, and their own problems were already
large and impinging on her. "I thought I'd better return home. I thought I'd
better return home after the rainy season because I couldn't help out at all [at
the samnak]. I thought I'd better live near my mother. Maybe I'd get better."
When the rainy season ended, Wābī asked Māechī Senī for permission to
leave the samnak and to go home. Senī and the others there had already
helped her enough, and she missed her mother's care. "My mother had said
when I went forth that people who go forth have no one to look after them

when they are sick. If I ever got sick I should remember that my mother would take care of me forever—that if she were still alive, she'd help me, she'd help all her children. I thought about these words of my mother a lot. I cried, thinking of them. I thought it would be better if I went home."

Wābī, suffering reverberations from the most profound disappointment she had ever experienced, a disappointment that was leading her to question the life she had chosen seven years earlier, a rewarding life that had given her valuable work, a place to live, food every day, and the closest friend she had ever had, wondered if she should put aside her robes. She longed for the security once provided by her mother. Deeply troubled, she decided to return home to visit her mother and to consider divestiture of her robes and living the householder life.

This visit home was uncomfortable. Living in the "hot" world of house-holders, Wābī struggled. "Once there I remembered the heat I'd felt when-ever I was home—I couldn't live there; I couldn't spend the night in that house. I went home one day, and I couldn't sleep the whole night. I went to stay in the temple. I was hot, hot, just like being in hell. I knew where heat came from, I'd already been to hell." Unwilling to burden Māechī Senī further and unable to live at home with her mother, Wābī's struggle in-creased. She could neither eat nor wash her clothes. She was too weak even to lift a glass of milk. "At first I thought, this is the first time this has ever happened to me. Before that, if I'd had a problem, I would respect the prob-lem, I would practice. Like the problem with Māechī Mīna, I could medi-tate—I could practice to take care of myself, to set my heart at ease, and the problem disappeared. I knew what to do and how to solve the problem. I could then work with [Māechī Mīna]. My mindfulness was weak, so I worked on my mindfulness. I practiced to improve my mindfulness."

But after the incident with the teacher, "I had no place to go, no place to be. My heartmind had no place to be. Practice had always been a refuge; now I had no refuge for my heartmind." She had lost the "perfect confidence" in the Buddha, Dhamma, and Sangha that a practitioner gains through seeing the Dhamma for one's self.[4]

Chapter 8

Perseverance and Striving: Resolution of the Crisis

A bhikkhu is angry and displeased with his companions in the holy life, resentful and callous towards them, and thus his mind does not incline to ardour, devotion, perseverance, and striving. As his mind does not incline to ardour, devotion, perseverance, and striving, that is the . . . wilderness in the heart that he has not abandoned.

—*Majjhima Nikāya* 16.7

In desperation, unable to engage in meditation, a mental and spiritual practice that had been both a major attraction to the holy life as well as a refuge and challenge to her for years, and lacking even a physical refuge, Māechī Wābī turned to her father and asked permission to stay at his temple while she thought things over and recovered from her illness. Once in the temple, she was able to take care of herself with some help from a younger brother who had been a novice there for four years. "Of all this suffering the worst was feeling that I was unable to help those around me. When I'd been sick I couldn't contribute at all," Wābī said of the time. Her father's temple was designed for monks, so she slept on a mat in the kitchen; no other appropriate accommodations were available for women at the temple. Though somewhat physically recovered, she was lonely for the company of other māechī: "I couldn't live there because there were no māechī at all. I just couldn't live like that. There was my father, and my younger brother, but I had no friends there. I need friends around, women, so we can be women-friends together."

Wābī then saw the world from the viewpoint of most māechī in Thailand as they live among monks. In temples designed for monks who are mistaken

86

as the sole core of Buddhism (instead of as *part* of one of the three traditional refuges of Buddhism: the Buddha, the Dhamma, and the Sangha), these women piece together lives on the margins of their male-dominated temples. Most māechī in this situation rely on food they buy or on the leftovers of monks, but Wābī went out to collect alms as she had when she lived at Māechī Senī's samnak: "Those people there—they'd never seen a māechī before I went alms-collecting there. I was the first ever to collect alms in that area. They looked at me and said things like, 'Eh? What is that, a man or a woman?' 'Why is that monk wearing white?' They didn't know māechī. They'd never seen māechī before. . . . The monks went first, then the novices, and finally me. . . . They gave to the monks, to the novices, and to me. They filled my alms bowl."

In this time of weakness, she felt that she was contributing in one significant way: by going on alms rounds. Even as she struggled to remain a māechī and to find meaning and purpose in that life, she introduced others to the possibility of going forth as a māechī: "I kind of wanted to hide, but then I thought: they've never seen a māechī before. It's like when I was a child, I'd never seen one—just once actually, and I determined in my heart I wanted to do that, to wear that white."

Her father recommended that she meditate seriously some more. She decided he was right, that she should rededicate herself to her practice. "So I left when I was a bit better, when I could take care of myself. . . . My father knew of a samnak with some knowledgeable practitioners . . . so I went to this place and I practiced very seriously for two months."

In losing refuges, Wābī gained them—stronger ones: as a young woman, in losing her family as refuge, she gained the refuge of Māechī Senī, her samnak, the wider community of māechī, and meditation—important aspects of the Buddhist path. She began to lose Senī's samnak as a refuge from the heat of human relations in the incident with Māechī Mīna. Later, when, as a result of the incident with her teacher, she could neither feel the value of meditation nor remain at her own samnak refuge, she came to understand that even aspects of the Buddhist path have the qualities of existing things—they too are *anicca, dukkha,* and *anattā.* When Wābī was accused by her teacher of teaching unrequested, she lost the most significant refuge she had found in the religious life. There was no way, even on retreat, even away from the people in her everyday life, that she could avoid the heat and hell of human relations and still be in contact with humans. Wābī found that there were no lasting, perfectly calm interpersonal relationships among and in which she could practice untouched by human concerns. When she began to meditate after months of refusing to do so, she started to build her life again, a life that recognized that she was part of the heat of human relations and thus could act more responsibly and ably within it when she recognized her own place in the heat. Every existing thing, even her samnak and meditation, changed, involved suffering, and lacked an essential self.

Wābī's crises with Māechī Mīna and with the teacher are deaths of her conception of herself as being morally pure and karmically superior. The purity she thought she had gained in the religious life was revealed as a limited purity. She thought she could live without bad action, but she learned she had bad karma just as all those with whom she had contact; human relations are very complex, and everyone acts less than perfectly sometimes. Even closely evaluated, careful, "perfect" actions rarely appear flawless in the complexity of intimate human relations. Wābī faced this when she realized Mīna's karmic situation was just like hers. She realized this more fully when she realized the teacher's karmic situation was just like hers.

Finding meditation again was one important element of her coming out of the crisis. Other important elements were the death of a person she greatly respected and a sign of tenacious loyalty as well as appreciation from Māechī Senī. Senī's father had died while Wābī was practicing at that temple, and Senī called Wābī out of her isolation to return to her samnak for the funeral. One of Senī's siblings wanted their father's cremation to take place immediately, but Senī disagreed, telling her family that they must wait for Wābī to come from the temple at which she was staying. "She told them that really even though I wasn't his child, he had loved me a lot, and she told how I had cared for him for a long time—longer than his real children—had cared for him more. I traveled back and then Māechī Senī could decide when the cremation was. I felt very sad with his passing away; it was as if he had been my only living relative." Despite having seen her mother and father recently, she still felt alone and alienated in the face of Senī's father's death and was greatly comforted by Senī's gesture, which cut through their inability to communicate about the source of her difficulties with a fundamental message of love, respect, and appreciation. She reflected on her life: "So when he passed away, I began thinking of my own life, how to manage myself, what would be good for me."

Once again, however, as things in her life stabilized, more things destabilized: she learned that her mother had been in a serious car accident and could not walk. Recovery would take a long time, and Wābī was requested to return home. It was the first time since going forth that she had returned home twice in a year. She was disturbed to find how difficult it was to live in the house with her mother and older sister: "It was impossible to live there caring for my mother—I felt it was so hot, the same as in hell, exactly the same as that time when I'd gone to hell."

She returned to Senī's samnak once again, leaving her mother in her elder sister's care. She compared her situation then to preparing a boat for ocean travel. She had been, she said, hoarding food and mending the leaks in her boat, but she had yet to take her boat anywhere—she had yet to put the boat to the use for which it had been created. The boat was in bad condition, and she had no compass. "If I went into the ocean with that boat and no compass I thought I'd end up drowning in the ocean, so I decided to look for the compass first, and that is wisdom—education both worldly and religious." She clearly discerned that she would go to some new place. Either separated physically and/or emotionally from those she loved and who loved her, "I came to know that those people couldn't help me get rid of my obstacles—no one except me could extinguish them. The Lord Buddha can't remove someone bound by all suffering, only you yourself can strip yourself from all suffering—you are the only one. A person can only point [the way]." Now able to meditate, Wābī sought direction—the wisdom that would be her compass. Wisdom meant not only the many kinds of knowledge gained in meditation such as knowledge of karma, the three characteristics, and the obstacles—but also secular knowledge. Wābī now sought knowledge of the world and of the people in the world. As she meditated, she learned where her earlier faith was weak and created a larger view of what Buddhism is: "This has to do with regaining my faith in Buddhism. For many years I knew some parts of Buddhism, but I didn't know the whole story. There are many aspects to Buddhism." Wābī knew Buddhist philosophy, stories, ethics, rituals, and symbols, but she did not know how individuals were differently Buddhist: "In the past I thought it wasn't necessary to know all different ways of being Buddhist. I thought meditation was enough. I thought you just found the things that helped you—for example, making merit, helping others. But now I see I must spend a long period of time practicing very seriously, examining my faith. I used to have a lot of faith. But three years ago I thought I might disrobe; my faith was shaken. I didn't think anyone could understand my heart. I saw then that faith isn't something that lasts, too. It changes, just like everything else. I knew I had a lot of obstacles.

"Faith is an issue of practice. Through practice you can get rid of your obstacles, you can know right from wrong. You train your heart so that you can know."

Her words here echo themes from "Effacement," a *sutta* of the *Majjhima Nikāya*. Most of the *sutta* consists of a list of negative problems and qualities that are, says the Buddha, counteracted with a list of positive solutions and qualities:

1. A person given to cruelty has non-cruelty by which to avoid it.
2. One given to killing living beings has abstention from killing living beings by which to avoid it.

3. One given to taking what is not given has abstention from taking what is not given by which to avoid it.

4. One given to be uncelibate has celibacy by which to avoid it.

5. One given to false speech has abstention from false speech by which to avoid it.[1]

Wābī had what she needed, because for every unhelpful quality there is its helpful opposite. Working to establish faith, however, was a new task for her:

> I tried to establish faith in my heart again. In the past I hadn't had to do that; I didn't have to know about that. I just had faith in my heart, so I didn't have to try to establish it. Trying to establish faith in my heart, I asked, "Why did I go forth? What is the purpose of going forth?" In the past, five rainy seasons ago, I would have said that you go forth because life is suffering. But it's not so simple anymore. This is very important for me. Education is my second story, religion is my first story. And the more I see of the world, the more I understand what Buddhism is. In order to get education, I have had to suffer a lot—it has been a story of crying for me. But in my quest for education I have also been able to understand more about faith so that I can understand the world better.

Reestablishing her faith meant exploring other ways of being a māechī— it led her to take another look at education. In her childhood, Wābī had been both attracted to and repulsed by education. While she had wanted to continue her education after she finished sixth grade, at the same time she had seen what happened to girls who left the village to become educated. Many returned to the village better educated, perhaps, but in ways that Wābī could not approve of: valuing appearance and material goods, thus wearing flashy urban clothes, with some girls returning alone and pregnant. Now education began to play a larger role in her thinking, and her attitude on that new role varied from victorious to defeated. While she could again meditate, a major religious victory, she sometimes saw her future, based on a quest for secular education, as resignation—she was now settling for less than she had dreamed of before. Meditation had lost its appeal when her meditation instructor had wronged her. Ironically, this meditation instructor, who had received a master's degree and thus was one of the best educated women Wābī had ever met, was at least partially responsible for her temporary inability to meditate and therefore indirectly responsible for her renewed quest for education.

This theme is also an echoing of "Effacement"—near the very end of the sutta, we are told: "What should be done for his disciples out of compassion by a teacher who seeks their welfare and has compassion for them, I have done for you." In explaining the passage, one translator notes: "The compassionate teacher's task is the correct teaching of the Dhamma; beyond that is the practice, which is the work of the disciples."[2] Wābī's practice was to be both continued meditation and secular education.

At this time she received a letter from the institute-established Dhammacarinī Samnak, inviting her to pursue her education, and live among the fifty māechī and fifty young girls who lived at the samnak, most of whom also studied or taught at the school, daily meditating, chanting, studying, and working. "My mother was very sick, my father's residence had burned down, the man who was essentially my grandfather had died, and I was just getting better from a long illness. I was suffering a lot of hardship. There was a lot going on. I thought disrobing might be better. That was when I was invited to come to Dhammacarinī."

When Wābī left Māechī Senī's samnak and went to Dhammacarinī, she acknowledged the complexity of the world and her power to act in that complexity, and she recognized how her actions affected others as well as herself. She also acknowledged the death of her limited view, her innocent but irresponsible refusal to see things as complex as they were. She could no longer see herself as without fault, a religious practitioner called to a quiet place away from the unpleasant heat of other people's involvements. Nor could she see herself keeping her newly gained wisdom to herself. She saw herself as a more complex person, and her call to serve others by teaching what she had learned required that she develop herself.

Through her struggle in losing and regaining her faith in her life as a māechī, she saw more clearly and could then act upon her duties to others. Wābī saw that she could help others with the knowledge that she had gained in her own suffering; she only needed to gain skills and credentials and continue her cultivation of awareness to do so.

Chapter 9

Confidence in a New Way of Living Dhamma

> *Friends, four things have been declared to us by the Blessed One who knows and sees, accomplished and fully enlightened. . . . What are the four? We have confidence in the Teacher, we have confidence in the Dhamma, we have fulfilled the precepts, and our companions in the Dhamma are dear and agreeable to us whether they are laymen or those gone forth.*
>
> —*Majjhima Nikāya* 11.3

When I taught English at the Institute of Thai Māechī's Dhammacarinī Samnak, I chose "well behaved" as the adjective most fitting to my students who were young girls; "extremely polite" was how I described the māechī. They began each class, as students do throughout Thailand, by standing up in unison and saying, "Good morning, teacher." At the end of class, they all stood up again in unison and said, "Thank you, teacher." Having left my shoes at the sidewalk of the open-air building, I would feel the cool of the painted cement on the soles of my feet while the rest of my body began to sweat in the tropical morning. Compared to most teachers at the school, I was quite physically active in the classroom. I leaped, with my small phrām robe flying, from one well used wooden desk-chair to another, encouraging the girls and māechī to use the English they were studying so diligently.

It is fair to say that most Caucasians sweat more than most Thais. As the mornings wore on, I would inevitably have to take out a white handkerchief and wipe my face. My students would smile in delight and turn their faces upward to check to see if the rotating electric fans hanging from the ceiling were on. Often the electricity went off, leaving me without relief. If the fans rotated dutifully, however, my students would turn their bright eyes back to me, waiting for the next bit of odd behavior from their English teacher, their local *farang* (foreigner). While every person has her or his problems and every community has its challenges, the norm at Dhammacarinī Samnak had to do with thoughtfulness, attentiveness, and right behavior.

The trifold glossy brochure for the school that is the main focus of the samnak features pictures of students studying, walking in meditation, sitting in meditation, working in the fields, and learning to sew. The emphasis here is on religious practice, learning, and discipline, and these emphases are evident whenever you talk with the teachers, founders, or students themselves. In fact, the purpose of the school, as presented in its published pamphlets, is threefold: to help māechī and children who do not have opportunities for education, receive both compulsory education and education in the Dhamma, to establish good religious heirs to help improve Buddhism and Thai society, and to cultivate the heartminds of these women and girls so that they are conscious of the individual's as well as the group's importance to the development of society.

One of the main reasons for the creation of the school was to provide an alternative to the rural-to-urban migration of young women. In an early proposal for Dhammacarinī School presented to possible financial contributors, the arguments for the samnak's school are founded on modern societal problems and the interconnectedness of all things—where modern Thailand meets Buddhist philosophy. "Interconnectedness," *paticcasamuppāda*, has been translated in many different ways, including dependent origination, law of causation, chain of causation, law of dependent arising, the chain of phenomenal cause and effect, the conditional arising and cessation of all phenomena, the twelve links of conditioned co-production, cause and effect, and conditioned genesis—it is one of the greatest realizations of the Buddha when he becomes enlightened, and it is part of what Wābī gained a better understanding of in her moment of realizing suchness. The founders of Dhammacarinī School note that the increasing migration to cities results in rural areas becoming more impoverished and urban areas becoming more congested. The urban congestion leads to unhelpful competition and feelings of vulnerability and danger when the city dwellers see their neighbors as people who may take what they have and claim victory over them in the race to succeed in the city. The confusion of progress and success with having material goods leads to more negative inclinations: greed, hatred, and delusion, the three inclinations that keep beings in samsara. Specifically, the pamphlet notes, materialism and the emotions it encourages lead to societal practices such as prostitution (and the high rate of HIV infection associated with it) and sweat shops. In these work situations, humans are used as implements for the production of pleasure and the wealth of others instead of encouraged to work on their own

spirituality, treasuring in a traditional Buddhist manner the opportunity beings have when born human.

Thailand's migration challenges are large indeed, especially for women.
Migration to urban areas by young Thai women is high, however, and with
good reason. A significantly higher percentage of people on the move to
urban areas is comprised of women because their ability to find work is good.
Job opportunities in the service sector attract rural people with few skills
outside of farming, and those job opportunities abound. They make money,
gain freedom and autonomy, and leave behind the constraints of the village.[1]
Further, they are able to send money to their family members still living in
the rural areas, and thus help those they love and enjoy reputations as good
daughters, granddaughters, and sisters.[2] But many women come to Bangkok
with no information on jobs and find themselves working in brothels or
unsafe factories. In such places of employment, women have little power to
improve the work situation or to move up and out of it. Better work requires
higher skill levels, which require more education, and women are less likely
to get an education because, as we saw with Wabī, cultural traditions value
men's education above women's and the Thai government offers more civil
service jobs to men than to women.[3]

In part to assist women such as these, who might otherwise migrate to
an urban area (probably Bangkok) and take low-level jobs, and thus suffer by
responding to less helpful desires than, for example, the desire to escape
samsara, Dhammacarinī School opened in 1990. The founders' analysis of
the societal problems and prescription for rectification links current social,
environmental, and emotional problems to the Buddhist principles of ignorance as the root of all problems in this world. Ignorance leads to desire; the
mere fulfillment of desires leads to continued rebirth in samsara. Only by
gaining wisdom and letting go of desires can one escape the cycle. Further,
rural areas such as that of Dhammacarinī Samnak are extolled as being better,
more peaceful and conducive to a good life; urban areas are condemned as
polluting people socially, emotionally, and spiritually.

The answer to the difficulties of materialism and other kinds of indulgences in sensual pleasures, predictably, is the middle way, a life neither
fraught with suffering nor steeped in sensual pleasure—the way the Buddha
put forth in his teachings and the way that is encouraged at Dhammacarinī
Samnak.

While a young boy or man from a poor family may best prepare for his
and his family's future by going forth as a monk and guaranteeing himself
an education and a place in a well established hierarchy or by joining the
military and guaranteeing himself work and training, girls and young women
do not enjoy these possibilities.[4] Opportunities for women are considerably
fewer—as we saw in Wabī's early life and in the life of her mother. Out of

a sensitivity to the disparate opportunities available to girls from poor families in Thailand, a monk called Lūangphǫ (an honorific) Im helped found Dhammacarinī School.[5] Having been sent a number of girls to live in his temple to gain merit and life experience (they could never expect, of course, to get an education there), Lūangphǫ Im decided to help found a place where girls with problems could go to study and to be cared for properly. He had been sensitized to women's issues by a video on development that pointed out how women are the first ones to help and encourage Buddhism, especially in relation to food. "Food," as he points out, "is the story of life, and food comes from women." Indeed, the Buddhist texts connect women and food from the very night of Gotama Buddha's enlightenment when, sitting under the Bodhi tree, he accepted milk-rice from a woman and was thus fueled in his meditation.

Initially, Lūangphǫ Im thought to start a school at his home temple in Bangkok, but the māechī living near the temple at that time did not want to be involved, pointing out to him that the reason they had gone forth was to live the religious life, a life outside of the everyday world, lacking in worldly concerns. Lūangphǫ Im called a meeting of some interested māechī—about twenty in all—from other temples, including Khun Māe Prathin Khwanon, the abbess of the samnak and head of the school when Wābī and I lived there and now president of the institute, and three other teachers and administrators at Dhammacarinī.[6] Because of the reluctance of the māechī at his own temple to help, Lūangphǫ Im could offer money—and not much else.

At that time, Khun Māe Prathin had already founded one educational program for māechī, which had failed. She was eager to try to establish another one, providing that she could correct some of the problems that had caused the failure of the first. These problems stemmed from the restriction of the student population to māechī alone, the lower level of the general health of māechī, and the hard work required in the then newly established samnak. Money was collected from many people and places, including individual donors and Pāknam Temple, a large temple in Bangkok that houses many māechī and still maintains its tie to Dhammacarinī Samnak. All agreed that impoverished girls and women needed more opportunities for education, especially opportunities that would encourage satisfaction in rural areas rather than those that would attract women to dangerous urban ones.

In the perspective of the founders of Dhammacarinī School, women who live in urban areas are more likely to adopt the values of the urban communities—values such as material advancement over spiritual development and physical beauty over spiritual beauty. Thus one main goal of the school is to allow its students to enjoy the benefits of the city—for example, greater educational opportunities—without suffering the drawbacks, which, in the view of the founders, include moral laxity.

Further evidence for the perceived connection of moral laxity and urban living is a connection between single women and prostitution. As Wābī found, women are expected to marry and bear children. If they do not marry, they may remain home and care for children in the family. If, however, they leave the home and go to an urban area, they may cease to remain upright women. In the proposal for Dhammacarinī School, fully one-third of the description of Thailand's social problems and how they arise focuses on the problems of the prostitution of children and women. The proposal claims that prostitution has become the norm in Thai society and that the people who make their living this way not only suffer from oppression (the women and children are often forced or deceived into the business) but from strains on their minds and bodies with indirect and direct results, including diseases such as AIDS. Māechī and prostitutes are often grouped together in the media and in discussions in Thailand, both because these are the two most visible groups of women who choose to be single and because women of both groups tend to have less education. What is true in the West may prove to be at least partially true in Thailand:

[A]ny free and independent woman signals a "loose woman." The freedom of women is equated with whoredom. A woman "on her own" is regarded as "free for men." Looseness is reduced to lewdness. Freedom is transformed from a positive state where women are free of all men (for example, celibates or lesbians) or even where women are free of some men (unmarried heterosexually active women, prostitutes), to a negative state. . . . [S]uch women are "free" to be tamed (which often means raped).[7]

Single women are often seen as loose, as women to be tamed by men. Most Thais assume that prostitutes are "bad" women who have lost their morality, not good women who have turned to this profession because Thai society has failed to give them safer, more acceptable, and more rewarding ways of earning money. Further, most Thais assume that prostitutes are immoral, despite the evidence that these women often use their money in ways that most Thais find admirable: they support their families and give money to monks.[8] Māechī who live among monks and serve them in temples are considered "tamed." An older māechī, it is concluded, has no one who cares for her, and younger māechī have failed in love. These women then are consigned to lives of servitude to monks; they can only hope that their next birth will be better. Few non-māechī and few māechī who live in monk-dominated temples comment on the increased freedom that a woman gone forth can enjoy—the freedom to live in a variety of temples or samnaks, to travel, to live among those she chooses—probably because fewer māechī in temples can enjoy these freedoms unless encouraged to do so by the abbot, who often maintains control.

In contrast to viewing māechī as women to be tamed, occasionally the grouping of female prostitutes and māechī is done with the hope of the "good" māechī having a positive impact on the "bad" prostitutes. In one training workshop on counseling for young Thai māechī, the forty māechī, most in their late teens, were brought to a prison for prostitutes.[9] Located on an island not far from Bangkok, the prison houses over 200 women; all are required to wear the same uniform, with slight differences based on how long a woman has been incarcerated there, and to follow a strict, daily regimen that includes twice-daily courtyard roll calls of all prisoners. While they receive training in various handicrafts, and many of the women appreciate this, most feel that they have been incarcerated unjustly, and their working counterparts fear incarceration in this particular prison more than they fear many other dangers in their work. The prison is known to deaden the souls of its residents. While the penitentiary is touted as a model, which is one reason the young māechī were taken there to visit, it routinely strips its residents of their dignity and individuality. They are subjected to sermons from government and religious officials that reinforce the general perception of prostitutes as bad women; the women prisoners claim that no visitors accept their own roles in the societal factors that lead women to prostitution and then lead to the punishment of prostitutes, not to the punishment of the men who hire them.

The māechī in training were to interview the prostitutes, showing how they could use the principles they had learned about counseling by having conversations with women who required such. Those who established the training program included this exercise on the ground that māechī, being women and not being under the same restrictions as monks, are better able to help women than are monks. Unfortunately, it was an extremely awkward hour or so for most involved. In a large, covered, open-air pavilion, chairs were lined up, sides touching sides, in long rows facing each other, creating a stilted, formal atmosphere for conversation. The sense of two irreconcilable people meeting confrontationally, reflected in the chair arrangement, was further enhanced by the differences in the clothing of the women. The traditional Buddhist māechī robes of pristine white contrasted sharply with the blue, Western-style dress of the inmates. Few māechī present, despite their training and fine intentions, could help the inmates become calm enough to discuss their serious personal issues—especially with the expectation that the conversations had to be tape-recorded. The māechī knew that the professors running the workshop planned to listen to and analyze the tapes to determine how much they had learned. The inmates looked at the tape recorders, in short supply, with suspicion. You could reach out and touch the awkwardness of this crowd of women, as the calming winds blew cool through from the surrounding forests and the birds sang loudly.

The most successful conversations for all involved drew on the common backgrounds of the māechī and prostitutes and invited empathy for what had led the women to be incarcerated on the island and how that island prison was debilitating rather than rehabilitating the women there. Among those who participated in the workshop were māechī from Dhammacarinī, who are seen as good examples of a new kind of māechī in Thailand: well educated, firm in their roles as religious women, and concerned about societal problems. In this instance, as is true at Dhammacarinī, māechī are seen as the societal agents to bring about the end of problems such as prostitution. Perhaps more forward looking is the model of māechī as fellow seekers of opportunities for women rather than as "good" women opposed to "bad" women prostitutes.

While Dhammacarinī School was founded partially to prevent young girls from becoming prostitutes, supporting the claim that the girls in the school would be prostitutes if they were not students is predictably difficult. More generally, Dhammacarinī School was founded to provide opportunities to those girls who live in difficult circumstances and thus lack the opportunity to become educated, trained, and mature. The founders recognize that Thai society both includes and depends on women, and that developing māechī will help women and children who lack the opportunity to cultivate helpful habits and high expectations of themselves and other members of their society. Assisting girls and women will assist all members of Thai society. At home, the girls who come to Dhammacarinī live impoverished lives, "struggling against the inclination to surrender themselves to the mercy of fate," as the school brochure points out. The brochure describes orphans, children in sweat shops, and young girls deceived into leaving their homes for work who are then sold as prostitutes. These children, the brochure notes, "should be in school to prepare themselves to take the next step to fight for their futures." The difficulties of the girls are lessened in the samnak so that they will not suffer so much that they cannot learn both worldly knowledge and Buddhist truths. Also, by easing the burden on the families by caring for and educating the girls (parents are invited to assist in the cost of educating their daughters, but they are not compelled to do so), by reminding the girls of their debts to their parents, and by sending the girls back to their rural villages, the program seeks to spread the Dhamma through the girls to their families. Parents, while often sad that their daughters must live apart from them, are comforted that their children have a chance to become better educated than they and thus may have better futures. The girls themselves, almost universally, claim that what they most appreciate about the school is the discipline and training in proper behavior. Says one young māechī, "Best of all, I like the etiquette (*māruyāt*). For example, when you feel anger or desire, there's no need to fill the desire or express the anger. You just work with it." On this topic, one māechī claimed that the best aspects of the school-samnak are the education and the community: "The people who live here, each has her niche and each knows what she is supposed to do. If all people do their duties, there's enough time for everyone to do good. Lots of temples don't have this kind of community—they're disordered, and people don't know what they should do and so they don't have any opportunity to do good."

Khun Māe Prathin, the abbess for some years, says:

> Parents like that the children understand their duties and what's possible for them. . . . The children learn to help and to help all over while being safe: we know where they are and they won't have bad friends. . . . And they must learn to discern right from wrong. The māechī turn their attention to study and practice, to chanting. And they concentrate on helping society—*this* one, here within the walls. They meditate and chant, near the forest, isolated from society, and so learn peace, and come to know what it's like and then when they go into society they can help. When one works, one must have mindfulness. Begin with the breath and know how the breath has a purpose in the body. [Knowing this,] calm, and mindful of the breath, one can help others with loving-kindness and compassion. Loving-kindness and compassion are cultivated.

Dhammacarinī School provides a context for Thai girls and māechī to create a world of women. They define themselves not against or in relation to men but outside of those considerations focused on men. One scholar notes that "in a heterosexist society . . . most of women's personal, social, political, professional, and economic relations are defined by the ideology that woman is for man";[10] the world created by the māechī and the girls at Dhammacarinī defines women only in relation to other women. Their daily life is with each other; they see (and serve) men only on special occasions. In this world, a māechī, the abbess, is at the top of the pyramid, with her long-standing friends and fellow founders of the school and samnak, each recognized for her unique contributions. Below these women are the other māechī, such as Māechī Wābī, formally organized according to how long they have been ordained and informally organized according to their gifts to the community. At the bottom of the pyramid are the girls who attend the school, divided into junior high and high school students. These girls are instructed on how to treat māechī with respect, and they are allowed to interact daily with māechī. With so much attention at the usual Thai temples dedicated to the correct treatment of monks, and with the much larger number of temples than samnaks, far more Thai children and young adults know how to treat the official male religious in Thailand than how to treat māechī; Dhammacarinī students are being trained to make a difference.

The closed, women-composed environment of Dhammacarinī allows an atmosphere that can encourage not only religiosity among women but respect for māechī and for friendship among women. The girls talk a lot with their friends about their dreams of marriage, but the people with whom they are currently making their lives are not young men, which is bound to have some effect. In fact, it already does. The new recruits to the school are often girls from the villages of the girls who live or have lived at Dhammacarinī. When they return home, either to live or on the annual month-long vacation, they make such a favorable impression on their old neighbors that other girls want to attend the school.

One can trace the increased networking of Thai māechī to the positive influence of Western feminism: the realization of the need for establishing the Institute of Thai Māechī was at least partially inspired by the questions of Westerners interested in women and Buddhism. One can also, however, trace the current problems of women in Thailand to a negative influence of Western feminism in the increasingly modernized country. The modern Western division between home and work and feminist enthusiasm for getting women out of the home to go to work creates a very difficult situation. While most residents of Thailand still farm, the percentage doing so has decreased drastically. In a farming family, women could work the fields and care for the children by dividing such labor casually among themselves throughout the day and by bringing the children out into the fields as they worked. In this circumstance, work in and outside of the home is not so clearly divided. More and more often, however, women work in factories and in the service sector, conforming to the modern Western division between work and home, and thus now face the difficulties in child care that have become so acute in the United States.

How is a woman to work in one place to earn money—the urban areas—and raise children in another place—their rural homes—with the money earned from the work? Many Thai women answer this question by leaving their children in the care of relatives, a solution more acceptable among Thais than among, for example, most Americans, but still considered problematic.

Dhammacarinī School also offers help in this area—the girls learn vocational subjects so that they may return to their rural homes and support themselves without moving to urban areas. While child care is still an issue if the women work in industries, it is less so because of the kin networks and geographical closeness of work and home. The success of these vocational programs, however, may be more in their functions of concentrating the girls' energy, keeping Thai traditions alive, and offering the girls caring contact with adults than in training the girls in helpful skills designed to keep them in their home villages. Most agree that what modern young workers need are the skills that will allow them to work in the manufacturing and service sectors. Notable in both of the Buddhist schools formed for girls is the high percentage of students that comes from the Northeast—the poorest section of Thailand with the smallest number of opportunities for nonrural employment and the worst conditions for farming.[11]

The school works to dissuade or at least to delay the migration of girls and young women to urban areas, but the schooling of young girls in a community made up of women from all over the country may help the girls form a support network that actually facilitates moves to urban areas because one of the most important factors in migration is sponsorship—the social contacts of rural and urban people. Some scholars of Thai migration suggest that:

> Contacts between villagers and urban dwellers play an important role in influencing migration decisions and shaping migration streams. The migration literature demonstrates that potential migrants typically consider few alternative destinations before moving. Their decisions concerning where and even whether to move are heavily influenced by the social networks linking them to other places. The important function of providing information about urban opportunities is often performed by the villager's kinfolk, but can be performed by close friends, co-workers, or employers as well. In addition to providing information about opportunities, urban social contacts also provide a variety of sponsorship functions once the migration has actually moved. Whenever a migrant arrives in a new community, he needs a place to stay, a job, and information about the community. He needs someone to "show him the ropes" and someone who will help "bail him out" if he gets into trouble. Having a social contact at the destination may ease the adjustment process and can spell the difference between migrating or not.[12]

The girls and māechī of Dhammacarinī come from all over Thailand and thus have different backgrounds. They and their relatives form a large group of people who can serve as contacts. Such a safe community as Dhammacarinī, rooted in religious principles and open to the sharing of information among its residents, could easily lead to the networking that facilitates urban migration.

In time, the effects of being educated in a school such as Dhammacarinī will be better known. After all, only about fifty young women have graduated from Dhammacarinī, and studies are needed on what these women do after they leave the school. However, we can examine some of the purposes of the

school and how it seeks to fulfill those purposes in light of other research that
has been done.

The two groups responsible for the program, the Institute of Thai Māechī
and the Dhammacarinī School committee, which arose out of the meeting
called by Lūangphǫ Im, developed the school in three stages. In its first two
years, 1990–1992, it arranged for personnel, established the buildings, found
the materials, and worked on the curriculum. At this first stage, only three
grades of school were offered, the approximate equivalent of grades seven to
nine in the United States. Working with the Departments of Religion and
Non-Formal Education in the Ministry of Education, the school established
a program to cover the material of three secular grades in two years and a
program to offer Dhamma education. Further, it arranged for teachers of
vocational skills such as sewing, flower making, and hair cutting. During
stage two, from 1992–1994, the high school education program was established, covering the final three grades of secondary education in Thailand.
Now, at stage three of the project, the school reaches out to more māechī and
to those whom māechī can serve by encouraging Dhammacarinī māechī to
attend training sessions and other meetings as well as summer service programs administered by the institute—the shift has changed from establishment of the school to outreach.

When the school was begun, the main problem, the founders and administrators agree, was cultural not financial. The students came from all over the
country and from all different sorts of situations in answer to a notification
of its opening sent out to many temples.[13] Because of the cultural differences,
there were many misunderstandings among the girls themselves over everyday practices related to cleanliness, disease, and cooking. The girls had to
learn to solve these problems. One of the results of these early difficulties is
the set of nineteen rules that are read aloud each week by the top student in
the highest class. The first rules remind the students generally of their responsibilities toward their own development and the development of the community; the later rules more specifically remind the students of the ways that
they can do this: by not wasting water and by wearing shoes, by hanging
laundry, and by disposing of garbage at appropriate places and times. For
example, most Thais remove their shoes upon entering a home but wear their
shoes in public buildings. Leaders of the samnak had to determine which
rooms and buildings on samnak grounds were to be entered with shoes on
and which with shoes off. Students encountered these sorts of difficulties
when living among people who shared the same country but not the same
daily practices.

Following the system of the Ministry of Education, the curriculum of the
school includes ordinary compulsory subjects including social studies, English, and Thai. The curriculum also includes Buddhist subjects including

those related to the life of a person gone forth. The girls are also given training, outside of the normal school months, in different skills such as sewing and flower making, the Thai art of cutting and reshaping flowers and parts of plants into ornate designs. During the school year they are required to help with the agricultural work of the samnak and are taught the skills required for that as well. By learning to depend on themselves, the girls learn how to nourish their own lives.

While the school is a major focus of the samnak, the residents of the samnak are not limited to the girls and maechi who attend the school. There are three other significant subgroups of women—the administrator and teacher maechi and phram, the maechi and phram who are only informally associated with the school, and the regular visitors. The administrator and teacher maechi number five. Several of the teachers commute weekly from their home temple in Bangkok, a difficult journey but one that they undertake until more maechi can be educated and can then take their places.

Maechi can be involved in the school and its students and activities as much or as little as they like. Some remember the samnak when its founders were clearing the land and digging the ditches necessary to drain its water. Such women remember when there was no idea for a school on its grounds—there was more than enough work simply helping to build the chanting and meditation hall and living quarters. Ms. Noi, a sixty-seven-year-old phram, has lived at Dhammacarini on and off for some years, and while uninvolved with most official activities of the school, she is supportive of girls being educated and offers her living area as a study center for maechi who need a quiet place. Ms. Noi is relieved to have the opportunity to make merit and to enjoy peace away from her alcoholic and abusive son, and away from other familial intrigues. Her son sold some of the family's land without consulting the family and set Ms. Noi's clothes on fire once when she was at a temple. Ms. Noi says, "It's hard to be poor, to work each day to get enough food to eat for that day. Poor. You get tired, you enter a temple so you can make merit. You chant a lot and so make merit. Living at home, you get tired, depressed, worried. I came to study Dhamma; Buddha gave a purpose for our days." She was glad to choose an all-women community because living with monks is *nagliat*, ugly. "To be the only woman in a group of monks would not be okay, it would make me very uncomfortable." She recommends that the girls who live there avoid marriage and go forth as maechi. One younger maechi, age thirty, notes that when a woman lives among monks, "you have to live always afraid of doing something wrong."

In some ways the samnak community makes spatially explicit a common situation of older women. Raymond notes of Western women: "[M]any old women do return literally to the worlds of women. In old age, women are each other's most constant companions. For many, it is the first time in their lives when they do not have to 'relate to' or take care of men and children."[14] It is not uncommon to see in the samnak a group of older māechī washing their robes together, sharing memories of their pasts and concerns about their current community.

The visitors are a motley crew, drawn by the peace, the multitude of religious women, and the needs of the girls and māechī. Ms. Warida, a retired math teacher, comes every two or three months for a few days to live in a room in the building she had constructed a few years ago. She likes to see programs that help the poor and likes this one especially: "Helping poor people is good. This program is especially good because now these girls won't be prostitutes, and they won't have to go begging for money." In a few years she plans to settle permanently in the building she only temporarily occupies now. After forty-two years of hard work in a Catholic school in Bangkok, she enjoys her freedom too much to consider seriously going forth as a māechī; the five or eight vows of a phrām, uncomplicated by close attention to minutiae of dress and behavior, are enough. Another occasional visitor is one of the early supporters of the school, a social worker partially funded in her work by the Buddhist activist Sulak Sivaraksa. Partially physically disabled now, this bright young woman continues to show her dedication to improving Thai society and helps in the decision making whenever she goes to Dhammacarinī.

Dhammacarinī's school is the first ever established by māechī for māechī—the first Buddhist school established for girls in Thailand. Its work teams encourage personal responsibility as well as cooperation among the residents; its gardens, mushroom hut, and trees and coal-producing kiln facilitate samnak self-sufficiency. The varied population encourages openmindedness and development of communication skills. Further, the mixture of māechī and girls allows a unique opportunity for training young people in respectful behavior toward women who have gone forth, as well as an opportunity for these girls to get a close-up view of the lives of women who eschew householder roles. Their almost exclusive reliance on women and girls to define themselves allows the māechī and young girls a unique opportunity for religious, social, and personal exploration. Just as women in the United States move to urban areas to free themselves from domestic shackles, these women and girls born into "unchosen communit[ies] of origin" leave their rural homes to "surmount moral particularities of family and place that define and limit their moral starting points."[15]

Dhammacarinī, as a community of choice of over 100 girls and women, offers its residents opportunities to explore new ways of being female in modernizing Thailand and new kinds of relationships to consider important and life forming. All-women communities such as Dhammacarinī Samnak, with its emphases on educational and religious development, provide grow-

ing opportunities for women, in some ways inviting them to redefine themselves and in some ways redefining Buddhism. While the Buddhism found
within these samnak walls is in many ways a Buddhism defined by monks
(e.g., the Dhamma texts used are those written and chosen by monks at the
national level, and one weekly sermon is given by a monk and listened to
over the radio), it is also a Buddhism persistently and visibly shaped and
created by women such as Khun Māe Prathin and Māechī Wābī. When a
woman has a religious difficulty, this and similar samnaks are places where
she can come to develop herself, talking, chanting, and meditating with other
women. Such a samnak is also a place where the gifts of a single woman can
be given—in the nurturing of the girls who attend the school as well as in the
repairing of the *sala* roof. Here in this community of choice, 100 women and
girls can work to realize the best of their characters, the best of those around
them, and the best of Buddhism.

Chapter 10

Possibilities and Resolution: Māechī Wābī and the Institute of Thai Māechī

Abandoning doubt, he abides having gone forth beyond doubt, unperplexed about wholesome states; he purifies his mind from doubt.

—*Majjhima Nikāya* 27.18

The benefits of living at Dhammacarinī Samnak for someone like Māechī Wābī are clear once you are familiar with the samnak. When Wābī was making her decision, however, the benefits were not obvious. She did not know much about Dhammacarinī besides what she had learned in its brochure. She knew no one who lived there with whom she might consult about it. But this lack of friends there had its own appeal. If she went to a place where no one knew her, perhaps she could forget about her own troubles. She explained, "If you don't know anyone, you don't have to explain anything. If they knew me, then when they saw my face they would know I was having problems, and they would ask me about them. 'What's wrong?' 'What problems are you having?' I really didn't want to speak about them."

One of the main reasons Wābī did not abandon her māechī vows and become a householder at the time of her crisis of faith was that there was another place to go—she could maintain her relationships with Māechī Mīna and Māechī Senī without confronting either about the problems she was having related to them and without submitting to continued difficulties with them by remaining in the samnak. She had great respect and love, as always, for Senī, but she was still alienated from her by the difficulties in her relationship with Mīna and with Senī's teacher. Dhammacarinī gave her another place to be, other people to be with, and a good reason for being there. She

106

could maintain her relationships without having to reveal unpleasant information to Senī about her teacher and follower. "I knew I needed to do something—that was clear. It was a clear and strong feeling."

The chance to pursue her education while remaining a māechī solved her problem: "From all this suffering came this opportunity I am now acting on—the opportunity I have to study more here." The positive results of the move were clear immediately and led her to reflect on the necessity of different kinds of training—formal secular education, insight meditation, and education in the hearts and minds of others: "Finally I came to [Dhammacarinī], and the state of my heart got better very quickly; I've gotten better from all those bad times." She determined that she would continue her secular education and daily meditation and plan in the future to spend the time necessary to gain the greatest benefits of insight meditation. Without such study, she felt, she could not benefit others. She compared her situation to mine; I had to get a Ph.D. first before I could reach out to others:

> Like you, without being able to help others, my life has no meaning, purpose, no benefit. The difference is that for me the meaning of my life has to do with insight meditation. I have to train seriously before I can give in that way. This is the way of helping others, isn't it? You have to train yourself first.

Training herself would include secular education, education in insight meditation, and studying the ways of others. "You have to understand emotions, and you have to understand what comes out of people's mouths—when it's important and when it's not. I've practiced insight meditation," she said. "You have to [have emotional understandings], and you have to know the details." Her incident with the teacher taught her that power without empathy is dangerous. "If a teacher doesn't have that kind of knowledge, they can't help. They don't understand the reality of the practitioner of insight meditation. They don't know how to help."

Several ironic turns came out of the healing from the incident. One was the renewed desire for secular education, for the education the meditation teacher had and Wābī did not: "I knew I wanted to become better educated. I wanted to know what—after I studied and became better educated—what kind of person I'd be." And there arose in her a desire to teach:

> My feeling of shock was very great because I had never considered teaching others before. After this incident I wondered what the feeling was like to want to teach others. What is it to call yourself a "teacher" (āčhān)? What is the feeling that arises when you call yourself a "teacher"? Or when you get a lot of education?

Because [Māechī Senī's teacher] had a lot of education, this woman—twenty years.

While Wābī didn't want to model herself after Māechī Noy, in a way she chose to do so by pursuing her education. And while Wābī had not meant, at that samnak, to elevate herself to teacher status, she is now quite consciously working toward that.

One aspect of her quest for education led her to me, a foreigner. When we were once discussing the incident with the meditation teacher, I sensed that she needed a break from the difficult topic so I asked her more about her plans for the future. I was surprised when she replied, "I want to study [meditation] with a foreigner." She laughed and noted, "It's strange, isn't it?"

In some ways it was indeed very strange to hear that a Thai religious wanted to learn about her religion from a foreigner. Almost every other Thai person with whom I spoke on this topic (and there was an obvious reason to discuss the subject: I was a foreigner studying Buddhism, so the subject came up often) had this basic attitude: any foreigner who came to study Buddhism in Thailand obviously had very good karma—good enough karma to bring that person from a country where there is hardly any knowledge of Buddhism to a country steeped in Buddhism. Foreigners who go forth as monks are often highly respected as monks and are turned to for advice; they are consistently referred to as people who have very good karma to have come to Thailand. (There are many more Westerners who go forth as monks than those who go forth as māechī. Monks, being better educated and supported by the government, often speak English, thus an English-speaking foreign man has more people with whom he can communicate easily and from whom he can learn. Māechī are much less likely to know English or another language other than their native one because of their lack of education. Further, texts of instruction on how to be a monk are translated into English, while the handbook for māechī is not.) So for a foreigner, coming to Thailand was evidence of his or her good karma. I never heard, however, any Thai people comment on how good their karma was to allow them to come into contact with a foreigner who now embraces Buddhism. They concentrate on the good fortune that the foreigner has to be able to learn from the real sources of Buddhist knowledge, the Thais. Only occasionally have I heard speculations that Westernized Buddhism, with its focus on meditation, might reinvigorate Buddhism, seen as being overconcerned with appearances and ritual and the memorization of texts.

I asked why Wābī wanted to study with a foreigner (by which she meant non-Asian), and I came to understand more of the real reasons she wanted to study English with me: "I want to know . . . well, Thai people, we're envious.

And I think I can find a foreigner who really knows the Dhamma and who doesn't have this quality. . . . I was very sad about when this meditation teacher talked with me." Senī's teacher's reaction to Wābī's teaching was complex, but one root of it had been envy. When the students called Wābī *ačhān*, the same term that they used for the teacher, the teacher had become angry. That anger, aimed back at Wābī in public, had created a lot of difficulties for different people—Wābī, Senī, some of the meditators—at least the ones who knew Wābī had been requested to teach—and certainly the teacher herself. When I asked Wābī if she did not think a foreigner would have this same problem, she replied: "I want to know if foreigners have this same problem that Thais have. I want to know." She stressed the importance of that teacher being a woman: "A person who teaches me has to be a woman because I can't tell a man the important things about my life."

One reason for Wābī's interest in envy may be her own earlier battles with pride. One of the main sources of her failing in her relationship with Māechī Mīna was that she excused Mīna's envy of her as being irrelevant, not worthy of her attention, and not inspiring her to consider Mīna's pain. In her pride at being a good māechī and acting out of duty, she ignored another's pain—until her meditation revealed her blindness.

Another attraction for Wābī to learn English was related to the name I use for her in this book. One day I asked her what name I should use in my writing instead of her real one. She suggested, fairly quickly, though shyly but then firmly—"Wābī." I asked her the meaning of the word *wābī*, and she replied that she did not know, but she told me where she had gotten the name.

When she lived at the samnak of Māechī Senī, she went through a period of having meditational visits by a being named Joey. "He didn't have red hair like a lot of foreigners, but he had a nose just like yours. He was a foreigner." While Joey did not exist in corporeal form, he did exist, and he was in love with her. He would come and cry and cry, and sometimes she would cry with him. He was deeply in love with her and wanted a relationship with her, but she told him that she really never wanted the family life; she never wanted to have children. She said that the only way they could be together was as people who have gone forth—he would have to go forth as a monk. He agreed. He said they could live religious lives beside each other. Throughout their acquaintance, he called her "Wābī"; she never knew what it meant until we looked it up in my dictionary; it means pond, lake, or swamp. Why he called her that is, predictably, a mystery; noncorporeal beings can be as complex and difficult to understand as corporeal ones. Wābī never asked him and offered no speculation on the answer.

Her meditation, and especially these incidents relating to foreigners, had led her to discuss with me her life and her difficulties in remaining a māechī.

Once I had heard the whole story more than once and had asked many
questions about it, I told her that I thought the incident with her meditation
instructor was the most important one of her life. She replied:

> Yes, the most important one, and also the one I'm most quiet about.
> I never tell about it. I don't generally want others to know. Nothing
> much good came of it. Finally I think I just decided I was a bad
> person because after I'd returned, I kept thinking of the things she'd
> said that weren't true. That I wanted to be a teacher myself. That I
> was a person who—she said many things.

This assessment, however, was just the first in a number of evaluations
of the experience. Not long after saying that, Wābī described the results
differently: "At first though, there was no good coming from this story, no
good ideas." She simply suffered. "Education was not necessary. This is how
I felt up until this incident. Then I felt I must study. I couldn't practice. The
second thing in my life: education. I thought I had to study."

I asked her, "And your faith in Buddhism?"

"Faith? I thought it was over, I thought there was no faith left, I thought
more faith couldn't come. I was scared of all practitioners, scared of teachers,
of all people who might be teachers. I'd see someone teaching others, and I'd
just quake in fear." Wābī was confused by the experience. Māechī Noy was
a good person and had taught well so that many people had benefited, but her
damage to Wābī was great. "I wasn't sure whether all teachers were like this
or not. I even began to wonder if Māechī Senī was like this too. What was
she really like? If she were like this, what would I do? I thought I had to take
care of myself, all right. I had no refuge for sure. No refuge. My faith was
gone, and I'd have to establish it myself. I would have to do what it took to
establish faith again. I didn't know how long that would take."

After she had spent so much time recovering from and pondering the
incident, she asked herself why it had occurred.

> "Why?" I asked myself, and I thought, "Because she still has ob-
> stacles [kilesa], and I still have obstacles. She and I both still had
> obstacles, and because I still didn't have little obstacles, this incident
> happened to me. I had a lot of obstacles, and so did she. If I had had
> fewer obstacles, this incident wouldn't have occurred to me. Okay,
> she said this thing once, yet I was sorry for all of three years, two
> or three years.

By the time Wābī went forth, the outside world, her home, had become
intolerably "hot"—heated by the emotions of others as they threw themselves

into the stories of their lives, responding to greed, hatred, and delusion. Wabī found peace in going forth, in surrounding herself with others who sought to ennoble their lives through religious goals and practice. Caring for others, cooking, cleaning, and meditating all contributed, in the peace of the samnak, to a life dedicated to duty and spiritual quest. When one of her compatriots, someone who had chosen the same path as she, repeatedly criticized her, she took refuge in the array of distractions available even in a samnak. When the animosity peaked, however, and when her meditation was strong enough to provide her with ways of interpreting the animosity that were helpful along her Buddhist path, she got a glimpse of the real fruits of the path—joyful insight into the workings of the Buddhist world: an experience of suchness and an understanding of the karmic workings over her lifetimes.

These experiences gave her something to give to the world, something to teach, but she felt that others might not be able to hear her teaching because of her lack of education. She deepened her practice but failed to act on her lack of education. Her meditation experiences revealed important Buddhist truths and attached images to these truths that she could use to understand her life. Not until she was alone and facing a representative of Buddhism who betrayed her, however, was she forced to reconstruct her faith and her life as a maechī.

In one sense, it was friendship and meditation that made Wabī a maechī, and it was betrayal and the inability to meditate that led her to rejuvenate herself as a maechī, to rededicate herself to her path and to find a way to continue her path despite the obstacles. She had to reject the home life several times: first, when she went forth, also when she was tempted to divest her robes, even when she was rejecting the love of Joey.

Buddhism, to Wabī, is fundamentally about meditation and how it helps her see clearly and act well. Buddhism is also about friendship: friendship with women similarly dedicated to a religious path. Her friendship with Senī became a refuge—a refuge she had to protect, even if that meant physically leaving the refuge of her daily company. And Buddhism is about finding a way to develop and contribute her own gifts—the way that led her to Dhammacarinī Samnak.

Twenty years ago, maechī were isolated from one another and had serious problems with status and organization. Most report that at that time women who went forth were often very old, tolerated at the margins of temples by monks. Now, at least partially because there is a central bureaucracy of maechī, the Institute of Thai Maechī, which is reaching out to women and establishing more all-women communities of maechī, such as Dhammacarinī Samnak, that can serve maechī such as Maechī Wabī, the situation of maechī in Thailand is changing. More women are going forth at younger ages, either temporarily or for life, and more maechī are becoming

better educated—both secularly and religiously. Māechī have more choices
of where, among whom, and how they will live, as well as how long they will
stay where they are. They are building friendships that support them as religious women—friendships that give them more options and more support
for different paths.

Māechī are becoming more of a social force; they are part of a resur-
gence of Buddhism growing in response, in part, to a perceived decay of the
sangha. People are increasingly questioning and becoming disenchanted by
the traditional representatives of Buddhism. In this climate of growing suspicion of monks and the state-approved monk hierarchy, and as more people
have a greater consciousness of women's place in society, it is no surprise
that a growing population of women dedicated to living religious lives is
beginning to be viewed as potential leaders.

While this movement is partially the work of the institute and shows its
effectiveness, the institute is not without its problems. Māechī, both members
of the institute and not, sometimes claim that it is ineffective and overly
interested in rules. Judging from the institute's booklet on discipline, *The
Discipline of Practice of the Foundation of the Institute of Thai Māechī*, the
most widely circulated document published by the organization, this view of
the institute is easily substantiated. It appears obsessed with, or at least overly
interested in, administrative details—more interested in superficial rules than
in deeper concerns. Little mention is made of meditation, spiritual development, and how to cultivate inner peace, strength, and clarity of perception.
Much is made of the requirement that a māechī must memorize certain rules
before going forth, that she must become familiar with and understand other
rules. The booklet begins with a delineation of which lists of rules of conduct
a māechī must memorize in order to qualify for identification as a māechī by
the institute. The booklet places great importance on appropriate behavior or
rules of etiquette. Drawings early in the booklet specify the code of dress for
both māechī and phrām, noting the number of buttons allowed on shirt and
undervest as well as the number and placement of pockets and darts. The
description of the institute that follows these details of apparel emphasizes
the administrative organization, noting divisions of the institute for education
and training, the publicizing of ethical conduct (*sīladhamma*), public relations, social benefits, financial concerns of the institute, and regulation of the
conduct of māechī. The requirements for holding each office and for mem-
bership on each committee are described.

While these lists and rules and details seem to substantiate the claim that
the institute is overly attentive to superficial details, a closer examination of
the book and familiarity with the institute reveal a more significant concern.
The institute wants to give to māechī and society so that māechī can give to
others. The administrative committee has duties both to increase the number

of Thai māechī helping people and to increase their ability to help people. The committee is, according to *The Discipline of Practice*, to "encourage things which ought to be encouraged, establish anew that which ought to be established anew." Many of the rules derive from the long-standing discipline for monks, the *Pātimokkha*, similarly emphasizing behavior such as the seventy-five rules of training, which include specifically enumerated rules against such minutia of behavior as sitting and laughing loudly in public, walking and laughing loudly in public, sitting and fidgeting with one's arms, and walking and fidgeting with one's arms, and walking and gesticulating with one's arms. To get at the heart of the institute, one must read the booklet with attention to context. The importance of the booklet is that it exists and is circulated and serves as a point of departure for discussions of māechī on their position, behavior, and mind-set, that it calls to mind a standard of behavior and areas of concern for a group of people that has been very isolated for years and is only now beginning to see that it, as a group, shares potential and strengths and weaknesses.

Further, it helps to consider the māechī for whom the booklet was written. Most members of the institute have a fourth-grade education and are from rural backgrounds; many have had as little exposure to different māechī in different temples and samnaks as Wābī had when she went forth. My survey of over eighty māechī at the annual meeting revealed that 50 percent of them had a fourth-grade education or less; 17 percent had finished high school. The booklet gives māechī who have just gone forth details of the behavioral changes expected of them in their new position in society. It also serves as a guide and explains the relationship that can be one of the most important for a newly gone forth māechī: the relationship with the person at the samnak who is assigned initially to make sure that the adjustment to religious life goes smoothly on all levels. Each new māechī or phrām is assigned a more experienced māechī or phrām to guide her when she enters a samnak. The more experienced māechī or phrām then answers her questions, such as how she can receive meditation instruction and what to expect, where the location is for the separate disposal facilities for menstrual pads (beside the school in a dense patch of forest in a tiny framed hole hiding the huge cavern beneath it), and whether or not the blue towel with a rose decoration on it is acceptable for use in the samnak where everyone else seems to have white, undecorated towels (no, it is not).

The yearly meeting of māechī is another aspect of the institute's rigid bureaucracy that can, at first glance, seem empty. At the April 1995 meeting that I attended, over 300 māechī from all over the country came to Bangkok for three days. One full day was devoted to lay-dominated merit-making activities when a representative of the Queen of Thailand, who officially supports the institute, was present. Such an activity is indubitably important—to make merit is to cultivate virtues such as generosity; and long merit-making ceremonies can certainly serve as opportunities for developing patience. Further, the institute is not wealthy and relies almost completely on such private donations. Still, the hours spent in formal giving to the institute and the final half-day of the conference spent in the traditional water-pouring blessing (a traditional Thai ceremony called *trūat nam*) by a senior monk can seem beside the point. More than one māechī rolled her eyes at me empathetically as I endured the time in the hip- and knee-straining mermaid position on the floor awaiting an opportunity to pour a bit of water over the hands of a much-respected monk. Many māechī arranged to miss such ceremonies. But the younger māechī especially were deeply appreciative of the legitimization they saw māechī given in those three days in the capitol city of Thailand by relatives of the queen, famous monks, and other notables. Many were delighted, too, to have an opportunity to see so many māechī in one place—they came from temples with only one or two māechī. Simply by spending several days in a sea of similarly white-clad, religiously aspiring women, the māechī were gaining self-confidence and learning different ways to live religiously. Further, as they went from activity to activity, they talked excitedly about the projects of other māechī whom they had met at the conference and compared their own experiences. For example, many had heard rumors before they arrived of a village-focused development program, established by a māechī in northeast Thailand, which funded cottage industries very inexpensively, allowing villagers to remain on their land to support themselves with environmentally friendly products to be sold abroad. They were eager to learn more from their new friends.

Māechī commiserated with the difficulties of gaining familial support for their choice to go forth, recommended meditation temples to each other, and shared washing hints. The white robes of the māechī are notoriously difficult to keep clean, especially if daily work includes gardening and cleaning, as it almost always does. During my time in Thailand, one well-known māechī in the institute began wearing brown robes in emulation of a māechī who had gone forth in Sri Lanka. Her decision was much discussed. While the brown was much easier to keep clean, its closeness to the color of monks' robes and the implicit shunning of the tradition of white robes (valued as a color symbolizing purity at the very least) were points against it. Just as much of the importance of the booklet on training for māechī lies outside of the strict rules delineated therein, so did much of the importance of the conference lie outside of the delineated activities. And many of the benefits from both the booklet and the conference are related to the education level and the isolation of most māechī.

Through its booklet and the annual meeting, the institute tenaciously pursues its original and long-term goals. More and more māechī know what other māechī are doing, how they live, and what rewards they find in the life of one gone forth. More māechī have opportunities to seek education—both secular and Buddhist. One focal issue of the institute ten years ago is such a small problem now that few mention it: while elderly māechī begging on the streets was an issue large enough in the early 1980s that one researcher devoted a large section of her dissertation to it and newspaper articles on the topic were prevalent, nothing much is said about them now. While I saw elderly, financially destitute māechī traveling between and living in samnaks and temples during my years in Thailand, I never saw one begging in the streets. It appears that the older māechī are more likely to be taken care of now, and that the notorious "fake" māechī are no longer the problem they once were. (Throughout the 1980s newspapers reported incidents of fake monks and māechī. One village established a rotating system of begging monks and māechī. Each month different householding villagers replaced those returning from Bangkok; they shaved their heads and donned robes in order to collect money in the urban area. Then they returned home to use the money for their home lives.)

Wābī's involvement with the institute, like that of many māechī, varies. While she has not attended an annual meeting, she has benefited from living in Dhammacarinī Samnak, owned and run by the institute. Formally, since I met her, she has graduated from high school. Informally, she has met many māechī and other people who have helped her understand Buddhism and the world. Further, she has attended short institute-run training sessions and outreach programs for the poor held during the hot season. Because of the fame of Dhammacarinī Samnak as an institute success and her position in the samnak as being among those who have been ordained the longest, she has often been among some of the leaders of the Institute. They come down to show off the samnak, and Wābī assists. In these ways, she is part of a fabric of women religious—she has a place and ways to contribute. She has friends and colleagues to help her and whom she can help.

Chapter 11

Meditation and Social Work: The Institute and Māechī Leaders

And what is the way leading to the cessation of suffering, it is just this Noble Eightfold Path; that is, right view, right intention, right speech, right action, right livelihood, right effort, right mindfulness, and right concentration. This is called the way leading to the cessation of suffering.

—*Majjhima Nikāya* 9.18

Listening to the māechī such as Māechī Wābī and to the people who know māechī, it appears that māechī are making a new role for themselves, combining the qualities of the ascetic role that are so admired of men in Thailand with those of the mother/nurturer role so admired of Thai women. They go forth, living simply and concentrating on spiritual development, and they help the people (especially women and children) around them. A growing number of māechī walk the spiritual path as contemplative-activists. What meditation provides in their personal lives, the role of māechī provides in their social lives. The somewhat exempt position of a māechī, no longer expected to marry and care for children, allows her to "cultivate emotional openness and responsiveness"[1] in a way denied other women who are more enmeshed in human relationships—the exemption allows enough safety for exploration. She is allowed, to a certain degree, "love without possessiveness, attention without bias, involvement without panic."[2] No wonder women turn to māechī for counseling, and no wonder māechī establish and involve themselves in various kinds of social service. Like Wābī, most māechī have dramatic stories about when they began to realize their obligations to others as being among their religious duties.

116

When I first met Māechī Dārunī, whose meditation insights we looked at earlier, she busily ran both a contemplative samnak for women who wanted to meditate seriously under her guidance and a sewing shop where women (many of whom, she said, were utterly uninterested in Buddhism) could learn how to sew clothing and make money doing so. She had founded the samnak ten years earlier and the sewing shop two years earlier. Knowing that she firmly believed that meditation was the most effective way to solve problems, I asked her why she bothered with the sewing shop, work that was demanding and troublesome. She told me the story of a young woman who came to her asking for permission to go forth as a māechī in her samnak.

It is standard procedure to request permission to go forth from the leader of a samnak, and Dārunī uses the occasion to find out as much as possible about the motivation behind the request. The young woman who came to her was clearly only telling part of her story in response to Dārunī's initial questions. When Dārunī noticed cuts on the woman's legs and asked where they had come from, the woman began to cry and told the whole story. Her family had sold her into prostitution, and she had been taken to Bangkok and kept in a brothel.[3] This is not uncommon in the area of Dārunī's samnak; the women there have a solid reputation, centuries old, of being among the nation's most beautiful. The poverty level is very high, employment opportunities are very low, and a military base had been established nearby, so there are many single men living in the vicinity who go to prostitutes as part of a normal night out with "the boys." Pimps working for the Thai mafia regularly scout the area for young women from poor families and offer the families money in return for their daughters' services. Once a daughter is in the care of a pimp, she is generally at his or her mercy. Not only does the pimp decide where she will work and live, he or she decides how much money each sexual encounter will reduce the debt the woman is paying him or her and how much room and board costs will increase the debt. These mathematics can be, as a worker for Empower, a prostitute support organization, once told me, "very creative."[4]

In the case of this young woman, she was taken to Bangkok and held in a brothel with little freedom to leave the building at all and no freedom to do so unaccompanied. She determined that she must free herself and return home, so she tied the sheets from several beds together and climbed out the window of the brothel. Her home-fashioned rope broke, however, and she landed in a pile of trash in the alley below, cutting her legs on glass. Depending on the kindness of a cab driver, she made her way to a nearby city (the pimp would be waiting for her at the Bangkok bus station that serves the area of her home, so she had to get to another city to leave from) and went home.

Pimps such as hers, however, often maintain local control by bribing law enforcement officers, and hers had done just that—police officers arrived at her house while she was out one day and told her parents that she had stolen from her employers. Having no money with which to convince the police to drop the charge and unwilling to return to her servitude or go far from her family, she thought about going forth as a māechī so that she would be protected from her troubles in the comparative anonymity afforded in a samnak. She could then remain in the vicinity of her parents, able to visit with them occasionally without risking being taken away by the pimp.

Hearing this woman's story convinced Dārunī that she needed to help local women get other jobs so that economics would not force them into brothels. Face to face with a woman who so desperately wanted to remain close to her family, a woman who was not moved to prostitution because of a thirst for material goods but out of economic necessity and filial duty, Dārunī could not accept the usual dismissal of prostitutes as materialistic women uninterested in living virtuous lives. She thus built a shop and eventually negotiated a contract with a department store so that forty women could sew on the machines that she had in the shop or take them home and help fulfill the contract. Dārunī says:

> It was my idea to help. Many people come here to go forth, many women, and when their period of going forth is finished, when they've disrobed—well, most don't have education. They're from farming families and don't have knowledge to work outside. So when they leave, the Dhamma I've taught them serves no purpose. So it's been a waste of time to teach them. I thought, "If I give them knowledge, they can have a decent living—they can use their knowledge." They're farmers, they have no knowledge, and I teach them the Dhamma, and when they return home, they've learned only the Dhamma. They have no money, no skills to earn money. I . . . became tired; the efforts were useless.
>
> I thought that they need work to have money, and then they can be good people. You need money and you need work. You can then help society—in [this area] and in Thailand.

Māechī Senī and Māechī Dārunī, both leaders of small rural samnaks, agree that of the problems people come to them about, economic and marital ones feature prominently, so they have learned to advise women and to help with these issues. Both māechī lend money for projects to help women become less economically dependent on men and to help families when a member is sick. Both support entrepreneurial businesses established by women. Senī funded the opening of a restaurant in Bangkok; Dārunī helped establish a plant nursery in her local village by providing business advice and money.

Senī's samnak has several sewing machines; if a woman wants to learn to sew in order to work at the factory nearby, she need only bring in cloth to be taught by one of the māechī. Dārunī also assisted in funding the building of a village well.

Once a māechī is seen as a local leader, she receives daily reinforcement of her choice to go forth. She hears from the women who come to her the stories of the difficulties of being a wife, mother, and daughter, enmeshed in the concerns of daily living. Just as her position as a māechī allows her to hear these problems safely, it also allows her to offer a safe place for women to deal with their problems. Often local women come to Dārunī's samnak to gain perspective on their home lives; besides local women, those from Bangkok often come to Senī's samnak for similar reasons.[5] For example, a wife finds herself overwhelmed by jealousy and terrified for her own and her children's economic future when her husband takes a "minor wife." While a first wife, whose marriage is legitimated by the government, has some legal rights and protections, a minor wife, a long-term lover, does not. But a minor wife can bring misery to the first wife, not only emotionally but financially if the husband chooses to live with the lover, abandoning his first family, as Wābī's did. Legal recourse is rarely considered in rural areas and is probably unaffordable in most cases. More than once I heard Thai women hope their husbands would go to prostitutes rather than take a minor wife—not only would their husbands then be more likely to remain emotionally intimate with them, they would be more likely to continue to and be able to support their families. Generally, it is cheaper to visit prostitutes than to support a lover.

A mother may watch as her child loses motivation and refuses to go to school and may be shocked to inaction by learning that her child is using drugs. Or a young woman may fall in love with a married man and see herself tortured by love with no hope of a more socially legitimate, dependable relationship. Women in situations such as these come to samnaks for refuge and perspective. Some practice meditation for hours a day very seriously, consulting the samnak leader or recognized meditation instructor to ensure spiritual progress and attending religious classes. Others take robes and quietly help with work around the samnak, listening to talks on Buddhism and meditating and chanting, but mostly finding peace in the discipline of the samnak and in the emphasis on things other than family and economic gain. Such time-outs from worldly enmeshment can help not only by giving a perspective and the ability to act more freely and responsibly, but the break itself can help dissolve difficult situations. Māechī give emotional and spiritual support by supplying a refuge for women and by counseling them.

Some of the women who go forth for this sort of respite and refuge are those who have become involved in unhelpful social relationships, following a stereotype for māechī in Thai society. If a woman goes forth as a māechī at a young age, she will very likely be teased to her face or behind her back as a woman suffering from heartbreak. This popular conception of young māechī trivializes the spiritual path māechī have chosen, the role they serve in society, and the significant damage that a love affair or heartbreak can do, especially to a woman in Thai society. One of the first māechī I met in Thailand was a young woman who had fallen in love with a married man. He claimed he loved her, too, but that he could not afford to divorce his wife and maintain two families. He asked her to be his lover, but of course this request was highly problematic: not only did she not want to be dishonest to the wife of the man and with her friends and acquaintances, living a hidden life not condoned by those around her, and not only did she not want to end up ostracized and alone, but she also had realistic economic concerns. She worked for the government and had a good job, but if she had a child by this man, would she have to give up the child to relatives so that she might work to provide for it? She saw that she needed to end the relationship, but that was not easily done—their love was compelling, and the man was persistent. By going forth as a māechī for three months in a town twelve hours away by train from where she lived, she removed herself from a situation that was dooming her, gained a useful perspective, and worked to rearrange her priorities. Her meditation practice was sincere, and, surrounded by women quietly emphasizing other aspects of human life besides those of romantic love, family, and economics, she was able to calm herself and adjust her life so that she could lead it more honestly and helpfully.

In these ways samnaks answer serious needs, especially those of women. Dārunī expressed it this way: "The most important thing I can teach people is to value their lives more, to develop their minds. If people develop their own minds, they'll use their daily lives well. When they want material things, radios, cars, it's a sign that their minds aren't developed." Of the women that come to her samnak to stay days, weeks, and months, Dārunī said,

> Everyone has problems. . . . People who stay longer, they have much suffering and cannot solve their problems. I teach . . . meditation in order that their minds have peace. Our duty is to help them have peace, in mind and body. Their duty is to stay, not contacting others, to stay in their rooms and practice. I teach [meditation] for their peace. Then when they leave, they are better people. They have peace; they have purpose. When they first come here, they may have ideas, but they cannot tell which are right and which are wrong. When they're overwhelmed by negative emotion, they can't know right from wrong. But here they can practice in peace and calm their minds and then they can consider right from wrong.

Both Dārunī and Senī daily counsel women who cannot take the time to stay at the samnak. They both report that much of their counseling has to do with interpersonal relationships and economics. Says Dārunī: "There are five things I teach them. . . . One, a religion for working: take the five precepts and keep them, don't be lazy about them. Two, save money every day. If you get ten baht a day, you must save one baht a day. Three, don't lie—to yourself or to others. First, you have to be honest with yourself. If you make a vow to yourself, you must keep the vow. Four, you must consider everything first before using your money. You must use your brain first. Five, tolerance, patience. . . . [People] have to . . . avoid speaking in anger."

The roots of public service for māechī are in their experiences as women removed from householder lives. Meditation can detach them from everyday enmeshment and open their eyes to the suffering and causes of suffering in themselves and those around them. It can help them develop compassion and think of effective responses to the suffering of those around them. Societally, as women removed from their families, māechī can develop roles for themselves that other women are unable to—because these other women are blind to them or because they have no time to develop these other roles. Whereas a woman with a family has concern for family members foremost in her mind and works daily to improve their circumstances, a woman who leaves the house and vows to consider religious development as the most important aspect of human experience can gain a perspective not only on her own interpersonal relationships but on the societal underpinnings that form the interpersonal relationships around her. Thus freed, she can concentrate on maintaining helpful relationships with those around her, learning from these relationships and contributing to her community by providing the refuge of meditation and peace to people who visit the samnak and sometimes by establishing social service programs that directly answer to the financial, social, and emotional problems that result from the inegalitarian roles of men and women. In such ways, māechī in modern Thailand form a small but significant group of mother/nurturer ascetics, contemplative-activists removed from the fast-running river of modern society, thus better able to assist those around them when they have difficulty navigating that river.

Does the institute support this aspect of māechī—the development of nurturing ascetics? Certainly through its encouragement of social progress, such as Dhammacarinī School, it does. At least one scholar has argued, however, that the institute, "while being helpful in supporting [māechī] and encouraging education, may not be helpful if [it does] not encourage the very art that [māechī] are gaining respect for, namely, meditation"—an ascetic aspect of the new role.[6] It is true that the institute formally encourages sitting meditation very little (in the daily schedule at conferences and training sessions, more time is devoted to the practice of chanting than sitting meditation, for example, and many more hours are given over to workshops). Evidence, however, indicates that the institute does not spend more time and energy encouraging meditation simply because there is little need for encouragement—most māechī are daily reinforced in their practice of meditation by the rewards of meditation itself. Many, like Wabī, were drawn to go forth in the first place by experiencing meditation.

Meditation, then, plays a role in the goings on of the institute, but not one on which much formal organization is focused. At the annual meeting of the institute, for example, one day was dedicated to workshops and presentations centered on the development of leadership and counseling techniques and other aspects of social service. When breaking into groups according to major area of interest, over half of the māechī joined the group on meditation. On the one hand, the institute only encouraged meditation as one topic among many; on the other hand, most of the people there chose to discuss that topic, and they clearly recognized the connection between rootedness in meditation and helpful social service.

So while the institute may be seen as being overly bureaucratic and rigid, paying too much attention to details of behavior, nevertheless, it allows for a flexibility in response that is helpful to its members and the people they serve. The institute surrenders power with ease to people who do not hold official positions but who wish to contribute. This agility allows a diverse group of leaders to respond creatively to immediate needs and the definition and attainment of short-term goals, as well as to long-term concerns. Famous, educated, socially conscious women such as Māechī Sunsanee Sthirasuta, Māechī Kanittha Vichiancharoen, and Ms. Kanok Samsen Vil all run programs for māechī through the institute, though none holds an official position.

In preparation for the annual institute meeting, for example, Māechī Sunsanee, a well-known, well-educated māechī from a family of high status who operates a retreat center and samnak on the periphery of Bangkok, ran a week-long preparation conference for promising māechī. Through a series of presentations and small group work, attendees were invited to explore issues related to women and Buddhism, the main social roles of māechī, religious education, and the future development of the institute. When Sunsanee first proposed the idea of such a preparatory meeting for the annual institute meeting to Māechī Waree and Māechī Laksana, secretary general and assistant secretary general of the institute, they eagerly supported it, consulting lists of members and other māechī to determine who should be specially selected to receive greater training in institute-related concerns by attending the conference.

Through Sunsanee, the institute could also be said to encourage meditation. Whenever she speaks, Sunsanee emphasizes the importance of knowing yourself, and of knowing what you are doing. Meditation played a large role in her own going forth, and she does not shy away from revealing details of her own life to clarify the benefits of the practice. Before she went forth, she had a successful professional life, was married to a wealthy man, and was a darling of the elite, but she felt "emotionally tired."

> I was never contented. If I had tens of thousands, I wanted hundreds of thousands; when I had hundreds of thousands, I wanted millions. I was always competing to get new things, larger and better things, but I didn't know who I was competing with. I was happy, but it wasn't true happiness. . . . All I got then was myself. All I saw was myself. I was selfish. My fame had to be better than others', had to be more, higher. . . . I had to be better than anyone else.
>
> I was exhausted, withered, like a pendulum swinging on the inside, not stable. . . . I wanted everything. . . . I went forth because I was tired in my heart—physically well and okay, dining in hotels and going to functions, always dressing well. But when I saw my friends driving a new car, I wanted a new car too. I was so tired. Back then my life was simply me always trying to give myself things. But now, here and now, it's a life that offers other people my good things.

The more she meditated, the more she saw how superficial her earlier happiness had been, how shallow her thinking had been. "I was taught to think, but I hadn't been taught to have a system of thinking that comes from a still mind—a system of a still mind." She knew how to apply her intellect to the problem solving dictated by her work and her status in an increasingly materialistic society, but she needed to learn the deeper problem solving and clarity of perception that one can learn in meditation. Her teacher taught her that "if you want to know other people's world, you have to know yourself clearly first. If you know your own nature, then you know the nature of all the things surrounding you." She took several years to ground herself in meditation and the life of a māechī, abandoning her marriage and professional life.

> Now I've studied these things: Where does anger come from? Does it stay long? Where does it go? Meditation is like this. We look at these things, we ask these questions, we look at desire: where is it from? What causes it? . . . Meditation is like creating anew . . . you recreate your mind in order to contemplate.
>
> You live every breath of your life in order to have continual mindfulness, in order to realize quickly, in order to know quickly,

realize quickly, have wisdom, know what you're doing, be conscious of what you're doing. . . . When you have these things, then
you have mindfulness and consciousness of what you're doing.

She reaches to her girlhood, as well as to her meditation practice, to explain
her service to others: "My mother taught me that the first spoonful of rice has
to go to the monks. And after that we eat. My mother taught us to give to
others first."

Her programs to help others, her services to māechī, especially young
māechī, include an annual meditation training session of twelve days, which
100 to 150 māechī attend. The session, "A Life Devoted to Dhamma: Meditation Training for Buddhist Māechī," has three main objectives: to help
māechī understand Buddhist practice, to help them understand their role, and
to introduce them to applications of Buddhist teaching to social and rural
development so that they will be better able to make practical and Buddhist
development projects of their own.

Her other social service programs include teaching university students
and adults meditation, training Thai boxers in compassion and positive attention, administering a program for handicapped children, and running a Sun-
day program that aims to strengthen families by structuring group play,
learning, and working activities on the grounds of her retreat center and
samnak. She teaches meditation to all volunteers in her programs, māechī and
laypeople. Further, she invites māechī from all over the country who wish to
study in Bangkok to live in her samnak as they do so. As one of the great
difficulties in seeking higher education for māechī is finding housing in the
expensive, crowded city, Sunsanee's assistance in this regard is greatly appreciated. Also, the māechī who come to live with her receive excellent
training by serving as her assistants. They learn the skills that Sunsanee
gained from her own education and from her life as a professional woman:
how to run conferences, organize retreats, invite important speakers, arrange
for their accommodations, and encourage communication.

The social service program of Sunsanee that has received the most attention, and which is another example of the focus of many māechī on the needs
of women and children, is her shelter for mothers and infants. She invites
unwed mothers fifteen years of age and older who lack the financial, emotional,
and social support to bring their children to this house on the edge of her
samnak grounds. By providing a safe home for the women and their infants,
she works to convince Thai women who would otherwise abandon their infants
at the hospital to keep and raise their children. She meets with the residents of
the house daily and teaches them meditation as well as group dynamics, urging
them to see themselves and others more clearly and to act effectively in their
interpersonal relations, while simultaneously providing them with a safe and

supportive environment in which to learn to be caring mothers and to otherwise explore the rewards of her teaching. The women practice meditation regularly. As they become more comfortable in their new home, they often become involved in Sunsanee's other programs, for example, working at the neighborhood nursery school and cooking for the meditation retreats.

Many of the women, she told me, have been raped, which is one reason they consider abandoning their infants before learning of the shelter. They have no love for the father of the infant, nor do they have positive feelings about the incident that brought about conception. After listening to the women recount their experiences, Sunsanee concluded that in reliving their violent experiences in their minds, they were often repeatedly experiencing the event, preventing healing. Practicing meditation, learning mindfulness, she finds, brings the women away from the painful memory and back to the present moment and so assists healing. "The rape is over. When you think about the dark moonlit night when you were sprawled on the ground—that thinking is now you raping yourself. That's living in the past. You're forcing yourself to live in the past, just as someone forced you into sex." Sunsanee uses metaphors of rape in diverse contexts. She once spoke about the best way to deal with the appropriately notorious Bangkok traffic problems:

> This is an example of how you have to put up with things you don't like. Bangkok is not good, but you have to be with it, live in it. You can complain about it every day—but it's no good raping yourself, forcing yourself to live the suffering again and again by complaining. You can't go anywhere else, so—you have to live in Bangkok, you suffer so much you think you have to complain every day, but a wise person will have mindfulness enough to live happily, not falling prey to what we call modernity. If every time you see a red light, you curse it—you have to think for yourself, how do I suffer in this state of city life? You'll have anger if you scold something. So you have to practice. If you curse everything every time you don't like something, then what comes out of it is your own grouchiness. You become a person who lives in conflict with your surroundings. If you're wise, you change. If you can't run red lights, you just have to accept the red lights. Live happily with what you don't like. . . . We are the definers of things—we define things. If we choose city life, then we define that situation of being in the city.

When she speaks with men she uses the metaphor of rape in a similar way: "One rape occurs every five minutes in Thailand. I turn to men and say, 'Don't rape anybody—especially yourself. You rape yourself when you force yourself to do something that's not right.' "

Sunsanee urges a balance of contemplation and work when she explains
the details of her shelter for women and infants:

> Our help is not just bodily. We help in such a way that we help the
> women be delivered both in soul and in body. We decide how best
> to save them, both in body and soul. This is very important—if you
> help them only in the body [such as simply providing a place for the
> women to live], you have to take on the burden yourself in the long
> run because those people you've helped can't stand up on their own,
> because they have taken up the habit of taking. That's why you have
> to help them get up and fight. Helping the women in this house, it
> isn't about teaching them just to take. A woman has been raped. And
> she comes to this place, and I tell her that she has to help us work
> immediately. Many social workers ask why Māechī Sunsanee is so
> strict.[7] Look at the differences between two approaches: You tell the
> girl, "You come here, live comfortably, whatever you want you tell
> us," with, "You own this place, we are colleagues, co-workers, help-
> ing each other." Which of these choices will help the girl be a
> member of the house better? The latter will give you 200 colleagues.[8]
>
> In this house we don't have to employ any social workers. We
> help each other. Making everyone help each other makes us proud
> of ourselves. What's helping each other? I mean by helping people
> put down, put aside, her state of having-been-raped. And live in the
> present.

She consciously creates her life so that others can see her as a role
model. "Living in [this retreat center], helping others—it's not just me practicing alone, it's persuading others to join me, and by this I help others. We
live in a country in which we have to persevere and give opportunities to
others to travel with us, to journey with us." She closely associates the benefits
of meditation and the ability to serve others: "A cool person[9] is a useful
person."

When considering current merit-making practices in Thailand, Sunsanee
notes among laypeople a pattern evident in the concerns of the institute; she
claims that a change has taken place: in the past, people gave material things
in order to make merit, but now people are inclined to make merit by helping
others—directly or indirectly. Says she, "I think there are more people willing to share. The wisdom of sharing is on the rise. They choose to make merit
with people who are ready to make merit with other people, through helping
others."

Besides Sunsanee, there are two other prominent women who, while
holding no official rank in the Institute of Thai Māechī, contribute through

their own intelligence, clear-sightedness, strength, and energy to benefit others in general and other māechī in particular, developing the role of māechī as mother/nurturer ascetics. Again, partly because of the flexibility of the organization, these women also have considerable influence: Māechī Kanittha and her half-sister, Ms. Kanok.[10]

When she talks about having gone forth, Kanittha notes how she had decided to go forth forty-five years ago but got involved in family affairs. Now that her children are married and she and her husband are amicably separated, largely due to concentration on work, she is free to live the religious life that she has wanted to live for a long time. She and her mother had always dreamed of becoming māechī together, but when her mother died at age seventy-two, that dream still had not been realized. When Kanittha's own seventy-second birthday approached, she felt the loss of that unrealized dream and wanted more and more to pursue the part of it she still could by going forth herself. Her children and husband and other family members objected. To communicate clearly her intentions, she prepared clothes and other necessities for going forth and wrote a small book urging her family members to shave her head and dress her in white for her funeral should she die before going forth. While her family continued to worry about her health and the dietary restrictions of māechī, they accepted the seriousness of her aspirations.[11]

Kanittha is a strong, outspoken woman. She is not as restrained in her movements as most māechī I have met, and she is as likely to talk about feminism, spousal abuse, rape, and lesbians as she is about Buddhist truths. She is a straight talker, laughs loudly when amused, and is passionate about her concerns. She has worked for years in various ways to improve conditions for women in her country, and she is dedicated to working as hard and as long as she can in response to the continuing need. On the varied compound Kanittha established that houses one emergency shelter for battered women and its associated child care center, there also stands the central office of the Association for the Promotion of the Status of Women, its library, a modest hotel with pool and recreation center, and māechī rooms attached to her small cottage. The diverse activities, functions, and people on the compound reflect Kanittha's diverse interests as well as her central concern: to make the world a better place, especially for women and children.

In a way similar to Kanittha's seeking the institute's approval for her drafting of a māechī law, she sought the approval of the Institute of Thai Māechī before moving ahead with the proposal that she and Māechī Amarit, a famous meditation teacher who runs several large samnaks in northern Thailand and who is well educated secularly as well, developed for a college for māechī. She envisions a college that will respond flexibly to māechī needs, allowing them to study Dhamma, Thai crafts, subjects required in Thai compulsory education, and other subjects of interest to māechī, ones that will allow them to serve members of their society better. Kanittha says, "Our new nun's college, it's different. It's to prepare you to be more useful to your community. It's a different thing."

In explaining her emphasis on service, Kanittha refers to Buddhism and Catholicism. When I asked her about her role models over the years, she meandered to an answer she wanted to develop: "I just liked the way of the Buddha, and I learned. And I read the . . . the *Therīgāthā* and all that." She paused and then continued:

> You know my role models might be the Catholic nuns. . . . I admired the Catholic nuns when I was in a Catholic convent school, and I always thought that Buddhist nuns should do something like the Catholics. They leave their families and sacrifice themselves for their community and all like that. At the same time, they practice their Dhamma and they serve other people. It is the Catholic way: they believe they serve God. . . . Really, I know them. And it's very kind of them to serve us. And they believe that God will love them, God will be pleased with them, so they serve God by doing charity work.

Besides referring to Catholic nuns in explaining her dedication to social service, Kanittha refers to the Buddha's advice: "Don't do evil things. Do good things. And purify your mind." "The precepts," she explains, "are the [most important thing]. Helping others is the second. The third is meditation, detachment." While her main work is running shelters for abused women and administering the Association for the Promotion of the Status of Women, which she established in 1974, Kanittha takes time to meditate at the contemplative samnaks of Māechī Amarit.

Ms. Kanok is another powerful woman who, holding no official position in the institute, is a leader of māechī and works through and with the institute to assist māechī in helping more. Kanok exudes much of the same fierce righteousness, vast energy, and competent dedication to improving the world as does her half-sister Māechī Kanittha, especially in her attention to women and girls. Kanok began running training workshops for māechī thirty years ago through the Girl Guide Association:[12] "You see, most of the māechī, they are people who are poor—they cannot help themselves economically or socially. And we feel that since we give training to young girls wherever they are, we should give them consideration too. We train girls in the slum areas, in the rural areas, in school, and we also train girls who [go forth], become māechī." She concentrates her training of māechī not in compulsory educational subjects but in traditional crafts such as sewing and cooking as well as the practical but not necessarily traditional subjects such as food preservation. A very down-to-earth woman, Kanok detests the practice of girls becoming educated through sixth grade and never using the knowledge they gain in school for their lives on farms. She trains māechī in traditional flower arrangement and in sewing Thai triangular pillows in an effort to invite the women to help preserve aspects of Thai culture.

Her more recent workshops have focused on training māechī in counseling—again, with a practical purpose in mind: to enable young girls to consult serious, religious-minded adults when in trouble. Because māechī generally live in rural areas where urban-trained counselors have no desire to go, Kanok seeks to train the māechī so that they are better able to contribute to their local communities in ways that help the girls there. She explains that the popular misconception is that the girls agree to leave their villages and families in order to seek a more exciting and financially rewarding life in the city as prostitutes. In her own visits to villages, however, she found that the girls go into prostitution not merely because of poverty but because of the low quality of interpersonal relations in their lives at home. "The mother and father do not get along, and the children do not want to be with the parents that are always fighting with each other. They have no one whom they can consult." Māechī trained in counseling could not only help the girls envision better lives for themselves than what they see in their parents, but they might be able to assist the parents as well.

Kanok, a former member of parliament, is dedicated to politics, the welfare of women in Thailand, and Thai culture. When I asked her why she chose to emphasize social work when she worked with māechī, she stressed the importance of keeping Buddhism alive. "I feel that if we don't make our māechī useful and if we don't make our people understand Buddhism, there will be no Buddhism in this country . . . I feel the nuns should help the monks in accomplishing the learning of Buddhism, real Buddhism, for the people." She emphasizes that in an increasingly materialistic culture, laypeople need the example of people who sincerely cultivate detachment, and she hopes that māechī can communicate to laypeople that they need only work to get what is enough: "If [you have] more than enough, it means you are trying to get from others . . . you make other people unhappy. Just like if you have a factory, of course, you do it for profit, but if [you do not cultivate detachment], you [always feel you] don't have enough profit. If you have a hundred, you want a thousand, if you have a thousand, you want ten thousand. It means you are trying to take it from the poor people."

Kanok agrees with Sunsanee that making merit now has more to do with helping people than it does with donating money to temples for buildings: "I believe in developing human beings. [Some others] believe in building [temple] walls, temple buildings.[13] I believe the people are very poor, why should we build a wall? That's not the right thing. . . . I want results. I want these māechī to be useful." She wants to prevent social catastrophes such as prostitution by educating those who might become involved so that they see the problems of contributing to society in ways that are less helpful. Even simple training in flower arrangement can contribute to this education because while arranging flowers the person is more disciplined and is thus more likely to see the advantages of being more disciplined. Why make merit building a wall when you can make merit helping a human being develop?

A major challenge in educating māechī, as Kanok sees it, is recognizing and responding to the difference between *using* māechī and *developing* māechī. She criticizes programs that do the former and not the latter: programs such as those sponsored by some monks that send untrained māechī into villages do not "raise the status of the māechī, but they use the māechī. I think that's wrong because you can use people who are well developed to develop other people; you cannot use the underdeveloped to develop other people." She stresses the importance of developing māechī: "I feel very sorry because this country is very poor. You eat your mangos, you throw [the pits] away, and in another few years, you could eat a lot of mangos from [the tree that's grown as a result of the discarded pit]. . . . But you have to pay attention to [the pit]. . . . The māechī are just like you and me: they are human and strong, they have hearts and brains, and they can do whatever you and I can do. Why don't we give them the opportunity to be useful?"

Like Māechī Kanittha, she sees problems in the approach differences of the respective organized churches toward Buddhist māechī and Catholic nuns: "If a Thai girl becomes a Catholic sister, she is taught how to do this and that. Why isn't it the same with Thai girls who are māechī in the Buddhist religion?" Kanok did not attend Catholic school, but her work in Girl Guides took her into the slums where a Catholic nun ran a program for impoverished girls. Eventually this Catholic nun went to a rural area and started a rice farm. "When she went there, she couldn't find anyone to drive the tractor. She drove the tractor herself. If a Buddhist nun did that, oh, the people would be shocked. I think education helps [Catholic nuns]."

She feels that girls should have māechī to consult, not just monks. Monks, faced with young girls consulting them every day, are less likely to keep their vows of celibacy. "It is the māechī who should go in and help the girls." Kanok founded the Buddhist Women's Association, a volunteer organization that, among other activities, gives awards to māechī who distinguish themselves in service.

Māechī Sunsanee, Māechī Kanittha, and Ms. Kanok are often sought out by journalists to represent māechī. Articles in the press that focus on māechī frequently quote these women and publish photographs of them. They are high-profile leaders, and through them Thais are becoming more familiar with the lives and purposes of māechī. They also help māechī gain broader perspectives on the world through their own service and through their training of māechī. Working with and through the institute, they encourage māechī as they make their new role in Thai society, a social role for spiritual women, a spiritual role for social women. As a result of the sort of path-breaking work done by the institute, Sunsanee, Kanittha, and Kanok, Wabī can live at Dhammacarinī Samnak, head a work team that grows food for the samnak, study English, and complete her high school degree. She can reach out to the young girls from Isān like herself who come there in hopes of building a future on a sound foundation. She can meditate and chant daily, and she can discuss the Dhamma with her fellow māechī to find richness and meaning in her life.

Chapter 12

Departure

Greatly increasing is the glory of him who exerts himself, is thoughtful, pure in character, analytical, self-restrained, vigilant, and lives according to the Dhamma.

—*Dhammapada* 24

It is 3:30 A.M., and I join the white-clad figures of māechī and phrām outside of the main building of Dhammacarinī Samnak. It is dark, but the area around the door is well lit from above, and I remove my white plastic shoes and step onto the cool glassiness of the white porch that surrounds the building. The morning air wafts against my skin appealingly but stinks of the recently established pig farm nearby. No bucolic dream is this. It is modern Thailand, and if the noisy night creatures were to pause all at once, we would be able to hear the low-pitched drone under the clanging and crashing of the ice factory down the road.

The downstairs is hardly lit at all. The large space divided according to the different activities that occur there is unobtrusively awaiting the less religiously focused engagements of the day to begin later. The two small conversation areas—one for more formal events, one for less—the storage space for school supplies, the sewing area, the library, and even the large classroom with its own altar lie in darkness as we make our way up to the main altar room.

We walk quietly up the stairs, not engaging in much communication but smiling if we catch each other's eyes. Māechī Wābī raises the skin where her eyebrows would be and looks significantly at my hands. I smile and shake my head: no, I have not brought Āromdī, the little black cat I adore, into the

132

meditation hall this time. I never should have done it yesterday. Even when he slept peacefully, hidden by my small robe as I meditated, I was utterly distracted by the loud purrs. I could neither stop admiring him nor stop wondering if others would hear and whether I would get in trouble. And I wondered what that trouble would look like if I, the only non-Thai here, were to be its focus.

The hard chill of the floor is replaced by the warm plushness of the red carpet after I climb the stairs and cross the huge room used for chanting, meditation, and most religious ceremonies and sit to the side of the raised platform on which the māechī will all line up, according to when they were ordained. The comparatively lower temperature of the early morning requires only a few of the windows that cover all four walls to be open, and the large ceiling fans rotate only very slowly above us.

Together we bow three times to the Buddha before us on the crowded and glittering altar, rearrange ourselves in posture appropriate for meditation, and lower our eyelids. As I lower mine, I see the figure of Wābī, in calm, alert posture, seated almost directly in front of the largest Buddha statue.

Our silent meditation is broken later when we begin to chant rhythmically and almost atonally in Thai and Pāli. More melodious chanting would be just one more sensual pleasure at which to grasp that, being grasped at, would keep us all in the samsaric round of suffering. But I still find most Buddhist chanting exquisite in its simplicity. Some of the māechī at the front, such as Wābī, no longer need to use the chanting pamphlets, but I certainly use mine. I marked some of the words months ago in English in pencil so I could remember exactly when we are inviting the gods to come for our chanting and when we are sending them off and away, a part of the ritual that I particularly enjoy. Now I look at these unnecessary textual notes and see how far I have come during my stay at the samnak. Many of the words now have become part of my everyday vocabulary.

When I first arrived at the samnak, I had little use for chanting. It was both boring and difficult—boring if I did not bother to try to discern the meaning but only focused on making the correct sounds (an unfortunately common practice among Thais when they chant in Pāli, I'm told), and difficult if I worked to discern the full meaning as I simultaneously tried to make the right sounds. But now the discipline of chanting several times every day joined the disciplines of getting up at 3:30 A.M., meditating, and restraining from abrupt and overly active movements, and from eating after noon. I have been calmed and formed by the disciplines and have a more considered outlook on my life, both in and out of the samnak.

I will leave soon. I will leave these thirty-six acres of samnak land enclosed by its high, solid-white wall. I will miss the large, golden, walking Buddha statue directly inside the gate and the traditional Thai roofs—their

pointed corners lifting upward and a row of flame-like curves along the top—
of the residences on that side of the samnak. I will miss the wordless, clat-
tering noise of the dining hall during the two meals a day. I will miss even
my awkwardness when, at each meal, one student or another approaches me
to take my plate when I get up and try to wash it myself.

I will miss the row of shade trees lining the entrance where yesterday I
found twenty or so white-robed māechī and schoolgirls dressed in loose black
pants and white shirts. They climbed in and around the trees, using an assort-
ment of saws, knives, and shears to prune them, collecting branches in small
bundles tied by bits of white cloth. These branches will be used later in the
cooking fires under the huge rice vat and two huge woks in the kitchen. I will
miss the casual chats I had with māechī and the young girls at the school as
we squatted in the grass with hand-held scythes, slowly cutting, overseen by
team leaders such as Māechī Wābī. I will miss one precocious māechī's
repeated bandaging of the wounds I acquired through my awkwardness with
the scythe. (She and two others eventually supplied me with gloves in an
effort to stop the bloodletting.) Perhaps what I will miss most about the
outside of the samnak, besides the raging purple clouds preceding the storms
of the rainy season, are the small signs hanging from trees: "Work is life,"
"Life is fighting, so you must live with patience," and "If you want knowledge, don't show disrespect to your teachers."

Before I was invited to live here and before coming to stay, I came from
Bangkok just to take a look. I was harried and damp with sweat. The private,
direct bus that seemed like such an excellent idea (a promise of a quick trip
with no changes required and little waiting) had broken down three times en
route. The final breakdown required that we all file onto the road and wait in
the hot sun until another small, equally unreliable bus, already filled, came
along (and, yes, it broke down twice, too) and allowed us to get on. My
conservative pumps complicated the back pain inspired by having to crouch
partially standing at the back of the bus, crammed now with two busloads of
people. Further, there was a monk at the back of the bus who was upset that
my skirt might brush his robes. The texts require a monk to wash his robes
repeatedly if so sullied by a woman. It is a lot of work, plus monks simply
should not be that close to a woman—ever. Two laymen had joined in his
concern, adding to my annoyance. I was hot and wet and in pain and could
cultivate not one thought of loving-kindness. Nor was I feeling particularly
respectful of the Buddhist texts. I thought that this monk and these two
laymen should simply rearrange their own seating so that the laymen protected the monk from contact. Why was it *my* responsibility to alter my
crippling position to accommodate *his* vows? No, I was neither filled with
generosity, loving-kindness, nor any other of the better states of the heartmind.

But when I arrived that first time at the samnak, I was shown into the small round building with the red conical roof (a motif in the buildings here) used to receive visitors. I was made to feel at ease in the cool of the building, and I was offered the traditional glass of water and allowed to rest before a māechī came to see why I had come. I was calmed in those moments as I have been calmed in these many months.

Tomorrow, Wābī, with whom I have spent so many hours in work and conversation, and I will say our final good-byes. She has taken much time from her crowded schedule to help me, and I am sure she will be at least a little relieved to have that time back. The mushroom hut that she established has been empty of mushrooms since my arrival. It is time to go down the road to the farm and acquire some bags of spores. The owner used to raise pigs, but as she became more and more serious about Buddhism, she found that she could no longer be part of the slaughter process. That owner will give Wābī some spores, and Wābī will let them grow in the wet darkness of the palm-leafed hut tucked inconspicuously behind the kitchen. And she will catch up on the rosters of the young girls on her work team and talk with all of them to make sure they are doing all right.

Wābī's duties here are great but not overpowering. The majority of the population of this samnak is involved in the samnak school, which has brought these girls from all over the country, and which brought Wābī here. The work required to maintain it demands the cooperation of both those who have gone forth and those who have not. But these two groups are also separated—even the young māechī who are students in the school and who sometimes only differ from their fellow students by their robes and the expectations of them. Wābī, like most of the māechī here, shares a room with one other māechī. The sixty-three girls, ages thirteen to eighteen, are housed ten to fifteen to a room in the school building itself or in the small building next door. Housing is one of the difficulties at the samnak: there is not enough. Since Wābī first went forth, she never shared a room before she moved here to continue her education. The māechī need private rooms for discipline, to help them avoid idle chatter and other laxities in practice and to enforce their self-reliance. The administrators of the schools are also disappointed that most of the girls sleep in the upstairs classrooms on the ten to fifteen low wooden beds with thin mattresses crowded wall to wall. The daily schedules of the girls and māechī differ as well: while māechī are expected to get up and chant and meditate at 3:30 A.M., the girls sleep until 5 A.M. and begin the day with fifteen minutes of physical exercise. In the morning, the māechī squeeze in an additional class on chanting before regular school classes begin, and at night, they have another session of required meditation and study. These differences in schedule force the māechī students to pay close attention to their use of time, as each day they have approximately three fewer hours for study than their fellow students who have not gone forth.

Wābī is one such māechī student who must balance her commitments. She attends classes regularly and heads an afternoon work team of students and māechī students daily. As one of the māechī who went forth long ago, she not only sits in the front of the upstairs sala for meditation and chanting but also takes on altar-related and chanting-leading responsibilities as necessary. Her agricultural knowledge inspired her to establish the mushroom hut and several vegetable gardens.

Her future is by no means secure, but she is certainly welcome to stay at Dhammacarinī Samnak, where she is much respected, for as long as she wants. Sometimes she hopes to go on a two-year meditation retreat to deepen her understanding of Buddhism, to deepen her practice, and to take more steps toward abandoning samsara in favor of nibbāna. Sometimes she talks of joining a male-dominated temple and, secure in the friendships of her many māechī friends from years of living among them, help teach the *sāmanen*, the young boys who live and study on the temple grounds. In either case, her years as a māechī have benefited her, despite or because of their challenges. The Institute of Thai Māechī has helped her become more educated both secularly and religiously, and mentors have helped her. And I have had the pleasure of becoming her friend.

Chapter 13

Conclusion

Māechī in Thailand, such as Māechī Wābī, Dārunī, Senī, Mīna, and Noy, are a unique group of women gaining influence in a fast-changing society. By dedicating themselves to Buddhism, these women obtain freedom, places to live, friendships to foster, religious meaning, and sometimes formal education. By remaining single and cultivating a role outside of the usual expectations for women, they develop useful perspectives. They also, by meditating, cultivate useful perspectives. All of these aspects of their lives ensure that they have gifts to give to the people around them. In addition, their national organization, the Institute of Thai Māechī, further assists in māechī development. What is the generosity and compassion that māechī work to cultivate? A look at the Vessantara Jātaka, one of the best-known Buddhist stories in Thailand, allows us one last glimpse at māechī in Thailand in general and Wābī in particular.[1]

A synopsis of the tale: Prince Vessantara lives with his wife Maddī and their two children, a son and a daughter, in a kingdom he will inherit. He is much loved and appreciated for his generosity, but when he gives away the white elephant which guarantees enough rainfall for the area in which it lives, the people become angry and ask his father to send him from the kingdom. His father complies, and Vessantara leaves, giving all of his worldly goods away before embarking on his long journey. Though Vessantara, his mother, and his father argue against his wife Maddī accompanying him, she chooses to go and brings their children. Eventually, after difficult traveling, the family reaches a forest and makes a home there, the couple living as celibates. One day when Maddī is out collecting food, an old brahmin comes and asks Vessantara for his children so that they can become his servants; Vessantara

137

gives his children to the man. Jūjaka Sakka, king of the gods, has been looking on, and he decides to protect Maddī from being given away similarly; he appears before Vessantara as a brahmin, asks for Maddī, and when Vessantara gives her to him, he quickly gives her back. By giving Maddī to Vessantara, he ensures that the two will stay together: she is a gift to Vessantara. The old brahmin brings Vessantara's and Maddī's children to Vessantara's father, Sañjaya, in hopes of obtaining money. He receives the money but dies overeating. Vessantara's father is overwhelmed by regret and goes out to seek Vessantara and Maddī to ask that they return to the kingdom. They agree to return, the children are reunited with their parents, and Vessantara rules the kingdom.

When Wābī first heard the story of Vessantara as a child visiting her local temple, she cried; over the years, the story has taken on many layers of meaning as she has lived, making her own stories. She finds the story rich in lessons. In contrast, when I first read the story of Prince Vessantara, I was appalled. As one friend noted when I described the story to her, it is like the apex of a bad dress rehearsal on generosity—all of the mistakes possible related to giving are made: giving too much, giving what is not one's to give, giving inappropriately, blindly giving. Prince Vessantara, the hero of the story, is renowned for his generosity, and he earns that reputation: when he is born, he immediately wants to give away something, anything, to those around him (so, of course, he turns to his mother to supply him with something to give). He gives away the prize elephant of his kingdom, the elephant that keeps his kingdom prosperous, its people well fed; his generosity thus seems to ensure the suffering of the citizens of his realm. He gives up his children for the sake of his own enlightenment, condemning them at least to a temporary period of pain before his father can rescue them from their cruel master and condemning his wife to the pain of losing her children. Particularly poignant is the scene near the end of the story, when Vessantara's and Maddī's children are reunited with their parents for the first time since their having been given away by Vessantara. Streams of milk from Maddī's breasts sprinkle them, and when she faints, the streams continue to flow into the children's mouths. Vessantara faints, his parents faint, and the 60,000 ministers all faint. Presumably, the fountainous breast milk continues to flow. Not only has the giving led to an evidently harmful degree of emotion (after all, equanimity—"coolness"—is highly valued in Buddhism), but Vessantara has gotten much credit for the giving, while Maddī appears to be at least as much of a model of generosity throughout the story.

In his eagerness to develop his generosity, Vessantara seems to lack compassion. When he approaches Maddī after he has been banished from the kingdom, he simply tells her to look for a new husband. He does not anticipate her distress at losing him, nor does he examine the difficulties of finding a new husband and the societal position of a widow. Maddī has to point out to him that death would be better to her than living without him. She has to explain the problems of a widow in their society—that a widow has no power to determine her life, that her sons can refuse her anything and torture and debase her, that a woman widowed is as defenseless as a kingdom without a king. When Maddī tells him her dream that warns of the loss of her children, he dismisses it as inconsequential so that he will be sure to have the opportunity to give the children away. The dream is described:

> A dark man wearing two saffron robes and with red garlands adorn-
> ing his ears came threatening her with a weapon in his hand. He
> entered the leaf-hut, and grasping Maddī by the hair, dragged her out
> and threw her flat on the ground. Then, as she shrieked, he dug out
> her eyes, pulled off her arms and splitting her breast took out her
> heart, dripping blood, and went off.[2]

Maddī is concerned about the nightmare that indicates she will lose that which is most important to her: her children. In her concern, she approaches Vessantara at night—an inappropriate time for celibates to talk. Vessantara understands the dream to mean that he will have an opportunity to "fulfill the Perfection of giving" by giving his children away and so he lies to Maddī saying it must have been something she ate; he does not want her to be an obstacle to his enlightenment.[3] Maddī, despite his belittling analysis of the dream, however, takes it seriously enough to warn him especially to take care of the children. She tells him that she will try to return early from her gathering expedition that day in order to look after them herself.

Maddī, in contrast to Vessantara, is a model of compassion. She is the mother/nurturer to Vessantara's renunciant. She gathers food for the family and supports Vessantara when he doubts himself, such as when he hears his father's assemblage approaching the hermitage and is concerned—Maddī then reassures him that nobody could overcome him.[4] She does what she can to ensure family unity. She suffers in sympathy with those around her when they suffer. When Vessantara thinks to go to the forest without his children, she also anticipates the comfort Vessantara will need in the forest—the comfort his children can provide. Vessantara's stalwart rule-abiding nature (generosity is one of the finest virtues, therefore he will give at every opportunity) is balanced by Maddī's nurturing, empathy, perceptiveness, and attention to particulars.

Maddī's dream parallels the meditation experiences and stories māechī learn from the women who visit them and ask for assistance. Maddī, while dreaming, is removed from her householder obligations and the net of her responsibilities. She is alone, beside her children but not engaged with them.

From this removed position, she gains a vital clue into her situation and the challenges ahead of her: she will lose that which is most important to her, "the very best gift."[5]

Sakka, king of the gods, gives us an indication of a helpful way to view Maddī and Vessantara. After Vessantara renounces his children, Sakka fears that he may give away Maddī. He is not concerned about Maddī if this happens—he is concerned about Vessantara, who would be left "alone, helpless, and without support."[6] Vessantara is, in a way, a renunciant even before he goes to live in the hermitage—he is a man always emptying himself, always giving up what he has, always renouncing. This aspect of Vessantara appeals to the renunciants who traditionally recount the story once a year, such as the monk who told Wabī the story and such as Wabī herself. Maddī, on the other hand, is the nurturer and the one attending to the particulars of each situation. Vessantara gives because his highest rule is to give. Maddī's actions are guided by compassion and particular circumstances. She joins Vessantara when he leaves, because to do otherwise would result in her suffering. She brings the children, because to do otherwise would result in Vessantara's suffering. Maddī is the mother/nurturer to Vessantara's renunciant.

Wabī appreciates Vessantara's generosity; she sees his willingness to renounce that which he loves the most as the quintessential response to the problem of the karmic rounds. She also relates to the peace he feels in giving—similar to the peace she gained in giving money at the temple before she went forth and the peace she gains through living the religious life, having given up her family. She also empathizes with Vessantara's banishment, mirroring in a way her own banishment from the householder life—though she tried to go back to it, return was impossible for her. She admires the faithful love of Maddī, who would follow her husband out of the kingdom. She relates to the children's abandonment by their father. As Vessantara sought his enlightenment by giving up his children, so did her father seek his when he went forth as a monk. Wabī understands the matrix of events that seems so horrendous—parentless children as slaves under a cruel master—as the karmic cycle. They suffer because this is samsara, the place of suffering. Understanding detachment (and thus, generosity) as the way to escape suffering, Wabī appreciates Vessantara's choice. She also relates to Maddī's suffering and her courage.

The brahmin Jūjaka, who asked Vessantara for his children, is similar to Maechī Mīna and Maechī Noy in Wabī's life. Jūjaka created the opportunity for Vessantara's ultimate renunciation, as Mīna and the meditation instructor created the opportunity for Wabī's ultimate renunciation—of meditation and of her conception of herself as a maechī. On the night of the children's departure, Vessantara's struggle to reach the Buddhist goal of equanimity contrasts with Maddī's deep pain and panic. She writhes, trying to learn the truth of what has happened to her children. He sits, valiantly fostering the equanimity he knows he must develop. They are both struggling with gaining a truthful, honorable perspective on their greatest loss—which will lead to their regaining all they had before and more. Sakka recognizes the need for both Vessantara and Maddī—which is why he ensures Maddī's continued presence with Vessantara by giving her to him as a gift. Vessantara is a good, giving renunciant—we know that from the start—but Maddī also holds qualities that are necessary, evidently for the survival not only of Vessantara but of herself and the children.

In some ways, then, Vessantara is strict generosity and Maddī is flexible compassion. Vessantara's generosity and Maddī's compassion both need wisdom to guide them, as do Wābī and the other māechī of Thailand. For the māechī of Thailand today, that wisdom comes from many sources: from meditation, greater opportunities for secular and religious education, and greater opportunities to learn from others who are creating similar paths to their own.

The balancing of Vessantara's strict code of generosity and Maddī's responsiveness to particulars not only helps us understand māechī as renunciants/nurturers in seeking wisdom, but these aspects also mirror the strict bureaucracy of the national organization of the Institute of Thai Māechī and its flexibility and responsiveness that allows for leaders such as Māechī Kanittha, Sunsanee, and Kanok to respond to the particularities of the moment.

Wābī's ultimate renunciations led to her creating a new path for herself as a māechī, as Vessantara's and Maddī's ultimate renunciation led to their regaining and ruling the kingdom. In the face of Thailand's challenges as it changes so rapidly, māechī appear to give up the concerns of the householder life, of the world, and this renunciation leads them to create their own new path—as renunciants who nurture. They nurture and mother their own family of woman renunciants as well as, in particular, the other women and children around them. On a societal level, māechī have gifts to offer because of the challenges presented to them—being largely denied education, they are seeking it. Denied respect, they are striving to earn it. Denied mainstream acceptance, they are offering their view from the outside. Without Jūjaka's inexcusable request for the children, Vessantara would never have made his ultimate act of generosity.

Women in Thailand are most universally admired when they are mothers, but as mothers they are often in impossible circumstances. Increasingly, women are alone in supporting their children and increasingly it is difficult to support their children while remaining at home. The money is in the urban areas, and the urban areas require that one leave one's children in one place and work in another. The image of Maddī lying on the ground in a dead faint as her children drink her breast milk resonates. Maddī at this point reminds us of Wābī's mother, working hard to support her own children and the children of her children, staying up late to make merit by cutting the hair of the elderly people of her village. She would not renounce the world except as an act of duty to her family. Maddī temporarily abandons the kingdom with her husband Vessantara; Wābī's mother went forth temporarily as a phrām when her daughter went forth as a māechī. Among those who can help overburdened women in Thailand while working on their own spirituality are the women who renounce the burden of the householder life by going forth. Their lives define a new kind of spirituality, a woman's spirituality.

This spirituality allows a laywoman to come to a māechī, to relieve her heart of her troubles in private conversation, and to listen to ways in which she can help her situation while feeling the warm touch of a human hand on her arm. She can hear the words counseling detachment while strengthened by human touch and empathy. Literally and sometimes figuratively, māechī can touch women in ways that male religious representatives, with their vows against seeing and touching women, cannot. Further, this spirituality seems not only to allow māechī to serve women but to demand that they do so. As they refine their own perceptions of the world through meditation and define their social position alongside the realm of householders by living in their own religious environments, they see women and the ways in which they can help them. And because they have something to give, and because gifts are necessarily to be given, māechī give their gifts.

If, in one perspective, the story of Vessantara's generosity is the quintessential worst dress rehearsal in which all of the errors are made, perhaps māechī generosity is a correction similar to Sakka's perception of Maddī as being necessary to Vessantara: māechī development of their practice and service to others is the victorious opening night traditionally said to follow the worst dress rehearsals.

Appendix

Approach, Transliteration, Pronunciation, and Translation

APPROACH

As a beginning student of Buddhism many years ago, my primary interest was in its philosophy as found in the oldest texts. I assumed then that Buddhism was a fixed, timeless, objective, coherent entity. As I dedicated my life to the study of this religion, however, I became more and more aware of the problems of representing a living tradition through its texts and ideals. I found that the lived tradition of Buddhism is, yes, textually defined but also, most assuredly, culturally defined and defining. After years of research on Buddhist texts, philosophy, and history, and after hundreds of interviews, months of archival research, and over a year living among māechī, I find that there is no one entity that is Buddhism nor one that is "māechī."

With my earlier model, I might have written this book by describing the phenomenon of māechī, keeping my eyes on this phenomenon as a whole. Then I might have found a representative of that phenomenon to depict it and acquainted the reader with it.

But how does one get at māechī when one discovers that there is no such entity? I found that the best way was to find a case and contextualize it vigorously. By looking at Māechī Wābī carefully and deeply and by examining the different aspects of her culture that played roles in her life, I found that I could begin to sort out māechī, women in Thailand, Thai culture, Buddhist texts, and Buddhist philosophy.

Thus in this book I use Wābī's life as a prism. The more one understands her life, the more one begins to understand the many aspects or colors of the

143

lives of other māechī. The reader is welcomed into Wābī's life and learns along the way about Thailand, gender in Thailand, Buddhism, meditation, māechī, and monasticism. My conclusions about māechī in general are not ones drawn from one woman's life. They are conclusions drawn from years of research and study, brought to readers through an examination of one woman's life. The biographical narrative is not the foundation of this book, although it allows a deep examination of the relationship of meditation to life. Rather, the narrative allows the reader to view some of the implications of societal and religious situations. Focusing on Wābī's life as a Buddhist allows Buddhism, and Thai Buddhism in particular, to live. It allows the women who are involved in it to live.

TRANSLITERATION, PRONUNCIATION, AND TRANSLATION

I use the transliteration system for Thai set forth by the U.S. Library of Congress. There are disadvantages to this, to be sure—for example, the five tones of Thai (as important to speakers and listeners of the language as are, say, vowels in English) are not represented. And for those who do not speak Thai, the pronunciations even of vowels and consonants are not immediately apparent for some of the words. Using this system, however, has consistency. If a reader wants to know more about a Thai word used, she or he can easily consult a chart for this system and a dictionary or two and be well on her or his way.

For personal names, I have used the transliteration preferred by the named person.

Those who do not speak Thai will find useful some hints about the pronunciation of one of the most often-used Thai words here. The vowel of the syllable "māe" in māechī is pronounced close to that of the vowel sound one uses to induce others to repeat themselves: "eh?" Further, "chī" rhymes with "gee." The tone of the first syllable is falling—it has the tone one associates with the "hey!" that one might utter involuntarily and self-righteously upon discovering that someone has cut in front of her or him in a long line. The tone of the second syllable is the normal tone—not particularly high or low, not falling as the first, and not rising as one uses in English in asking a tag question such as, "You wanted the green one, right?" Taking a few moments to pronounce this word ("meh"[falling tone]-chee") will help the reader become acquainted and comfortable with it and at least in a small way with the importance of tones in this language. The name of the woman focused on in this book is Wābī, pronounced "wah-bee."

For turning other transliterated Thai words into reasonably close approximations of how they are pronounced, the reader will want to remember a few things:

ā is pronounced as in "ah."

ī is pronounced *ee* as in "meet."

ū is pronounced *oo* as in "loot."

u is prounounced similarly but less drawn out in time.

An "h" following a "k," "p," or "t" only adds aspiration, more outbreath; it does not alter the sound of the consonant substantially. Thus *tham* is pronounced not with the English "th" sound but with the initial sound of the word "take."

The language of the oldest Buddhist texts recognized by Theravāda Buddhists (as by most Thai Buddhists) is a language similar to Sanskrit, called Pāli. For approximating the pronunciation of these transliterations, the reader will want to remember these things: "c" is pronounced "ch," as in "church" (important in the pronunciation of *Dhammacarinī* and *anicca,* for example).

Vowels listed above under the Thai transliteration are pronouced similarly, except "u" is pronouced short and flat like "u" in "cut."

Also similarly, consonants followed by an "h" are aspirated—pronounced with more air being emitted.

Finally, I translate *būat* as "to go forth." While the phrase may appear awkward at first, there are good reasons for this translation. "Go forth" is a phrase often used in Buddhist texts, a shortened version of "to go forth from home to homelessness." It is important because of the implications that one does indeed leave the home life in order to follow the most respected Buddhist path. Also, the phrase points to one of the unique qualities of Thai culture: the juxtaposition of amazing fluidity and rigidity. There is great rigidity on the occasion of certain ritually understood acts. To go forth as a māechī is to abandon utterly one way of living life. To repeat the phrase that refers to that abandonment is to indicate its straightforward, unambiguous, defining role. To repeat the phrase is to mirror the Thai reality. One alternative that many scholars use is the term *ordain,* but to ordain does not necessarily mean to abandon the life of the householder, nor does it express the rigidity of the categorization that follows the ritual of going forth.

Endnotes

ACKNOWLEDGMENTS

1. *Dīgha Nikāya* 31.24.

INTRODUCTION

1. Transliterated from Thai, the name of the samnak is *Thamachārinī*, but I will transliterate the name from its Pāli origins.

2. I conducted my interviews in Thai. I recorded almost all of the formal interviews and then translated and transcribed them simultaneously. Words attributed to Māechī Wābī and others, then, are their words translated into English by me. I learned much in informal conversations, of course, but in this book I never quote a person directly unless the person said those words. For more on my approach and on transliteration and pronunciation issues, please see the appendix.

I include helpful Thai and Pāli words in this text and in the glossary. Pāli is the language of the canon of Theravāda Buddhism—the kind of Buddhism predominant in Thailand. I exclude the diacriticals on Pāli words that are now part of the vocabulary of most educated Westerners.

CHAPTER 1

1. "Siddhattha Gotama" in Pāli, "Siddhartha Gautama" in Sanskrit—the first being his personal name and the second being his family name.

2. See the discussion in Chapter 6 for more on these forms of meditation.

3. Peter Harvey, *An Introduction to Buddhism* (Cambridge: Cambridge University Press, 1990), 42–43.

4. For the classic article on merit making and status in Thailand, see Hanks' "Merit and Power in the Thai Social Order," *American Anthropologist* 64 (1962): 1247–61.

5. From *Passionate Journey: The Spiritual Autobiography of Satomi Myōdō*, translated and annotated by Sallie B. King (Albany: State University of New York Press, 1993), 5. For an analysis of images of men and women in ancient Indian Buddhism, see especially chapter 4 of Rita Gross's *Buddhism after Patriarchy: A Feminist History, Analysis, and Reconstruction of Buddhism* (Albany: State University of New York Press, 1993) and Karen Christina Lang's "Lord Death's Snare: Gender-Related Imagery in the Theragāthā and the Therīgāthā," *Journal of Feminist Studies in Religion* 2: 2 (fall 1986): 63–80.

6. Different Buddhists recognize different texts as trustworthy. The texts I refer to here and elsewhere in this book are those recognized by the Theravāda school of Buddhism, the school that dominates Thailand and the tradition that Wābī follows. As the oldest texts of Buddhism, they are the most dependable source of the teachings of the Buddha.

7. *Dīgha Nikāya* 16.5.9.

8. Marilyn Friedman, *What Are Friends For? Feminist Perspectives on Personal Relationships and Moral Theory* (Ithaca: Cornell University Press, 1993), 217.

9. Carolyn Heilbrun, *Writing a Woman's Life* (New York: Ballantine Books, 1988), 51, 20, 52–53.

10. Carolyn Heilbrun, *Writing a Woman's Life*, 65.

11. Rita M. Gross discusses the story of Gotama Buddha's abandonment of his wife and newborn child and its implications for feminist Buddhists in chapter 3 of her *Buddhism after Patriarchy*.

12. Gananath Obeyesekere gives a psychoanalytic view of the meanings of shaving one's head in his *Medusa's Hair: An Essay on Personal Symbols and Religious Experience* (Chicago: University of Chicago Press, 1981).

13. Cook, "The Position of Nuns in Thai Buddhism" (Master's Thesis, Australian National University, 1981), 173.

14. Liz Wilson, "Seeing through the Gendered 'I': The Self-Scrutiny and Self-Disclosure of Nuns in Post–Asokan Buddhist Hagiographic Literature," in *Journal of Feminist Studies in Religion* 2: 1 (spring 1995): 46.

15. Phrām also refers to a male ritual role. See Stanley Jeyaraja Tambiah's *Buddhism and the Spirit Cults in North-East Thailand* (New York: Cambridge University Press, 1970).

16. The seventh precept is separated into two precepts.

17. Young boys go forth not as monks but as *sāmanen*, shaving their heads and eyebrows, and wearing monklike robes but taking only ten precepts. The novices often do a considerable amount of work at a temple and are given education, room, and board.

CHAPTER 2

1. It is not a new problem; a passage from the Buddhist texts describing the ideal monk is preceded by this description: "There are persons who are faithless and have gone forth from the home life into homelessness not out of faith but seeking a livelihood, who are fraudulent, deceitful, treacherous, haughty, hollow, personally vain, rough-tongued, loose-spoken, unguarded in their sense faculties, immoderate in eating, undevoted to wakefulness, unconcerned with recluseship, not greatly respectful of training, luxurious, careless, leaders in backsliding, neglectful of seclusion, lazy, wanting in energy, unmindful, not fully aware, unconcentrated, with straying minds, devoid of wisdom, drivellers" (*Majjhima Nikāya* 5.32).

2. Charles F. Keyes, *Thailand: Buddhist Kingdom as Modern Nation-State* (Boulder: Westview Press, 1987), 205.

3. A. Thomas Kirsch, "Economy, Polity, and Religion in Thailand," in *Change and Persistence in Thai Society*, eds. William Skinner and A. Thomas Kirsch (Ithaca, N.Y.: Cornell University Press, 1975), 178.

4. Charles F. Keyes, "Mother or Mistress but Never a Monk: Buddhist Notions of Female Gender in Rural Thailand," *American Ethnologist* 11 (1984): 227.

5. For more on this practice, see Marjorie A. Muecke, " 'Reproductive Success' among the Urban Poor: A Micro-Level Study of Infant Survival and Child Growth in Northern Thailand" (Ph.D. dissertation, University of Washington, 1976), 373–86.

6. Keyes, "Mother or Mistress but Never a Monk," 229.

7. Keyes, "Mother or Mistress but Never a Monk," 229, citing P. Van Esterik, "Laywomen in Theravada Buddhism," in *Women in Southeast Asia*, ed. P. Van Esterik, Occasional Paper #9 (Dekalb: Northern Illinois University, Center for Southeast Asian Studies, 1982), 65.

8. Keyes notes that by the fifteenth century, monks were considered fields of merit: "The most positive moral act a layperson could perform was to provide support in the form of food, clothing, shelter, and medicines to the sangha [monks]. Through such acts, the laity 'made merit' (tham bun, in Thai), which would be experienced as a positive reward in the future, either in this life or in a subsequent lifetime" (*Thailand*, 35). Also see Cook, "The Position of Nuns in Thai Buddhism"; P. Van Esterik, "Laywomen in Theravada Buddhism."

9. Keyes, "Mother or Mistress but Never a Monk," 229.

10. Van Esterik, "Laywomen in Theravada Buddhism," 74.

11. Stanley Jeyaraja Tambiah has explored some of the political connections of this temple in *The Buddhist Saints of the Forest and the Cult of Amulets* (New York: Cambridge University Press, 1984), ch. 11.

12. Rita Gross, in her *Buddhism after Patriarchy*, gives information on the historical precedents of monastic codes protecting religious women from "demanding monks who might ask nuns to do housework for the monks or to give them food and clothing," 37. Also see Nancy Auer Falk, "The Case of the Vanishing Nuns: The Fruits of Ambivalence in Ancient Indian Buddhism," in *Unspoken Worlds: Women's Religious Lives*, eds. Nancy Auer Falk and Rita M. Gross, 207–24.

13. For a particularly eloquent explanation of some of Max Weber's ideas on this topic, from which I draw here, see S. N. Eisenstadt's introduction to Max Weber's *On Charisma and Institution Building: Selected Papers*, ed. and trans. S. N. Eisenstadt (Chicago: University of Chicago Press, 1968).

14. Literally, "king of the sangha."

15. Records do not reveal the number of samnaks separate from temples in existence at the time. The māechī I interviewed on the point were doubtful that any all-māechī samnaks existed separately from temples then.

16. Mahamokut Buddhist University is a highly reputable university for the Thai religious, almost exclusively attended by monks.

17. Rita Gross writes of parallel incidents that led to Jutsun Kushala, a Vajrayāna teacher, returning to teaching after many years of raising a family: "Her brother the Sakya Trizen and the Dalai Lama asked her to teach again because they were so frequently besieged by questions about female teachers from Western students." Rita Gross, *Buddhism after Patriarchy*, 99.

18. According to the Theravāda Buddhist texts, a woman going forth as a bhikkhunī must have bhikkhunī present as she takes her vows. With no living bhikkhunī, it is impossible to go forth in a ceremony as described in the texts. Nancy J. Barnes provides a solid discussion on this issue and the state of religious women in various Asian countries in her article, "Buddhist Women and the Nuns' Order in Asia," in *Engaged Buddhism: Buddhist Liberation Movements in Asia*, eds. Christopher S. Queen and Sallie B. King (Albany: State University of New York Press, 1996), 259–94.

19. E-mail to International Network of Engaged Buddhists 6 September 1996.

20. Tomomi Ito, "Buddhist Women in Dhamma Practice in Contemporary Thailand: Movements Regarding Their Status as World Renunciates," *Journal of Sophia Asian Studies* 17 (1999): 162. This article gives a helpful overview of the current political and status considerations of today's religious women in Thailand.

21. Professor Chatsumarn Kabilsingh is a famous spokesperson for the reestablishment of the bhikkhunī line; her mother went forth under the Mahayana tradition in Taiwan and recognizes herself as a Theravāda bhikkhunī.

22. *Khunying* is a term indicating that the person is of a particular high status. It is an honorific journalists continue to use for Māechī Kanittha, despite her having given up the householder world to which it applies.

CHAPTER 3

1. For an excellent discussion of Hindu renounciants emphasizing both maternal qualities and renounciant values, see Meena Rani Khandelwal's "Reconsidering *Sannyasa:* The Lives and Reflections of Female Hindu Renouncers in Haridwar, North India" (Ph.D. dissertation, University of Virginia, 1995).

2. Marilyn Friedman, *What Are Friends For?*, 221.

CHAPTER 4

1. Charlotte Linde, *Life Stories: The Creation of Coherence* (New York: Oxford University Press, 1993), 6.

2. Gabriel Moran, "Alternative Developmental Images," in *Stages of Faith and Religious Development: Implications for Church, Education, and Society*, eds. James W. Fowler, Karl Ernst Nipkow, and Friedrich Schweitzer (London: SCM Press, 1991), 161.

3. Donald K. Swearer, "Control and Freedom: The Structure of Buddhist Meditation in the Pāli Suttas," *Philosophy East and West* (1973): 435. Also see Amadeo Sole-Leris's *Tranquillity and Insight: An Introduction to the Oldest Forms of Buddhist Meditation* (Boston: Shambhala Press, 1986), a particularly concise, text-based description of these forms of meditation. For scholarship examining the relationship of these types of meditation as less complementary and more in tension, see Paul Griffiths's "Concentration or Insight: The Problematic of Theravāda Buddhist Meditation Theory," *The Journal of the American Academy of Religion* 49 (December 1981), 605–24.

4. Bhikkhu Ñāṇamoli and Bhikkhu Bodhi, introduction to *The Middle Length Discourses of the Buddha: A New Translation of the Majjhima Nikāya* (Boston: Wisdom Publications, 1995), 39–40.

5. *Majjhima Nikāya* 74.10–12.

6. In the interest of purifying themselves of the wrongdoing of the year, of thanking the Mother of Waters, and of community and romantic fun, people gather at waterside after dusk to launch small boats. Generally, the boats are made of banana leaves or paper (catastrophically, styrofoam was popular for awhile, but environmentalists are helping it become less so) and hold a lighted candle, a flower, incense, and a coin.

7. Michael Carrithers, *The Forest Monks of Sri Lanka: An Anthropological and Historical Study* (Delhi: Oxford University Press, 1983), 56–57.

8. *Dīgha Nikāya* 22.5; Liz Wilson points out that most such meditations in Theravada texts are meditations on a woman's body and that the experience, then, is different for the practitioners, depending on their gender: "[U]nlike the monk who, as

observing subject, contemplates with horror a body that is not his own, the loathly nun who performs this meditation is both the observing subject and the observed object. In order to occupy the subject position, she turns her gaze on her own body as object. Surveying her own body as an ideal object of meditation, the loathly nun achieves the enlightened subjectivity made normative by exemplary men of insight. She thus incorporates within herself both the male and female roles characteristic of the monks' stories." Liz Wilson, "Seeing through the Gendered 'I', 58–59.

9. It is also a natural antidote to fear. According to the Buddhist texts, the Buddha originally taught loving-kindness meditation when practitioners were scared of meditating alone in the woods.

10. It needed no motivation or instigation.

11. See especially *Majjhima Nikāya* 4.27.

12. *Majjhima Nikāya* 7.17.

13. Thanks to Wimonkarn Kosumas for pointing this out to me in conversation.

CHAPTER 5

1. *Majjhima Nikāya* 129.8-16.

2. Robert Coles, *The Call of Stories: Teaching and the Moral Imagination* (Boston: Houghton Mifflin Co., 1989), 115–166. For a concise Western approach to the relationship of imagination and compassion, see Lawrence Blum's "Compassion," in *Explaining Emotions*, ed. Amelie Oksenberg Rorty (Berkeley: University of California Press, 1980), 507–18. For more on the cultivation of attentiveness and its contribution to the moral life, see Arne Johan Vetlesen's *Perception, Empathy, and Judgment: An Inquiry into the Preconditions of Moral Performance* (University Park: Pennsylvania State University Press, 1994) and Tom Kitwood's *Concern for Others: A New Psychology of Conscience and Morality* (New York: Routledge, 1990). The relationship of imagination, meditation and attention, and compassion in the Buddhist context is explored in greater detail in Chapter 6.

3. Robert Coles, *The Call of Stories*, 125.

CHAPTER 6

1. For a text-based examination of the ethical implications of some Tibetan Buddhist meditations, see Georges Dreyfuss's "Meditation as Ethical Activity," *Journal of Buddhist Ethics* [electronic journal] 2 (1995). He makes the important point that "the modern academic study of Buddhism does not address meditation adequately. Whereas we seem to find little problem to describe the myths, rituals, and narratives of Buddhist tradition, we seem to find it much more difficult to explain meditation in terms that are accessible to the educated public." Our inability to do this leads to a

paltry understanding of what Buddhism is and what it offers its followers. The examination of meditation in this chapter is my own attempt to rectify this problem, complementing the work of Dreyfuss. Harvey Aronson, also using a text-based approach, argues against too much emphasis on meditative cultivation of love (*mettā*) and compassion (*karunā*) as motivations for social action. Instead, he claims that the motivation for social action is simple compassion (*karuññā*) and sympathy (*anukampā*), qualities that non-meditators have as well as meditators. See Aronson, "Motivations to Social Action in Theravāda Buddhism: Uses and Misuses of Traditional Doctrines," in *Studies in the History of Buddhism*, ed. A. K. Narain (Delhi: B.R. Publishing, 1980), 1–12.

I am greatly indebted to the work of Martha Nussbaum in the following discussion.

2. What one scholar refers to as "ceremonial Buddhism"—see Paul David Numrich's *Old Wisdom in the New World: Americanization in Two Immigrant Theravada Buddhist Temples* (Knoxville: University of Tennessee Press, 1996), 61.

3. See Beesey's "Women and Buddhism in Thailand: A Changing Identity for Religious Women," in *Radical Conservatism: Buddhism in the Contemporary World—Articles in Honor of Bhikkhu Buddhadasa's 84th Birthday Anniversary*, Thai Inter-Religious Commission for Development and International Network of Engaged Buddhists (Bangkok: The Sathirakoses-Nagapradipa Foundation, 1990), 311–45; and see J. Van Esterik's "Women Meditation Teachers in Thailand," in *Women in Southeast Asia*, ed. Penny Van Esterik, Occasional Paper #9 (Dekalb: Northern Illinois University, Center for Southeast Asian Studies, 1982), 42–54.

4. Martha C. Nussbaum, "Introduction: Form and Content, Philosophy and Literature," in *Love's Knowledge: Essays on Philosophy and Literature* (New York: Oxford University Press, 1990), 47.

5. These themes of clarity and moral obligation are present throughout Buddhist literature; for an in-depth Western treatment of the relationship between clear perception and moral obligation, see especially Martha C. Nussbaum's "The Discernment of Perception: An Aristotelian Conception of Private and Public Rationality" and " 'Finely Aware and Richly Responsible': Literature and the Moral Imagination," in *Love's Knowledge*, 54–105, 148–67.

6. Martha C. Nussbaum, " 'Finely Aware and Richly Responsible': Literature and the Moral Imagination," in *Love's Knowledge*, 160.

7. *Majjhima Nikāya* 5.4, 5.4, 5.29.

8. Nussbaum, "Introduction," in *Love's Knowledge*, 22.

9. Nussbaum, "Flawed Crystals: James's *The Golden Bowl* and Literature as Moral Philosophy," *in Love's Knowledge*, 127.

10. For this metaphor and others, see *The Book of the Kindred Sayings: Saṃyutta-Nikāya*, Part II, trans. Mrs. Rhys Davids (London: Pali Text Society, 1972), 118ff.

11. *Majjhima Nikāya* 6.6.

CHAPTER 7

1. For a traditional Theravāda view of these kinds of difficulties, see ch. 20, "Purification by Knowledge and Vision of What Is and What Is Not Path," in Bhadantacariya Buddhaghosa's *Visuddhimaga*, translated as *The Path of Purification* by Bhikkhu Ñāṇamoli, 2d ed. (Colombo, Sri Lanka: A. Senage, 1964).

2. Lucien Hanks, "Merit and Power in the Thai Social Order," in *American Anthropologist* 64 (1962): 1247–61.

3. Steven Collins, *Selfless Persons: Imagery and Thought in Theravada Buddhism* (New York: Cambridge University Press, 1982), 89.

4. Bhikkhu Ñāṇamoli and Bhikkhu Bodhi, trans., *The Middle Length Discourses of the Buddha*, 1180, footnote 89.

CHAPTER 8

1. *Majjhima Nikāya* 8.14.

2. Bhikkhu Ñāṇamoli and Bhikkhu Bodhi, trans., *The Middle Length Discourses of the Buddha*, 1184, footnote 113.

CHAPTER 9

1. Fred Arnold and Suwanlee Piampiti, "Female Migration in Thailand," in *Women in the Cities of Asia: Migration and Urban Adaptation*, eds. James T. Fawcett, Siew-Ean Khoo, and Peter C. Smith (Boulder: Westview Press, 1984), 143–64

2. Employed women are more likely to send money to their rural homes than employed men. A fine source of information on women and migration in Thailand is Gordon F. De Jong's, Kerry Richter's, and Pimonpan Isarabhakdi's article, "Gender, Values, and Intentions to Move in Rural Thailand," *International Migration Review* 30: 3 (fall 1996): 748–70.

3. De Jong, Richter, and Isarabhakdi, "Gender, Values, and Intentions to Move in Rural Thailand," 752.

4. Only a few women are allowed in the Thai military, and those only at the lowest levels.

5. "Lūangphọ" is an honorific that indicates a higher status than the usual "Phra" used as an honorific for monks. This gentleman's more formal name was Lūangphọ Rachdilok.

6. "Khun Mãe" is an honorific reserved for those mãechi who are deemed worthy of particular respect. Most abbesses of samnaks are referred to as "Khun Mãe."

7. Janice G. Raymond, *A Passion for Friends: Toward a Philosophy of Female Affection* (Boston: Beacon Press, 1986), 62.

8. The best article on how female prostitutes in Thailand support the basic institutions of Thai society, such as family and religion, is Marjorie A. Muecke's "Mother Sold Food, Daughter Sells Her Body: The Cultural Continuity of Prostitution," *Social Science & Medicine* 35: 7 (1992): 891–901.

9. Prostitution is illegal in Thailand, but only prostitutes are arrested for the crime; rarely, if ever, are their clients arrested.

10. Raymond, *A Passion for Friends*, 11.

11. The other Buddhist school for girls was founded on the model of Dhammacarinī and is located near Chiang Mai.

12. Theodore D. Fuller, Paul Lightfoot, and Peerasit Kamnuansilpa, "Urban Ties of Rural Thais," *International Migration Review* 24 (fall 1990): 535.

13. In 1995, about 10 percent of the girls were from the north, about 10 percent were from the south, about 50 percent were from the northeast, Isan, and the rest were from the central region, where the school is located.

14. Raymond, *A Passion for Friends*, 63.

15. Marilyn Friedman, *What Are Friends For?*, 251.

CHAPTER 11

1. Nussbaum, "Introduction," in *Love's Knowledge*, 44.

2. Nussbaum, " 'Finely Aware . . . ' " in *Love's Knowledge*, 162.

3. The best article on this practice is Marjorie Muecke's "Mother Sold Food, Daughter Sells Her Body, 891–901. In it, Muecke points out that prostitution "enables women, through remittances home and merit-making activities, to fulfil traditional cultural functions of daughters, conserving the institutions of family and village-level Buddhism, as well as of government," 891. Another treatment of the practice is Pasuk Phongpaichit's *Rural Women in Thailand: From Peasant Girls to Bangkok Masseuses* (Geneva: International Labour Office, 1980. See also Khin Thitsa's *Providence and Prostitution: Image and Reality for Women in Buddhist Thailand* (London: Change International Reports, 1980).

4. Empower, with offices in Bangkok and Chiang Mai, is the only organization currently working with prostitutes nonjudgmentally to offer them education. If the prostitutes want English lessons to enable them to speak with their clients more easily, Empower provides those lessons. Empower also offers emotional support and counseling.

5. Not much time has passed since Māechī Senī taught meditation in Bangkok, so the ties between her and the women living in the city remain strong.

6. Allan Beesey, "Women and Buddhism in Thailand, 338.

7. Māechī Sunsanee refers to herself in the third person fairly frequently.

8. Over 200 women have spent time in the house.

9. A person who has "cooled" the hot emotions—who eliminates greed, anger, and delusion.

10. Both Māechī Kanittha and Ms. Kanok are *khunying*, a category of high-status women. The respect of this status is reflected in newspaper reports on Māechī Kanittha when they refer to her as "Māechī Khunying Kanittha," retaining the secular honorific in spite of her having gone forth from the secular world.

11. Their concern about health appears to be well founded. I discovered that many Theravada monks and māechī who have lived the religious life for more than a decade had blood sugar complications such as diabetes and hypoglycemia. Because of the restrictions on eating times, monks and māechī go seventeen hours or so a day without solid food; the drinks they are allowed or can afford (milk is very expensive) are seldom enough to prevent the resultant irregular level of blood sugar that, maintained for so long, brings on grave physical difficulties.

12. Another name for the Girl Scouts Association.

13. A way to gain merit.

CHAPTER 13

1. Margaret Cone and Richard F. Gombrich point out: "Even the biography of the Buddha is not better known" than the *Vessantara Jataka*. See *The Perfect Generosity of Prince Vessantara: A Buddhist Epic*, introduction, trans. Margaret Cone and Richard F. Gombrich (New York: Oxford University Press, 1977), xv. For a sparkling and thorough analysis of the Vessantara Jataka, see Steven Collins's *Nirvana and Other Buddhist Felicities: Utopias of the Pali Imaginaire* (New York: Cambridge University Press, 1998), 497–554.

2. Cone and Gombrich, trans., *The Perfect Generosity of Prince Vessantara*, 54.

3. Cone and Gombrich, trans., *The Perfect Generosity of Prince Vessantara*, 54. Steven Collins explores the depths of Vessantara's struggles. By the end of the story, all five precepts have been violated. Vessantara's apprecation of renunciation is not acted upon in a simple manner. Collins, *Nirvana*, 528.

4. Cone and Gombrich, trans., *The Perfect Generosity of Prince Vessantara*, 87.

5. One refrain throughout, especially the last half of the story, is that "children are the very best gift." Cone and Gombrich, trans., *The Perfect Generosity of Prince Vessantara*, 74.

6. Cone and Gombrich, trans., *The Perfect Generosity of Prince Vessantara*, 75.

Glossary

All words are Pāli, unless otherwise noted.

āčhān (Thai)—a term of respect for a teacher or professor

anattā—not self, lack of essence

Ānanda—joy, pleasure, or bliss, the name of Gotama Buddha's close attendant

anicca—change

anukampā—sympathy, compassion, pity

arahant—one who has attained *nibbāna*, has extinguished his or her obstacles

Ārom dī (Thai)—in this case, the name of a cat, but the name derives from a phrase describing someone of good temperament

bāp (Thai)—unhelpful, wrong, sinful

bhikkhu—Theravāda Buddhist monk

bhikkhunī—nun, comparable to a monk in Theravāda Buddhism

bindapat (Thai from the Pāli)—the collecting of food by those who have gone forth

būat chī (Thai)—to go forth as a *māechī*

būat phra (Thai)—to go forth as a monk

Buddho—the awakened one, referring usually to Gotama Buddha, often repeated internally as a form of meditation

dhamma—this word has an extraordinary number of meanings. In this book, it generally refers to the Buddhist truths.

dhammatā (Thai: *thammadaa*)—suchness, a reference to the seeing clearly of things as they are: changing (anicca), not having an inherent self (anattā), and causing pain (dukkha)

dukkha—suffering, misery, woe, pain, ill, sorrow, trouble, discomfort, unsatisfactoriness, conflict; one of the three characteristics of samsara

farang (Thai)—foreigner, usually referring to a non-Asian

gāebūn (Thai)—fulfilling a vow or making a thankful offering

157

gap khão (Thai)—"with rice," food designed to be served with rice

Isãn (Thai)—northeast Thailand

Jãtaka—a story of one of the previous incarnations of the Buddha

karunã--compassion

kãruñña—compassion (differentiated by Aronson as "simple compassion")

khun mãe (Thai)—honorific for a mãechī high in status; an abbess, for example

kilesa—obstacles to the spiritual path

loy grathong—a water festival celebrated in parts of southeast Asia

Luang Pǫ (Thai)—honorific for a monk with a high status, such as an abbot

lũksit (Thai)—pupil or disciple

mãechī (Thai)—woman who shaves her head and eyebrows and wears a long skirt and long-sleeved white shirt covered with a white robe, similar to that of Buddhist monks, and who generally takes eight precepts; a nun

mãruyãt (Thai)—etiquette, politeness, the right thing to be done according to form

mettã—loving-kindness

nãglīat (Thai)—ugly, inappropriate

nak būat (Thai)—one who has gone forth, usually refers to a monk

nak patibat (Thai)—practitioner

nãmarūpa—name and form; mind and matter; feelings, perceptions, mental formations, consciousness, corporeality

nibbãna—release from the cycle of rebirth, samsara

Pãli—the language in which the canon of Theravãda Buddhism is written

paticcasamuppãda—interconnectedness, dependent origination, law of causation, chain of causation, law of dependent arising, chain of phenomenal cause and effect, the conditional arising and cessation of all phenomena, the twelve links of conditioned co-production, cause and effect, conditioned genesis

phrãm (Thai)—a woman who wears white, usually a white skirt, a white blouse, and a small white robe, usually shorter than that of a mãechī. She does not shave her head or eyebrows and may take five or eight vows. Often a woman who is living the religious life temporarily.

pubakãrī—one who does a kindness, a favor, looks after someone

puñña—auspicious, fortunate

sabãichai (Thai)—at ease, one's heart (*chai*) *is* comfortable (*sabãi*)

saddhū—"it is good"; similar in use to "Amen"

samatha—concentration, one-pointedness of mind, mental discipline *samnak* (Thai)—spaces such as offices, residences, and institutes, but among māechī, it refers to the space of māechī within or outside of temple grounds; a nunnery.

samsara—the cycle of birth and death; release from this cycle is nibbāna.

sangha—an assemblage; usually refers to Buddhist monks

sañña-khandha—perception

tham būn (Thai version of the Pāli)—to do a good thing, to do something auspicious, performing a helpful or skillful action, one that, in the natural workings of the law of karma (cause and effect), will result in good.

Theravāda—literally "the way of the elders"; refers to the oldest kind of Buddhism found mostly in South and Southeast Asia and so sometimes is called Southern Buddhism. Another division of Buddhism is the more recently developed Mahāyāna, found mostly in East Asia and so referred to as Eastern Buddhism. A further kind of Buddhism is Mantrayāna or Vajrayāna, also called Northern Buddhism and found mostly in Tibet and Nepal.

Therīgāthā—a text of hymns of senior nuns incorporated into the Khuddaka Nikāya

trūat nam (Thai)—a water-pouring ceremony

vipassanā—insight meditation

yokhī, yokhīnī (Thai; the Pāli is *yogī*)—practitioner

Bibliography

Arnold, Fred, and Suwanlee Piampiti. "Female Migration in Thailand." In *Women in the Cities of Asia: Migration and Urban Adaptation*, edited by James T. Fawcett, Siew-Ean Khoo, and Peter C. Smith. Boulder: Westview Press, 1984, 143–64.

Aronson, H. B. *Love and Sympathy in Theravāda Buddhism*. Delhi: Motilal Banarsidass, 1980.

———. "Motivations to Social Action in Theravāda Buddhism: Uses and Misuses of Traditional Doctrines." In *Studies in the History of Buddhism*, edited by A. K. Narain. Papers presented at the International Conference on the History of Buddhism at the University of Wisconsin, Madison, USA, August 19–21, 1976. Delhi: B. R. Publishing, 1980.

Barbour, John D. *Versions of Deconversion: Autobiography and the Loss of Faith*. Charlottesville, Va., and London: University Press of Virginia, 1994.

Barbre, Joy Webster, Amy Farrell, Shirley Nelson Garner, Susan Geiger, Ruth-Ellen Boetcher Joeres, Susan M. A. Lyons, Mary Jo Maynes, Pamela Mittlefehldt, Riv-Ellen Prell, and Virginia Steinhagen (The Personal Narratives Group), eds. *Interpreting Women's Lives: Feminist Theory and Personal Narratives*. Bloomington and Indianapolis: Indiana University Press, 1989.

Barnes, Nancy J. "Buddhist Women and the Nuns' Order in Asia." In *Engaged Buddhism: Buddhist Liberation Movements in Asia*, edited by Christopher S. Queen and Sallie B. King. Albany: State University of New York Press, 1996, 259–94.

Bartholomeusz, Tessa. "The Female Mendicant in Buddhist Srī Lankā." In *Buddhism, Sexuality, and Gender*, edited by José Ignacio Cabezón. Albany: State University of New York Press, 1985, 37–64.

———. *Women under the Bo Tree*. Cambridge: Cambridge University Press, 1994.

Bateson, Mary Catherine. *With a Woman's Eye: A Memoir of Margaret Mead and Gregory Bateson*. New York: Morrow, 1984.

Beckford, James. *Religion and Advanced Industrial Society*. Boston: Unwin Hyman, 1989.

———. "The Sociology of Religion and Social Problems." *Sociological Analysis* 51: 1 (1990): 1–14.

Beesey, Allan. "Women and Buddhism in Thailand: A Changing Identity for Religious Women." In *Radical Conservatism: Buddhism in the Contemporary World—Articles in Honor of Bhikkhu Buddhadasa's 84th Birthday Anniversary*. Thai Inter-Religious Commission for Development and International Network of Engaged Buddhists. Bangkok: The Sathirakoses-Nagapradipa Foundation, 1990, 311–45.

Bennett, Milton J. "Towards Ethnorelativism: A Developmental Model of Intercultural Sensitivity." In *Cross-Cultural Orientation: New Conceptualizations and Applications*, edited by Michael Paige. Lanham, Md.: University Press of America, 1986.

Bhikkhu Ñāṇamoli and Bhikkhu Bodhi, trans. *The Middle Length Discourses of the Buddha: A New Translation of the Majjhima Nikāya*. Wisdom Publications, 1995. (Cited in the text as *Majjhima Nikāya*.)

Blum, Lawrence. "Compassion." In *Explaining Emotions*, edited by Amelie Oksenberg Rorty. Berkeley: University of California Press, 1980, 507–18.

Bobilin, Robert. *Revolution from Below: Buddhist and Christian Movements for Justice in Asia: Four Case Studies from Thailand and Sri Lanka*. Lanham, Md.: University Press of America, 1988.

Boddy, Janice. "Spirits and Selves in Northern Sudan: The Cultural Therapeutics of Possession and Trance." *American Ethnologist* 15: 1: 4–27.

Braude, Ann. *Radical Spirits: Spiritualism and Women's Rights in Nineteenth-Century America*. Boston: Beacon Press, 1989.

Buddhaghosa, Bhadantacariya. *The Path of Purification*. Translated by Bhikkhu Ñyāṇamoli. 2d ed. Colombo, Sri Lanka: A. Semage, 1964.

Buddhavisate, Sukjai. *Sotanpap La Botbaat Kong Matchee Ny Sangkhom Thai: Kuksagrani Wat Soithong* ("The Status and Role of Matchee in Thai Society: The Case of Wat Soithong"). Dissertation, Chulalongkorn University, 1984.

Carrithers, Michael. *The Forest Monks of Sri Lanka: An Anthropological and Historical Study*. Delhi: Oxford University Press, 1983.

Clifford, James, and George E. Marcus, eds. *Writing Culture: The Poetics and the Politics of Ethnography*. Berkeley: University of California Press, 1986.

Cohen, Paul T., and Gehan Wijeyewardene. "Spirit Cults and the Position of Women in Thailand." *Mankind* (Special Issue 3). 14: 4 249–62.

Coles, Robert. *The Call of Service: A Witness to Idealism*. Boston: Houghton Mifflin Co., 1993.

———. *The Call of Stories: Teaching and the Moral Imagination*. Boston: Houghton Mifflin Co., 1989.

Collins, Steven. *Nirvana and Other Buddhist Felicities: Utopias of the Pali Imaginaire*. New York: Cambridge University Press, 1998.

———. *Selfless Persons: Imagery and Thought in Theravāda Buddhism*. New York: Cambridge University Press, 1982.

Cone, Margaret, and Richard F. Gombrich, trans. *The Perfect Generosity of Prince Vessantara: A Buddhist Epic.* New York: Oxford University Press, 1977.

Cook, Nerida. "The Position of Nuns in Thai Buddhism: Parameters of Religious Recognition." Master's thesis, Australian National University, 1981.

Davids, Caroline A. F. Rhys., trans. *The Book of Kindred Sayings:* Saṃyutta Nikāya, part II. London: Pali Text Society, 1972.

De Jong, Gordon F., Kerry Richter, and Pimonpan Isarabhakdi. "Gender, Values, and Intentions to Move in Rural Thailand." *International Migration Review* 30:3 (fall 1996): 748–70.

Dhammapada: Wisdom of the Buddha. Translated by Harischandra Kaviratna. Pasadena, Calif.: Theosophical University Press, 1980.

Dreyfuss, Georges. "Meditation as Ethical Activity." *Journal of Buddhist Ethics* 2 (1995).

Fairclough, Gordon, and Rodney Tasker. "Separate and Unequal." *Far Eastern Economic Review* 14 (April 1994): 22–23.

Falk, Nancy Auer. "The Case of the Vanishing Nuns: The Fruits of Ambivalence in Ancient Indian Buddhism." In *Unspoken Worlds: Women's Religious Lives in Non-Western Cultures.* edited by Nancy Auer Falk and Rita M. Gross. San Francisco: Harper and Row, 1980, 207–24.

Fowler, James W., Karl Ernst Nipkow, and Friedrich Schweitzer, eds. *Stages of Faith and Religious Development: Implications for Church, Education, and Society.* London: SCM Press, 1991.

Frank, Gelya. "Anthropology and Individual Lives: The Story of the Life History and the History of the Life Story." *American Anthropologist* 97: 1 (March 1995): 145–48.

Friedman, Marilyn. *What Are Friends For? Feminist Perspectives on Personal Relationships and Moral Theory.* Ithaca, N.Y.: Cornell University Press, 1993.

Frye, Marilyn. *The Politics of Reality: Essays in Feminist Theory.* Freedom, Calif.: The Crossing Press, 1983.

Fuller, Theodore D., Paul Lightfoot, and Peerasit Kamnuansilpa. "Toward Migration Management: A Field Experiment in Thailand." *Economic Development and Cultural Change* 33 (1985): 601–21.

———. "Urban Ties of Rural Thais." *International Migration Review* 24 (fall 1990): 534–62.

Gallagher, Eugene W. *Expectation and Experience: Explaining Religious Conversion.* Atlanta, Ga.: Scholar's Press, 1990.

Gilligan, Carol. *In a Different Voice: Psychological Theory and Women's Development.* Cambridge, Mass.: Harvard University Press, 1982.

Griffiths, Paul. "Concentration or Insight: The Problematic of Theravāda Buddhist Meditation Theory." *The Journal of the American Academy of Religion* 49 (December 1981): 605–24.

Gross, Rita M. *Buddhism after Patriarchy: A Feminist History, Analysis, and Reconstruction of Buddhism*. Albany: State University of New York Press, 1993.

————. "The Householder and the World Renunciant: Two Modes of Sexual Expression in Buddhism." *Journal of Ecumenical Studies* 22 (winter 1985): 81–96.

Gunn, Janet Varner. *Autobiography: Towards a Poetics of Experience*. Philadelphia: University of Pennsylvania Press, 1982.

Hanks, Lucien. "Merit and Power in the Thai Social Order." *American Anthropologist* 64 (1962): 1247–61.

Hardacre, Helen. *Kurozumikyo and the New Religions of Japan*. Princeton, N.J.: Princeton University Press, 1986.

Harvey, Peter. *An Introduction to Buddhism: Teachings, History, and Practices*. Cambridge: Cambridge University Press, 1990.

Heilbrun, Carolyn G. *Writing a Woman's Life*. New York: Ballantine Books, 1988.

Horner, I. B. *Women under Primitive Buddhism: Laywomen and Almswomen*. London: George Routledge and Sons, Ltd., 1930.

Hyde, Lewis. *The Gift: Imagination and the Erotic Life of Property*. New York: Random House, 1983.

Irvine, Walter. "Decline of Village Spirit Cults and Growth of Urban Spirit Mediumship: The Persistence of Spirit Beliefs, the Position of Women and Modernization." *Mankind* 14:4 (1984): 315-24.

Ishii, Yoneo. "Church and State in Thailand." *Asian Survey* 8: 10 (1968): 864–71.

————. *Sangha, State, and Society: Thai Buddhism in History*. Translated by Peter Hawkes. Honolulu: University of Hawaii Press, 1986. Monographs for the Center of Southeast Asian Studies, Kyoto University.

Ito, Tomomi. "Buddhist Women in Dhamma Practice in Contemporary Thailand: Movements Regarding Their Status as World Renunciates." *Journal of Sophia Asian Studies* 17 (1999): 147–81.

Jelinek, Estelle C. *The Tradition of Women's Autobiography from Antiquity to the Present*. Boston: Twayne Publishers, 1986.

Johnson, Mark. *Moral Imagination: Implications for Cognitive Science for Ethics*. Chicago: University of Chicago Press, 1993.

Kabilsingh, Chatsumarn. *Bhikkhuni yang nuiyuu ryy?* [So there are still Bhikkhuni?] Nakhon Pathom 2518.

————. "Buddhism and National Development: A Case Study of Buddhist Universities." In *Religion, Values, and Development in Southeast Asia*, edited by Bruce Matthews and Judith Nagarta. Singapore: Institute of Southeast Asia Studies, 1986.

————. "The Future of the Bhikkhuni Sangha in Thailand." In *Speaking of Faith: Cross-cultural Perspectives on Women, Religion, and Social Change*, edited by Diana L. Eck and Devaki Jain. New Delhi: Kali for Women, 1986, 139–48.

————. "The Religious Position of Buddhist Women in Thailand." In *Buddhist Ethics and Modern Society*, edited by C Fu et al. 259–64.

————. *Thai Women in Buddhism*. Berkeley, Calif.: Parallax Press, 1991.

Keyes, Charles F. "Buddhism and National Integration in Thailand." *Journal of Asian Studies* 30 (May 1971): 551–667.

————. "Charisma: From Social Life to Sacred Biography." *Journal of the American Academy of Religion* Thematic Study 48: 3–4 (1982): 1–22.

————. "Death of Two Buddhist Saints in Thailand." *Journal of the American Academy of Religion Thematic Study* 48: 3–4 (1982): 149–80.

————. "Mother or Mistress but Never a Monk: Buddhist Notions of Female Gender in Rural Thailand." *American Ethnologist* 11 (1984): 223–41.

————. "Structure and History in the Study of the Relationship between Theravāda Buddhism and Political Order." *Numen* 25 (August 1978): 156–70.

————. *Thailand: Buddhist Kingdom as Modern Nation-State*. Boulder: Westview Press, 1987.

————. "Theravada Buddhism and Its Worldly Transformations in Thailand: Reflections on the Work of Stanley Tambiah." *Contributions to Indian Sociology*. New Delhi 21: 1 (1987): 123–45.

Khandelwal, Meena Rani. "Reconsidering *Sannyasa*: The Lives and Reflections of Female Hindu Renouncers in Hardiwar, North India." Ph.D. dissertation, University of Virginia, 1995.

Khin, Thitsa. "Nuns, Mediums, and Prostitutes in Chiengmai: A Study of Some Marginal Categories of Women." In *Women and Development in Southeast Asia I*, edited by C. W. Watsorup. Canterbury: University of Kent, Center of Southeast Asian Studies, 1983, 34–XX.

————. *Providence and Prostitution: Image and Reality for Women in Buddhist Thailand*. London: Change International Reports (Women and Society), 1980.

Kirsch, A. Thomas. "Economy, Polity, and Religion in Thailand." In *Change and Persistence in Thai Society*, edited by William Skinner and A. Thomas Kirsch. Ithaca, N.Y.: Cornell University Press, 1975, 172–96.

————. "Text and Context: Buddhist Sex Roles, Culture of Gender Revisited." *American Ethnologist* 12: 2: 302–20.

Kitwood, Tom. *Concern for Others: A New Psychology of Conscience and Morality*. New York: Routledge, 1990.

Lang, Karen Christina. "Lord Death's Snare: Gender-Related Imagery in the Theragāthā and the Therīgāthā." *Journal of Feminist Studies in Religion* 2: 2 (fall 1986): 63–80.

Langness, L. L. and Gelya Frank. *Lives: An Anthropological Approach to Biography*. Novato, Calif.: Chandler and Sharp, 1981.

Lewis, I. M. *Ecstatic Religion: An Anthropological Study of Spirit Possession and Shamanism.* Harmondsworth: Penguin, 1971.

Lim, Mah Hui, and Douglas Porpora. "The Political Economic Factors of Migration to Bangkok." *Journal of Contemporary Asia* 17: 1 (1987): 76–89.

Linde, Charlotte. *Life Stories: The Creation of Coherence.* New York: Oxford University Press, 1993.

Marcus, George, and Michael Fischer. *Anthropology as Cultural Critique.* Chicago: University of Chicago Press, 1986.

Mauss, Marcel. *The Gift: Forms and Functions of Exchange in Archaic Societies.* Translated by Ian Cunnison. New York: Norton, 1967.

Moran, Gabriel. "Alternative Developmental Images." In *Stages of Faith and Religious Development: Implications for Church, Education, and Society,* edited by James W. Fowler, Karl Ernst Nipkow, and Friedrich Schweitzer. London: SCM Press, 1991, 149–61.

Muecke, Marjorie A. "Make Money Not Babies: Changing Status Markers of Northern Thai Women." *Asian Survey* 24 (1984): 459–70.

———. "Mother Sold Food, Daughter Sells Her Body: The Cultural Continuity of Prostitution." *Social Science & Medicine* 35: 7 (1992): 891-901.

———. "The New Thai 'Nun': A Paradigm Shift from Buddha to Chamatevi." Manuscript presented at the annual meeting of the American Anthropological Association in Washington, D.C., on November 19, 1989.

———. " 'Reproductive Success' among the Urban Poor: A Micro-Level Study of Infant Survival and Child Growth in Northern Thailand." Ph.D. dissertation, University of Washington, 1976.

Murcott, Susan. *The First Buddhist Women: Translations and Commentary on the Therīgāthā.* Berkeley, Calif.: Parallax Press, 1991.

Myōdō, Satomi. *Passionate Journey: The Spiritual Autobiography of Satomi Myodo.* Translated and annotated by Sallie B. King. Albany: State University of New York Press, 1993.

Numrich, Paul David. *Old Wisdom in the New World: Americanization in Two Immigrant Theravāda Buddhist Temples.* Knoxville: University of Tennessee Press, 1996.

Nussbaum, Martha C. *Love's Knowledge: Essays on Philosophy and Literature.* New York: Oxford University Press, 1990.

———. *Poetic Justice: The Literary Imagination and Public Life.* Boston: Beacon Press, 1995.

Obeyesekere, Gananath. *Medusa's Hair: An Essay on Personal Symbols and Religious Experience.* Chicago: University of Chicago Press, 1981.

Passionate Journey: The Spiritual Autobiography of Satomi Myōdō. Translated and annotated by Sallie B. King. Albany: State University of New York Press, 1993.

Paul, Diana Y. "Buddhist Attitudes toward Women's Bodies." *Buddhist Christian Studies* 1 (1981): 63–71.

———. *Women in Buddhism: Images of the Feminine in the Mahāyāna Tradition*. 2d ed. Berkeley, Calif.: University of California Press, 1985.

Phongpaichit, Pasuk. *Rural Women in Thailand: From Peasant Girls to Bangkok Masseuses*. Geneva: International Labour Office, World Employment Programme Research (Working Papers), 1980.

Poole, Fitz John Porter. "Metaphors and Maps: Towards Comparison in the Anthropology of Religion." *Journal of the American Academy of Religion* 53: 3 (1986): 411–60.

Porpora, Douglas, and Mah Hui Lim. "The Political Economic Factors of Migration to Bangkok." *Journal of Contemporary Asia* 17: 1: 76–89.

Rabīab Patibat Khōng Sathāban Māechī Hāeng Prathēt Thai. [Discipline of Practice of the Institute of Thai Matchee]. Bangkok, 1975.

Rahula, Walpola. *The Heritage of the Bhikkhu: A Short History of the Bhikkhu in Educational, Cultural, Social, and Political Life*. Translated by K. P. G. Wijayasurendra. New York: Grove Press, 1974.

Ramitanondh, S. "Family Life in a Northern Thai Village: A Study of the Structural Significance of Women." *Journal of Southeast Asian Studies* 11: 1 (1980) 224–25.

Ratchadworamunee, Phra. *Phočhonānugrom Phutthasat* [A Dictionary of Buddhism]. Bangkok: Department of Buddhist Affairs, 1992.

Raymond, Janice G. *A Passion for Friends: Toward a Philosophy of Female Affection*. Boston: Beacon Press, 1986.

Reynolds, Craig. "A Nineteenth Century Thai Buddhist Defense of Polygamy and Some Remarks on the Social History of Women in Thailand." Proceedings, Seventh Conference of the International Association of the Historians of Asia. Bangkok: Chulalongkorn Press, 1977, 927–70.

Reynolds, Frank E. "The Many Lives of Buddha: A Study of Sacred Biography and Theravāda Buddhism." In *The Biographical Process: Studies in the History and Psychology of Religion*, edited by Frank E. Reynolds and Donald Capps. The Hague: Mouton, 1976, 37–61.

Rhys Davids, Mrs., trans. *The Book of the Kindred Sayings: Saṃyutta-Nikāya*, Part II. London: Pali Text Society, 1972.

Rorty, Richard. "On Ethnocentrism: A Reply to Clifford Geertz." *Objectivity, Relativism, and Truth: Philosophical Papers*, Vol. 1. New York: Cambridge University Press, 1991, 203–10.

Sanday, Peggy R. "Female Status in the Public Domain." In *Woman, Culture, and Society*, edited by Michelle Zimbalist Rosaldo and Louise Lamphere. Stanford, Calif.: Stanford University Press, 1974, 189–206.

————. "Toward a Theory of the Status of Women." *American Anthropologist* 75: 5 (1973): 1682–1700.

Sax, William S. *Mountain Goddess: Gender and Politics in a Himalayan Pilgrimage.* New York: Oxford University Press, 1991.

Sharma, Arvind. "How and Why Did the Women of Ancient India Become Buddhist Nuns?" *Sociological Analysis* 38 (fall 1977): 239–51.

Shaw, Miranda. *Passionate Enlightenment: Women in Tantric Buddhism.* Princeton, N.J.: Princeton University Press, 1994.

Singnathanitiraksa, Bradong. "Botbat Kong Matchee Thai Ny Ganwapana Sangkom" [Role Expectation of Thai Matchee in Social Development]. Master's thesis, Thammasat University, 1973.

Sole-Leris, Amadeo. *Tranquillity and Insight: An Introduction to the Oldest Forms of Buddhist Meditation.* Boston: Shambhala Press, 1986.

Springer, J. Fred, and Richard W. Gable. "Modernization and Sex Roles: The Status of Women in the Thai Bureaucracy." *Sex Roles* 7 (1981): 723–37.

Suwanbubbha, Parichart. "A Comparative Study of the Status and Roles of Theravāda Buddhist and Roman Catholic Nuns: A Case Study of the Community of Bangkok." Master's thesis, Mahidol University, 1983.

Swearer, Donald K. "Control and Freedom: The Structure of Buddhist Meditation in the Pāli Suttas." *Philosophy East and West* (1973) 23: 435–55.

Tambiah, Stanley Jeyaraja. *The Buddhist Saints of the Forest and the Cult of Amulets: A Study in Charisma, Hagiography, Sectarianism, and Millenial Buddhism.* New York: Cambridge University Press, 1984.

————. *Buddhism and the Spirit Cults in North-East Thailand.* New York: Cambridge University Press, 1970.

————. *World Conqueror and World Rencouncer: A Study of Buddhism and Polity in Thailand against a Historical Background.* New York: Cambridge University Press, 1976.

Tantiwiramanond, Darunee, and Shashi Pandey. "The Status and Role of Thai Women in the Pre-Modern Period: A Historical and Cultural Perspective." *Sojourn* 2: 1, 125–49.

Tedlock, Barbara. "From Participant Observation to the Observation of Participation: The Emergence of Narrative Ethnography." *Journal of Anthropological Research* 47: 1 (1991): 69–94.

Thapar, R. "Renunciation: The Making of a Counter-Culture?" in *Ancient Indian Social History: Some Interpretations*, edited by R. Thapar. New Delhi: Orient Longmans, 1987; London: Sangam, 1996.

Thitsa, Khin. *Providence and Prostitution: Image and Reality for Women in Buddhist Thailand.* London: Change International Reports, 1980.

Thongthiraj, Took Took. "Toward a Struggle against Invisibility: Love between Women in Thailand." *Amerasia Journal* 20: 1 (1994): 45–58.

Thorpek, Susanne. *Voices from the City: Women of Bangkok.* London: Zed Books, 1987.

Tsomo, Karma Lekshe, ed. *Sakyadhītā: Daughters of the Buddha.* Itaca, N.Y.: Snow Lion Publishers, 1988.

Van Esterik, J. "Women Meditation Teachers in Thailand." In *Women in Southeast Asia,* edited by Penny Van Esterik. Occasional Paper #9. Dekalb: Northern Illinois University, Center for Southeast Asian Studies, 1982, 42–54.

Van Esterik, P. "Laywomen in Theravada Buddhism." In *Women in Southeast Asia,* edited by P. Van Esterik. Occasional Paper #9. Dekalb: Northern Illinois University, Center for Southeast Asian Studies, 1982, 55–78.

Vetlesen, Arne Johan. *Perception, Empathy, and Judgment: An Inquiry into the Preconditions of Moral Performance.* University Park: Pennsylvania State University Press, 1994.

Vichit-Vadakan, Juree. "Women and the Family in Thailand in the Midst of Social Change." *Law and Society Review* 28: 3 (1994): 515–24.

Walsh, Maurice, trans. *The Long Discourses of the Buddha: A Translation of the Dīgha Nikāya.* Somerville, Mass.: Wisdom Publications, 1987, 1995. (Cited in the text as *Dīgha Nikāya.*)

Watkins, Joanne C. *Spirited Women: Gender, Religion, and Cultural Identity in the Nepal Himalaya.* New York: Columbia University Press, 1996.

Weber, Max. *On Charisma and Institution Building: Selected Papers.* Translated and edited by S. N. Eisenstadt. Chicago: University of Chicago Press, 1968.

Wilson, Liz. "Seeing through the Gendered 'I': The Self-Scrutiny and Self-Disclosure of Nuns in Post–Asokan Buddhist Hagiographic Literature." *Journal of Feminist Studies in Religion* 2: 1 (spring 1995): 41–80.

Women in the Cities of Asia: Migration and Urban Adaptation. Edited by James T. Fawcett, Siew-Ean Khoo, and Peter C. Smith. Boulder: Westview Press, 1984.

Wuthnow, Robert. *Learning to Care: Elementary Kindness in an Age of Indifference.* New York: Oxford University Press, 1995.

in *Tradition,* No. 4 (Autumn 1970), 29-35.

Turner, Graeme. *Film as Social Practice.* London: Routledge, 1988.

Tudor, Andrew. *Theories of Film.* New York: Praeger, 1973.

Van Zoonen, L. "Feminist Perspectives on the Media." In *Mass Media and Society,* ed. James Curran and Michael Gurevitch. London, 1991.

Walkerdine, Valerie. "Video Replay: Families, Films and Fantasy." In *Formations of Fantasy,* ed. Victor Burgin, James Donald, and Cora Kaplan. London: Methuen, 1986.

Williams, Linda. *Hard Core: Power, Pleasure and the "Frenzy of the Visible."* Berkeley: University of California Press, 1989.

Williamson, Judith. *Decoding Advertisements.* London: Marion Boyars, 1978.

Wollen, Peter. *Signs and Meaning in the Cinema.* London: Secker and Warburg, 1969.

Woollacott, Janet. "Messages and Meanings." In *Culture, Society and the Media,* ed. Michael Gurevitch. London: Methuen, 1982.

Index

Abhiddhamma, 22, 69
Abstinence: from food, 19; sexual, 19
Āčhān, 79, 107, 109
Actions: bad, 88; karmic results, 64;
  motivation for, 152n1; past, 83;
  right, 116; roots of unwholesome,
  71; social, 152n1
Alms, 87
Altars, 2
Ānanda, 18
Anattā, 51, 87
Anger, 43, 52, 53, 72, 109, 156n9;
  counteracting, 53; forgiveness and,
  54–55; loving-kindness and, 53;
  origin of, 53; past lives and, 66;
  persistence of, 54; presence of, 53;
  removal of, 54; rootedness in
  previous lives, 52; of teacher at
  Māechī Wābī, 79, 80
Anicca, 87
Aronson, Harvey, 152n1
Arts, traditional, 4
Association for the Promotion of the
  Status of Women, 34, 128

Beatings, 50, 64
Betrayal, 111
Bhikkhu, 33, 86
Bhikkhunī, 33, 150n18; categories of,
  25; māechī as substitute for, 35;
  ordination problem, 33, 35;
  permission to become, 18; restart-
  ing lineage of, 33, 150n21
Binthabāt, 3

Body: blows to, 50; fur covering, 79;
  parts falling off, 49, 50; shaking,
  50
Boredom, 20
Bowonniwet Temple (Bangkok), 30
Breathing, 99
Buddha, 87, 133; in meditation, 2;
  refusal to allow bhikkhuni, 18
Buddhism: aspects of, 89; come-
  and-see aspect, 83; defilements,
  obstacles, or roots of unwholesome behavior, 43; definition by
  men, 27; disenchantment with
  representatives of, 26, 112;
  division of world into name and
  form, 49; eight precepts, 19, 81;
  establishment, 27; five precepts,
  19, 39, 81; as foundation for
  honorable life, 4; goal of
  equanimity in, 140, 141; government-defined, 27; heartmind in,
  9; hierarchies in, 83; ignorance
  as root of problems, 94;
  influence in society, 27; lack of
  input from women, 27; lived
  tradition of, 143; Mahāyana, 33;
  reality under-standing in, 49; ten
  precepts, 19; Theravāda, 25, 26,
  33, 49, 50, 51, 148n6, 150n18,
  151n8; traditional refuges of, 87;
  understanding through meditation, 68; village support for, 3;
  Westernized, 108
Buddhist Women's Association, 130